THE MEDIUM OF THE VIDEO GAME

The Medium of the

VIDEO

GAME

EDITED BY MARK J. P. WOLF

UNIVERSITY OF TEXAS PRESS

AUSTIN

Chapter 2, "Super Mario Nation," reprinted by permission of American Heritage, Inc., September 1997.

Portions of Chapter 3 appeared originally in "Inventing Space: Toward a Taxonomy of On- and Off-Screen Space in Video Games," *Film Quarterly* 51.1 (Fall 1997). Used by permission of the University of California Press. © 1971 by The Regents of the University of California.

Requests for permission to reproduce material from this work should be sent to Permissions, University of Texas Press, P.O. Box 7819, Austin, TX 78713-7819.
www.utexas.edu/utpress/about/bpermission.html

∞ The paper used in this book meets the minimum requirements of ANSI/NISO z39.48-1992 (R1997) (Permanence of Paper).

Library of Congress Cataloging-in-Publication Data

The medium of the video game / edited by Mark J. P. Wolf.—1st ed.
     p.   cm.
Includes bibliographical references and index.
ISBN 0-292-79150-x (pbk. : alk. paper)
1. Video games—United States.   2. Video games—History—United States.   I. Wolf, Mark J. P.

GV1469.3 .M43   2002
794.8'0973—dc21

2001037625

This book is dedicated to all the video game designers, players, collectors, researchers, and curators whose interest in the video game has spurred the development of the medium.

Contents

Foreword, *Ralph H. Baer*   ix

Acknowledgments   xvii

Introduction, *Mark J. P. Wolf*   1

I. The Emergence of the Video Game   **11**

  1. The Video Game as a Medium, *Mark J. P. Wolf*   13

  2. Super Mario Nation, *Steven L. Kent*   35

II. Formal Aspects of the Video Game   **49**

  3. Space in the Video Game, *Mark J. P. Wolf*   51

  4. Time in the Video Game, *Mark J. P. Wolf*   77

  5. Narrative in the Video Game, *Mark J. P. Wolf*   93

  6. Genre and the Video Game, *Mark J. P. Wolf*   113

III. The Video Game in Society and Culture   **135**

  7. Hot Circuits: Reflections on the 1989 Video Game Exhibition
     of the American Museum of the Moving Image,
     Rochelle Slovin   137

  8. Play It Again, Pac-Man, *Charles Bernstein*   155

  9. Archetypes on Acid: Video Games and Culture,
     Rebecca R. Tews   169

Appendix: Resources for Video Game Research, *Mark J. P. Wolf*   183

Index   193

About the Contributors   201

Foreword

Ralph H. Baer

As you will discover presently, *The Medium of the Video Game* deals in a thoughtful and scholarly manner with a great many aspects of video games. Because video games are now so much a part of our cultural landscape, it is sometimes hard to realize that they have not always been around—but they haven't.

Mark asked me to write this foreword because I was there at the very beginning of this saga. So here it is, but be forewarned! It's not easy to distance oneself from a parochial view of who did what, when, and where.

First of all, the concept of playing video games did not just appear from nowhere. It had to be invented. So, we might take a minute to consider the nature of inventions.

Let us just consider two specific classes: those inventions relating to a novel system concept and those that basically revolve around a novel method—resulting in a better product. The former class of inventions is one that "connects-the-dots"; the latter is generally in the nature of an "improvement."

Not too many people appear to understand this difference between the process of making an invention based on a novel system concept versus an invention that results in a better, or even novel, product. Of course, quite frequently inventions that "connect the dots" also have novel, even exciting, "method" content. That tends to confuse the issue.

To illustrate the point: the idea of running a computer under the control of a disc drive—a Disk Operating System, or DOS—is an example of a conceptual breakthrough . . . connecting the dots. Every last one of our present-day desktop and laptop computers still runs that way twenty years later. (Let's not get hung up on who claims to be the "Father of DOS." Hint: It wasn't B.G.) Every year there are faster, more capacious disc drives out there doing their job faster because engineers keep coming up with improvements—better methods.

Stepping back in history, it's instructive to take a look at electric power generation as an example: technologically, everything was in place to generate, distribute, and utilize electricity for industrial and home applications in the late 1800s. But it was Edison who conceived of putting all the elements together and acting upon his idea, or concept, and who built central power stations, created a switched distribution network, and, last but not least, developed usable light bulbs; the fact that Edison put it all together allows us to call him the "Father of the Electric Power Industry."

It's the concept, stupid! . . . as the current phrase goes, slightly paraphrased.

Along the way Edison and his staff developed many novel ways of generating, transmitting, controlling, and using the electric currents delivered by the system of his original concept. One of the technical improvements was the design of a higher voltage generator which delivered power more efficiently than previous designs. Some of the design specifics of that generator undoubtedly qualify as inventions. But those specifics didn't make Edison the "Father of the electric industry"; connecting the dots—putting it all together—is what constituted Edison's breakthrough.

With these definitions in mind, we can move on to the question of who invented video games.

Let's start with Steve Russell and others at MIT who bootlegged spare time on a DEC-1 computer in the early sixties and wrote software routines that eventually became space ships and missiles under the "player's" control. Did Russell or his associates invent video games?

Complex question, that. In the first place, in the sixties the term "video" was reserved for displays featuring a raster scan system. By definition, a video signal was comprised of an analog representation of the brightness levels along a raster line and was always associated with horizontal and vertical synchronization signals. It also may have had color components, usually present in the form of another analog signal, the color subcarrier signal.

Now, did the display of the PDP-1 have any of these characteristics? No, it didn't. Its display was of the vector type, which generated images by moving the electron beam around inside the CRT much as one might move a pencil over a piece of paper to draw the outlines of a figure. There was no raster.

So: Does that mean that Steve Russell did not design and play a video game? Well, yes and no. The term "video game" was not coined until the mid-seventies. But did Russell and his compadres play games under control of a computer and using a CRT display? You bet they did! Does that make Steve Russell the inventor of CRT games? Well, not really. CRT displays operating under electronic control and allowing human interaction were used by the military for training in missile guidance and other purposes both in this country's services and others during and after WWII. So that's not new. Were these applications truly "games"? That depends a lot on who's asking the question!

What Steve Russell and associates did was certainly highly creative and displayed a unique level of skill and insight into the ways of making a slow computer with limited facilities do their bidding. They certainly connected some dots! Had they applied for patents covering interactive game playing such as *Spacewar!* on a computer and CRT display, they would most certainly have been awarded a number of patent claims which might have become valuable years later. But they didn't . . . after all, theirs was an unauthorized, after-hours project. There were good reasons why they did not think in terms of protecting their code: Who but a select few had access to a refrigerator-sized, $100,000 computer? So they freely gave their code away and with that any chance of material rewards for their creativity, as least as far as I know.

Then there was Willy Higginbotham. In 1958, during an open house demonstration for visitors at Brookhaven National Labs, Higginbotham hooked an oscilloscope up to an analog computer. With this setup he dazzled onlookers by graphing the path of a dot which acted like a bouncing ball; the latter could be launched by pressing a button; the ball then "bounced" repeatedly—a more-or-less standard physics demonstration.

Much has been made of this simple but entertaining demo of basic ball dynamics. In fact, revisionists have turned that demonstration into a ping-pong game. It was nothing of the kind. But was it a game? More specifically, was it a video game?

I don't know. But even if it was a "video game," what became of it? The answer is: Nothing! In fact, it would never have seen the light of day again if it hadn't been dug up many years later by attorneys who were trying to "prove" that the concept of video games was "old" and not an invention by such interlopers as yours truly.

Nolan Bushnell is another key player in our story. His interest in playing interactive games displayed on a computer screen started when he was a student at the University of Utah, where he, like many other students, played *Spacewar!* The young Bushnell had the definitely novel concept of putting a pay-and-play *Spacewar!*-like game in an arcade environment. Having worked in an arcade at a Salt Lake City amusement park one summer, he "connected the dots."

He persevered and eventually designed and built a freestanding arcade game called *Computer Space,* which started the arcade video game business in 1971. And although *Computer Space* was not a commercial success—it was too expensive and too complicated to play, I am told—it was nevertheless the first video arcade game. Nolan Bushnell connected the dots.

Now, I come to my own story:

People frequently can't resist telling others, in my presence, that I was involved in creating the first video game. Hearing that bit of imprecise information, the listener invariably asks: "What game did you invent?" Hoping, no doubt, to hear me say *Pac-Man, Space Invaders, Donkey Kong,* or some other personal favorite.

When I reply that I didn't actually invent any of these games, but that I came up with the concept of playing games on a home TV set, the listener's eyes glaze over. Video games have become so much part of our culture that people tend to think that they have always been around.

They haven't. And when the idea of playing games on a home TV set first occurred to me in the early fifties, the reception was cool, to say the least. As another engineer and I worked on designing and building a TV set at Loral in 1951, I kept thinking: "How can we differentiate our TV set from everybody else's?" I had a suggestion: "How about making it play some simple games?" I was told to forget about that dumb idea.

I didn't forget the idea. By 1966, there were over 60 million TV sets in U.S. homes alone, to say nothing of those in the rest of the world. What were they good for if there was nothing on that anybody wanted to watch?

Being a television engineer by degree, I appreciated the fact that if TV sets weren't mass-produced, they would be expensive. They are really low-cost raster-scan graphic displays, although people didn't think of them that way in the 1960s.

The more I thought about using a standard home TV set to play games, the better I liked the idea. It definitely had legs. On September 1, 1966, I sat down and wrote a four-page paper describing my ideas for playing interactive games using an ordinary TV set. I had a fellow engineer witness and date those four pages, and we went to work.

At the time, I ran the Equipment Design Division at Sanders Associates, a large military electronics firm in New Hampshire, which became a

Lockheed company in the early eighties and is now a BAE System division. My operation was big—I had more than five hundred engineers, techs, and support people. I could afford to put a technician on the bench for a couple of weeks to determine the feasibility of that concept without rippling the overhead. No one need know.

There was no relationship between what was normally going on in my division and this early video game activity. I just decided to act on my long-held views of what to do with a TV set other than watch the standard fare. My immediate concern was to look into the technical feasibility of coming up with a novel and attractive product (for a price). What to do with it all if it panned out—that could wait.

It didn't take us long to figure out how to move a couple of spots around on the screen under player control. Pretty soon we were able to make some very neat demonstrations to the corporate director of patents and Sanders' director of R&D. Playing chase games and shooting at the screen turned them on. They supported me with funding and saw to it that patent applications were taken care of early in the game.

The work went forward. At various intervals the executive VP, my boss, would inquire whether I was still "screwing around with that stuff." It was difficult to see the payback at the time. Years later, when the millions came in via the patent licensing and the infringement litigation route, everybody "reminded" me of how supportive they had been of my video game efforts.

By 1968—two years and many bucks later—the now official project had gone through five sets of ever-improving game devices. Our "consoles" now allowed us to play ping-pong games, handball, volleyball, light-gun shooting-games, and quiz games as well as various forms of chase games, a golf game using an actual golf ball and putter, board games, and so forth.

By now, we had filed numerous patent applications with the U.S. Patent and Trademark Office in Washington, DC. During one of the conference meetings with one of the patent examiners there, I set up a small GE TV set and one of our early game boxes which I had brought along. I began playing games while my Sanders patent attorney associate was haggling with the examiner about the details of one of our patent applications. At first, the examiner objected, but within a half-hour the curious were streaming in from all over the floor to look at and play "TV games." Word got around fast that morning. The consensus was: "Man, this is different and it's fun!"

What we presented to the patent office was the concept of playing interactive games on a home TV set, along with numerous ideas for technical ways of making it happen cost-effectively. The use of CRT monitors, as later used in arcade games, was also part of our earliest patent applications. So was the concept of playing games over the "cable." By 1967, all of these concepts had been "reduced to practice," the patent office's way of saying that we had actually designed and built all of this stuff by then.

The U.S. patent office reviewed the relevant "patent art" and decided to "allow" more than a few important claims. The examiners clearly recognized that we had connected a new set of dots.

Our final, switch-programmable demonstration unit was housed in a box covered with brown, wood-grained adhesive paper to dress it up a bit: our Brown Box. In 1968 and 1969 we showed that box to all of the U.S. TV set manufacturers then in business in the hope that one of them would see fit to take a license. RCA, Sylvania, GE, Motorola, Zenith, and Magnavox all paraded through New Hampshire. Everyone was impressed; no one moved off a dime.

Finally, Magnavox took a license in 1971. We helped them engineer a production version of our Brown Box which was called *Odyssey*—Magnavox's Model ITL-200. They chose not to incorporate our method of producing colored backgrounds—too expensive; they didn't want sound, either—also too expensive. In the design process, they changed our switch-programming system to plug-in carts, which was a great idea.

In March of 1972 Magnavox's exclusive dealerships all over the country staged coordinated demonstrations of the new product line for the year. I attended one early demo in New York at Bowling Green in Central Park. Odyssey was the hit of the show. I was elated! Sitting among the dealers in the audience, I was hard-put not to jump up and down and yell: "That's my baby!"

On the other side of the country in Burlingame, California, at the Airport Marina Hotel, a product-line show was under way in late May. Nolan Bushnell was one of the visitors who came and played the Odyssey unit hands-on. He must have liked the idea of the Odyssey ping-pong game because he instructed newly hired employee Alan Alcorn to build a coin-op video game version of ping-pong. Alan designed several clever and novel features into this ping-pong machine. He could do these creative things because he was not constrained by the price limitations of a consumer product.

That machine was, of course, *PONG,* and *PONG* launched the arcade video game industry with a bang. Nolan Bushnell deserves the credit for this feat, without a doubt. He connected the dots. In my estimation, that makes him the "father of the arcade video game industry."

A few years later Nolan Bushnell signed up Atari as Magnavox's first licensee under our patents—several of which had been issued by then. In a series of lawsuits stretching over twenty years, these patents were upheld in various federal courts. A lot of money for licenses and infringement changed hands over those years. At the conclusion of the first trial in Chicago in 1976, Federal District Judge John Grady read his decision from the bench. He singled out my '480 patent as the "pioneering patent in this art," the field of home video games. That patent was first filed in January of 1968. It was based on the work we did during the first year of our project, 1966–1967, to define game concepts and convert them to hardware. Since holding the first patent in a new field makes you legally the original inventor of that conceptual landscape—at least under U.S. patent laws—I am the official inventor of home TV games, signed, sealed, and delivered by the U.S. Patent and Trademark Office.

That's what happened as a consequence of a simple idea I had way back and finally got around to pursuing in 1966. I knew nothing about Steve Russell's or Nolan Bushnell's work. I was just a guy with a TV engineering degree who wanted to do something with all those 60 million TV sets out there besides tuning in Channel 2, 4, or 7. And I did. If that makes me the "father of the home video game industry"—well, OK.

It's all about connecting the dots.

The instant success of *PONG* is legendary and certainly doesn't need retelling here. There is also no doubt that the appearance of *PONG* machines during 1972 helped sell Odyssey home TV games. It was the only way to approximate the *PONG* experience at home. Nearly 100,000 Odyssey units wound up in people's homes including some fifteen or twenty thousand light guns and optional carts. The home video game industry was launched!

Because Atari's *PONG* was an instant success, other arcade manufacturers quickly copied the design, and *PONG*-like machines proliferated by the next year. That game business has been roaring ahead ever since, with just a few "bad" years now and then. Nolan Bushnell got a nice big order for a home TV game version of *PONG* from Sears in 1974. That helped Atari rise like a rocket. There was no stopping them in the 1970s. By then, "video games" were permanently engraved on the map of the home entertainment industry.

Which, of course, still leaves the question of who "invented" video games? The short answer still is: "Let me tell you . . . It's a long story. . . ."
I'll let you be the judge.
End of the story! Enjoy the book!

D 240 1 D

United States Patent [19]

Baer

[11] **3,728,480**

[45] **Apr. 17, 1973**

[54] **TELEVISION GAMING AND TRAINING APPARATUS**

[75] Inventor: **Ralph H. Baer,** Manchester, N.H.

[73] Assignee: **Sanders Associates, Inc.,** Nashua, N.H.

[22] Filed: **Mar. 22, 1971**

[21] Appl. No.: **126,966**

Related U.S. Application Data

[63] Continuation of Ser. No. 697,798, Jan. 15, 1968, abandoned.

[52] U.S. Cl..................**178/6.8,** 178/6, 178/DIG. 1
[51] Int. Cl...**H04n 7/18**
[58] Field of Search.......................273/101.1, 101.2; 315/22, 26, 30, 10, 18; 178/DIG. 4, 7.83, DIG. 6

[56] **References Cited**

UNITED STATES PATENTS

2,489,883	11/1949	Hecht	250/217 CR
2,552,022	5/1951	Watson et al.	315/26
2,595,646	6/1952	Doba, Jr. et al.	328/187
2,648,724	8/1953	Enslein	178/6 TT
2,956,116	10/1960	Singleman	178/6 TT
3,014,724	12/1961	Cryder et al.	178/7.83
3,046,676	6/1962	Hermann et al.	35/25
3,151,248	9/1964	Glaser et al.	273/101.1
3,401,331	9/1968	Mussulman	178/6 TT
2,621,246	12/1952	Clayden et al.	178/DIG. 6
1,180,470	6/1959	France	

FOREIGN PATENTS OR APPLICATIONS

OTHER PUBLICATIONS

Radio and Television News; August 1956, pp. 63.
Radio Electronics, May 1956, pp. 38.

Primary Examiner—Richard Murray
Attorney—Louis Etlinger

[57] **ABSTRACT**

The present invention pertains to an apparatus and method, in conjunction with standard monochrome and color television receivers, for the generation, display, manipulation, and use of symbols or geometric figures upon the screen of the television receivers for the purpose of training simulation, for playing games, and for engaging in other activities by one or more participants. The invention comprises in one embodiment a control unit, connecting means and in some applications a television screen overlay mask utilized in conjunction with a standard television receiver. The control unit includes the control means, switches and electronic circuitry for the generation, manipulation and control of video signals which are to be displayed on the television screen. The connecting means couples the video signals to the receiver antenna terminals thereby using existing electronic circuits within the receiver to process and display the signals. An overlay mask which may be removably attached to the television screen may determine the nature of the game to be played or the training simulated. Control units are provided for each of the participants. Alternatively, games, training simulations and other activities may be carried out in conjunction with background and other pictorial information originated in the television receiver by commercial TV, closed-circuit TV or a CATV station.

46 Claims, 26 Drawing Figures

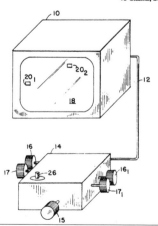

Acknowledgments

First, I would like to thank all the contributors, Ralph H. Baer, Charles Bernstein, Brian L. Johnson, Steven L. Kent, Rochelle Slovin, and Rebecca R. Tews, for their contributions to this book. Thanks also to Keith Feinstein for his great hospitality at Videotopia and for interesting discussions about video games. Chapter 2 originally appeared as an article in *American Heritage*, and portions of Chapter 3 appeared in *Film Quarterly*, so I would like to voice my appreciation to those two periodicals. Also, gracious thanks to Jim Burr at the University of Texas Press for providing patient and valuable editorial guidance. For lists of various video game cartridges, I would like to thank the video game community on the Internet, where some of the best video game research exists. Thanks also go to Bernard Perron for his enthusiasm for the project, Kevin Ruddy of the Video Arcade Preservation Society, David Winter in France for his *PONG* information, Richard Wolhers for reference assistance, Robin Lionheart of the Open Directory Project, Leonard Komblevicz for letting me borrow his Wonder Wizard game system, Phil Abramoff for taking me through *Tomb Raider* and *Tomb Raider II*, and to Wes Vokes, who introduced me to *Adventure* for the Atari 2600 when we were kids. And, of course, a big thanks goes to my parents, Joseph and Dorothy Wolf. And, as always, thanks be to God.

THE MEDIUM OF THE VIDEO GAME

Introduction

Mark J. P. Wolf

The year 2001 marks the thirtieth anniversary of commercial video games, which began with Nolan Bushnell's coin-operated *Computer Space* arcade game in 1971. Initially seen as an experiment, novelty, or toy, the video game grew into an item of mass consumption during the 1970s and quickly expanded through the 1980s and 1990s into a multi-billion-dollar-a-year industry. During its first thirty years, the video game market has rapidly expanded and has proven to be powerful competition for film and television, and as films like *Super Mario Bros.* (game, 1985; film, 1993), *Street Fighter* (game, 1987; film, 1994), *Mortal Kombat* (game, 1992; film, 1995), *Wing Commander* (game, 1990; film, 1999), and *Tomb Raider* (game, 1996; film, 2001), and so on, have shown, a source of material for films and television as well. During the 1990s, home computers and CD-ROM drives took over a large sector of the gaming market, although game systems such as Super Nintendo, Virtual Boy, X-Box, Sega Dreamcast, PlayStation 2, and others continue on in the game-console tradition. Newer technologies like DVD-ROM now feature games, and "level editors" allow players to design and play their own levels of games like *Doom* (1993). And stand-alone arcade-style video games found in malls are also featuring games of increasing speed and complexity, moving into ever more detailed three-dimensional environments, virtual reality, and simulator games.

Despite three decades of development, there has been relatively little scholarly study of these games, or even an acknowledgment of the medium of the video game as a whole. Acceptance of the medium as an art form is still in its early stages. Yet film and television industries realized the potential of the new medium as early as the mid-1970s, when they sought to have a hand in the video game market; CBS Electronics and 20th Century Fox made their own game cartridges, and several dozen movies and television shows were planned to be adapted into game cartridges for the Atari 2600 system alone.[1] As audiovisual entertainment whose content is largely representational, video games have a lot more in common with film and television than merely characters, settings, and plotlines. During production, producers of video games sometimes hire the same special effects houses that film and video makers use for animated sequences and motion-capture sessions. In the area of exhibition, video games compete for audiences at the same sites as film and TV: most multiplex theaters have video games in the lobby, if not separate side rooms devoted to them; home video game systems use the television set itself, encouraging their owners to play game programs instead of watching broadcast programs; and video rental companies, such as Blockbuster Video, also rent games and game systems. In record stores, alongside compact discs of film soundtracks, there are now CDs like *Duke Nukem: Music to Score By* and the soundtracks to *Myst* (1993), *Riven* (1997), and other games. And there's even competition at the Academy Awards, with the 1998 nomination of an animated sequence from the game *Oddworld: Abe's Exoddus* for Best Animated Short.

Theoretically, many of the same issues and concepts in film theory can also be applied to video games, and video games are themselves becoming more like film and television, embedding video clips within the games, or like many laserdisc, CD-ROM, and DVD-ROM games, relying on video sequences almost entirely. Many games now use recorded sounds rather than just computer-generated ones, and they have elaborate opening and closing sequences, in an attempt to create a more cinematic experience (including long crawls of end credits). And as graphics grow more representational and detailed, product placement and imbedded advertising may also become as common in video games as they are in movies (for example, Sega's *Top Skater* (1997) features over a dozen billboards for Coca-Cola). Video games are also rated just as films are, due to violence, nudity, and adult themes. Whereas films are rated by the MPPDA (Motion Picture Producers and Distributors Association), many video games are now rated by the AAMA (American Amusement Machine Association). Naturally, then, video game theory finds its roots in film and television theory.

Video Games and Film and Television Theory

As media, video games are already widespread and unique enough to deserve their own branch of theory. Currently, they are best approached and analyzed using conceptual tools developed in film and television theory and media studies. The study of video games overlaps these fields in many theoretical areas, including those of the active spectator, suture, first-person narrative, and spatial orientation, point of view, character identification, sound and image relations, and semiotics. Video games often rely on a knowledge of cinematic conventions (for example, in the construction of space and narrative action, continuity editing, the use of off-screen space, and concepts of point of view), and the possibility of one-on-one interaction means video games can extend them in ways that film cannot. While films traditionally position the spectator to identify with the main character through point of view and other techniques of suture, the actions of the player's on-screen surrogate character in the video game are controlled by the spectator/player, who vicariously experiences the game through the on-screen surrogate as a participant and not just an observer. Though we may refer to film spectatorship as "active," due to the viewer's ongoing attempt to make sense of the film, the video game player is even more active, making sense of the game as well as causing and reacting to the events depicted. Many games depict their diegetic worlds from a first-person perspective, and much of what occurs is due to the intervention or curiosity of the player, although in other games, quick thinking and fast reactions are required during game play. Only when a player becomes attuned to the design of the game and the algorithms by which it operates will success be possible; thus a certain manner of thinking and reacting is encouraged. In both film and video games, an inherent worldview is embodied in how actions are followed by outcomes and consequences; when a criminal is caught at the end of the film, we can read it as a cautionary tale, and likewise, other actions can appear to be condoned or encouraged. While film or TV may influence behavior, in the video game, the player is called upon not just to watch but to act; simulation becomes emulation, and sympathy becomes empathy. Alternate endings and branching storylines also help to define the inherent worldview by rewarding or punishing certain behaviors. A look at the medium of the video game may also bring to light certain unacknowledged assumptions in areas of theory dealing with reception, spectatorship, narrative structure, and the nature of the diegetic worlds seen on-screen and one's experience of them.

The study of video games also adds new concepts to existing ideas in moving imagery theory, such as those concerning the game's interface, player action, interactivity, navigation, and algorithmic structures. The interface bridges the gap between the diegetic world and that of the player.

Whether by mouse, joystick, trackball, gun, head-mounted display, or keyboard, some additional means of inputting player actions must be integrated into the design of the game. Informational graphics and nondiegetic displays are combined with game play in a variety of ways, each of which has a particular effect on the gameplay experience. Likewise, the way players' actions are transmuted to their on-screen surrogates are often designed to be as transparent or intuitive as possible, though not always. Navigation of the diegetic world also frequently figures as an important element of game play, and maps and mapping are common. Navigation also enhances the feeling of a consistent, three-dimensional space, through which one can freely move or at least have the illusion of moving. And finally, the algorithmic structures controlling the game's events and characters are gradually discerned, and knowledge of how they function is often needed for success in the game. While figuring out these structures, or solving puzzles or challenges posed by the game's author, players try to think like the designer or programmer, which sometimes forces them to momentarily take on the author's way of thinking. The interactive nature of video games, the possibility of many different outcomes, and the illusion of effectiveness and power on the part of the player can make video games potentially more attractive to people than more passive media; indeed, video games have even been shown to be clinically addictive.[2] Public debate as to the effects of video game violence occurs alongside debates regarding violence in film and television.

Examination of all of these elements will enrich moving imagery theory, pointing out unacknowledged assumptions which may lead to a better understanding of traditional media and the way they are received by an audience. And, audiences accustomed to interactive media like video games and the Internet may also begin to regard traditional passive media in different ways as they come to seem more passive and linear or more manipulative by comparison. Yet at the same time, the illusion of freedom one has in a partially navigable video game world can serve to obscure the points of view and assumptions which in some ways are even more present than they are in an on-screen world in film or television. Worldviews and ideas may be more effectively intertwined with the diegetic world in a video game, because a player's experience seems less directed than that of the viewer of a linear, noninteractive work. If knowledge of how film operates on the spectator is still incomplete, consider how much more incomplete is the knowledge of how video games operate on players, and what their effects are. Video games have become well integrated into other cultural forms and media, and yet are often overlooked as a cultural influence, despite a long and prominent presence in American culture.

....

Cultural Importance of Video Games

Historically, the video game has occupied several other important positions in culture; it was, in the early to mid-1970s, the first computer that could be used by the public in the form of stand-alone games in the arcade. And shortly after arcade games, home video game systems became the first entrance of the computer into the average American household. Some early systems even used the term "computer" as a selling point; the Atari 2600 was released officially as the Atari VCS CX2600, the "VCS" standing for "Video Computer System." In this way, the video game helped to build a positive, fun, and user-friendly image of the computer, which helped to usher in the era of the home computer only a few years later. In the long run, game cartridges were a good marketing tool for early home computer systems. Many people at the time wondered if they really needed a computer, or what they would use it for, since typewriters, board games, calculators, ledgers, and other technology already served their needs. Games made the computer a recreational device instead of merely a utilitarian one.

The video game was also the first medium to combine moving imagery, sound, and real-time user interaction in one machine, and so it made possible the first widespread appearance of interactive, on-screen worlds in which a game or story took place. Simple as they were at first, they fascinated the public, and quickly grew into a major industry. Nolan Bushnell's *Computer Space* brought him around $500 in royalties in 1971; a little over twenty years later, in 1992, the video game industry grossed over $5.3 billion, an increase of more than ten-million-fold. Sales in 1998 were 22 percent higher than 1997 sales, making 1998 a record-breaking year, with $6.3 billion in U.S. video games sales alone. The year 1999 broke the record again with a total of $6.9 billion. Worldwide sales are substantially higher, and the annual sales for individual companies can be in the billions of dollars; in fiscal 1997–98, Nintendo of America made $4.0 billion and Sony Computer Entertainment of America made $5.3 billion.[3] Not only does the video game industry now make more money than the film industry, but video games often take up more of the audience's time than films do. Whereas a movie can be viewed in its entirety typically in under three hours, video games, with their multiple levels, fast-action challenges, and puzzle solving, can require many hours of game play even when players have become familiar with them.

Today, the on-screen or diegetic worlds found in video games have grown tremendously in detail, size, and interactive potential. The shapes these diegetic worlds and the manner in which they are depicted have been heavily influenced by those of film and television, but have not remained limited to them. As video game graphics increase in resolution and rendering speed, and film and television move into the digital realm, the gap between them continues to close. Gradually, films are joining video games in the realm of computer graphics, not only through the growing use of digital effects in film and the use of video clips and film language within games, but with films like *Toy Story* (1995), *Antz* (1998), and *A Bug's Life* (1998), which are all entirely computer generated. *Toy Story* was also adapted into a Super Nintendo game, the graphics of which, although of much lower resolution, still managed to retain quite a bit of detail from the film's characters. Live-action films also have their equivalent in full-motion video games like *Johnny Mnemonic* (1995), *Star Trek: Borg* (1996), and others. Actors, storylines, and cinematic conventions are crossing over into video games, and many of the familiar titles, series, and franchises are often found in both.

The medium of video games itself has evolved with astonishing speed, and it is still changing—rapidly. Its growth is most striking when compared with that of other media; for example, film was still largely black and white and silent after its first three decades. In the same span of time, video games advanced from *PONG* to 64-bit and DVD-ROM-based games, and it is difficult to predict what they will be like even five years from now. With a rich three decades of history already behind video games, the medium is ripe for study.

Difficulties in Studying the Video Game

Why, then, has the video game largely been ignored in academic media studies? One reason might be its status as a "game," which separates it from traditional media such as books, film, radio, and television, despite its audiovisual nature and often narrative basis. Early games were also very simple graphically and narratively, and rather limited in subject matter. Since then, however, both graphics and storylines have improved, warranting more analysis and comment. Greater complexity and depth give the video game designer more opportunity to embody a message, worldview, or philosophy into a game in the same way these elements can be incorporated into novels and films. While it is true there are still a good number of games which are the gaming world's equivalent of slapstick comedies or plotless action films, more serious work continues to emerge and develop. The social effects of video games may also be difficult to pin down exactly—not that those of film and television are any easier to determine—but considering the position video games occupies culturally, it cannot be denied that an influence is present. And considering the amount of attention given to marginal films and TV programs, certainly video games are deserving of scrutiny under the academic microscope.

Perhaps the main reason for the neglect of the video game is that it is more difficult to study than traditional media. Admittedly, the video game as a "text" is much harder to master. Whereas someone can listen to a piece of music, read a novel, or sit and watch a film from beginning to end and be satisfied that he or she has seen all there is to see of it, this is usually not the case with a video game. Indeed, game-playing skills may be required to advance beyond the first few levels, or some puzzle-solving ability may be needed just to enter a locked door encountered early on in the diegetic world. Instead of fixed, linear sequences of text, image, or sound which remain unchanged when examined multiple times, a video game experience can vary widely from one playing to another. Even if a player has the right skills, there are often courses of action and areas of the game which are still left unexplored even after the game has been played several times. Mastery of the video game, then, can be more involved (and involving) than mastery of a film; in addition to critical skills, the researcher must possess game-playing or puzzle-solving skills, or at least know someone who does. Guides and cheat books are also sometimes available.

More time is also needed to experience a video game. Whereas movies are generally no more than a few hours in length, video games like *Riven* (1997), *Tomb Raider II* (1997), *Final Fantasy VIII* (2000), *The Longest Journey* (2000), and so on, can average forty or more hours to complete, not including all the possible endings they may contain. Sometimes it is not even clear how many choices a player has, and discovery of alternate narrative paths or hidden features (known as "Easter Eggs") is also a part of game play. It may take a good amount of playing time and attention to detail to say for certain that one has seen and heard everything a game has to offer (that is, all the screens, sounds, and video clips). Often, one needs to grasp an underlying logic in order to do so.

This book examines the video game as an artistic medium which has developed quickly in a short span of time. The first part, "The Emergence of the Video Game," begins in Chapter 1 with a look at the properties of the medium itself and the range of games that the term "video game" has been used to cover, along with explanations and definitions of some video game terminology and technology. In Chapter 2, Steven L. Kent offers an overview of the first twenty-five years of video game history.

The second part of the book, "Formal Aspects of the Video Game," features four chapters in which I examine the use of space, time, and narrative, and finally, how the video game challenges existing notions of genre, along with a descriptive list of video game genres. When possible, examples in this section will be taken from games that are more common, familiar, or easier to find; thus many examples will be taken from Atari 2600 games and more common games like *Myst* (1993), although unusual games will also be noted when necessary. Typically, I will also focus mainly on stand-alone arcade games and home video game systems, as video gaming is their primary purpose and function; the home computer came on the scene relatively late and subsumed the functions of the video game as it did the typewriter and calculator. On the other hand, some games, like First Star's *Spy Vs Spy* (1984), were only available as home computer software; likewise, networked games are played mainly on home computers, so mention of computer games will be made as well.

The third part of the book, "The Video Game in Society and Culture," looks more broadly at the social and cultural function of the video game. In Chapter 7, Rochelle Slovin, director and founder of the American Museum of the Moving Image (AMMI) in Astoria, New York, relates her experiences of museum exhibitions of video games. In Chapter 8, Charles Bernstein's "Play It Again, Pac-Man," an essay commissioned by the museum, takes a look at the American attraction and addiction to video games in the late 1980s. And finally, in Chapter 9, Rebecca R. Tews examines approaches that psychological research has taken toward the video game and suggests that Jungian archetypes may provide a key to understanding the role that video games play in culture. And finally, the appendix, "Resources for Video Game Research," includes some books, articles, websites, and suggestions for those interested in video game research.

Although "video game studies" is not yet an accepted field of academic study in the way cinema studies or television studies are, the video game has had a great impact on society and culture, and its influence on life in the late twentieth century should not be ignored. It continues to grow and mature, and has not yet shown signs of leveling off technologically. Aesthetically, a canon of "classics" is already developing. The video game's rapid growth, widespread appeal, and uniqueness as a medium behoove us to pay it closer attention and give it the examination and analysis that it is due.

....

Notes

1. Besides all the arcade video games based on movies, there are many home video games based on film and television. For the Atari 2600 alone, game cartridges based on movies include the following: *48 Hours, 9 to 5, Butch Cassidy and the Sundance Kid, China Syndrome, Deep Throat, Dragonslayer, E.T. the Extra-Terrestrial, Escape From Alcatraz, Excalibur, Fantastic Voyage, Friday the 13th, Ghostbusters, Ghostbusters II, Gremlins, Jaws, Karateka, Marathon Man, Poltergeist, Porky's, Raiders of the Lost Ark, Star Trek II: The Wrath of Khan, Star Trek III: The Search for Spock,* five different games based on the *Star Wars* films, *Texas Chainsaw Massacre, The Day the Earth Stood Still, The Last Starfighter, Towering Inferno, Trail of the Pink Panther,* and *Tron Deadly Discs.* Game cartridges for the Atari 2600 based on television shows include the following: *$25,000 Pyramid, A Game of Concentration, Dukes of Hazzard, Emergency!, Family Feud, Flipper, Jeopardy, Joker's Wild, Knight Rider, M*A*S*H, M*A*S*H II, Magnum PI, Mission Impossible,* and *Password,* as well as games based on *Romper Room, Scooby Doo, Star Trek, The A-Team, The Flintstones, The Incredible Hulk, The Price Is Right, Tic-Tac-Dough,* and *Wheel of Fortune.*

2. See S. Fisher, "Identifying Video Game Addiction in Children and Adolescents," *Addictive Behavior* 19.5 (Sept.–Oct. 1994), pp. 545–553; C. A. Phillips, S. Rolls, A. Rouse, and M. D. Griffiths, "Home Video Game Playing in Schoolchildren—A Study of Incidence and Patterns of Play," *Journal of Adolescence* 18.6 (Dec. 1995), pp. 687–691.

3. The dollar amounts come, respectively, from the following: Lou Kesten, "Past, Present, and Future," in *Video Game Quest: The Complete Guide to Home Video Game Systems, Video Games, and Accessories,*" ed. Jon C. A. DeKeles (DMS Publishers, 1990), pp. 1–2 and 1–3; "Rating Video Games: A Parent's Guide to Games," U.S. House Committee on the Judiciary, Committee on Governmental Affairs (Washington D.C.: U.S. Government Printing Office, Dec. 9, 1993); and Jennifer Klinger, "Videogame Sales Reach Record Highs in 1998," *GameWEEK* 5.6 (Feb. 10, 1999), pp. 1 and 9. Sales figures for Nintendo and Sony come from Ben Rinaldi, "1998 in Review: Top U.S. Sales Performers," *GameWEEK* 5.3 (Jan. 20, 1999), cover and pp. 14–15.

1

The Emergence of the Video Game

The Video Game as a Medium

Mark J. P. Wolf

J t took a while for both film and television to attain the status of an artistic medium, and likewise the video game has been slow to gain recognition in academia as an artistic medium, even after almost thirty years as a commercial industry and forty years of its existence. After appearing as an experiment and novelty and then developing into a toy, the video game took only a little over decade or so to grow into an item of mass consumption. Early games were graphically simple, and the medium as a whole did not have a widespread impact on popular culture until the latter half of the 1970s. Also, the video game's status as "game" put it in a different category from traditional media, despite its audiovisual nature and often narrative basis. Whereas works in traditional media are made up of fixed, linear sequences of text, image, or sound (or combinations of them) which remain unchanged when examined multiple times (apart from effects of wear and tear), events experienced in a video game will vary widely from one playing to another. Film viewers can watch a film from beginning to end and be satisfied that they have seen the film in its entirety, but a video game player must often have some amount of skill to advance through higher levels of a game, and there are often courses of action and areas of the game which are still left unexplored even after several times through. Mastery of the video game, then, can be more involved (and involving) than mastery of a film; in addition to critical skills, the researcher must possess game-playing skills, or at least know someone who does.

Although one can refer to film viewing as "active," meaning that the viewer is attentive to what is being shown and is applying imagination and critical thinking to make sense of or "read" a film, video game play requires input—physical action of some kind—from the player in order to function, and often quick reactions within a very limited time frame. Only when a player becomes attuned to the way in which a game operates will success be possible; thus a certain manner of thinking and reacting is encouraged, sometimes at the reflex level. In a film, all the steering of on-screen events is done for us by the filmmaker, whereas a video game leaves more possibilities open. The manner in which and the degree to which a film or a video game is a vicarious experience differs greatly.

Like the cinema before it, the video game became enormously successful financially within its first decade. The uniqueness of the video game medium has also opened up a new realm of interactive entertainment which has yet to be thoroughly examined and analyzed the way cinema and television have been. At present, film and television theories examining the use of moving imagery and sound are fairly well suited for analyzing video games, although some additions are needed to address areas where video games differ from traditional media (for example, the interface, interactivity, navigation, and algorithmic structures). In order to see where video games fit into the spectrum of other media, it is necessary to first consider the boundaries defining the medium of the video game.

Defining the Video Game

Defining the limits of what is meant by "video game" is more complicated than it first appears. Rather than attempt to create a single, definitive statement declaring the essence of the video game, we can begin with a narrow, precise definition and gradually widen its scope out to a broader definition, passing through various definitions found in popular usage along the way. Different aspects, such as technology, art, and the nature of the experience need also be considered in defining the term. In its strictest sense, we might start by noting the two criteria present in the name of the medium; its status as "video" and as "game."

Elements one would expect to find in a "game" are *conflict* (against an opponent or circumstances), *rules* (determining what can and cannot be done and when), use of some *player ability* (such as skill, strategy, or luck), and some kind of *valued outcome* (such as winning vs. losing, or the attaining of the highest score or fastest time for the completing of a task). All these are usually present in video games in some manner, though to differing degrees. In video games, the scoring of points, adherence to the rules, and the display of the game's visuals are all monitored by a computer instead of by human beings. The computer can also control the opposing characters within a game, becoming a participant as well as referee. One might also suggest that it is really the computer programmer, the person who wrote the program, that gamers are playing when they are "playing the computer," since the programmer's algorithms determine the actions of the computer-controlled players. In many cases, however, where brute computational force or speed is concerned, the idea that the computer programmer is the player seems a less tenable position (for example, supercomputer chess programs like IBM's *Deep Blue* and *Deep Thought* can certainly beat any of their programmers in chess).

Most video games are one-player games in which the player faces computer-controlled opponents and situations. Due to the almost instantaneous speed at which a computer can process user input, respond with reactions, and display the action on-screen, video games are often designed to require fast action and reflexes, much like sports or games like pinball or table tennis. Fast action is, for some, so integral to the gaming experience that narrower definitions of "video game" exclude text adventures, adaptations of card games and board games, contemplative puzzle-based programs like *Riven* (1997) and *Myst III: Exile* (2001), or any of the *Ultima* or *Zork* series, all of which generally do not require quick reflexes. Another element is the *identity* of the computer as a player. Keith Feinstein has suggested that the playing of a video game has a necessarily emotional element to it, similar to that of struggling against a playmate of comparable skill and ability. In his view, the computer must be more than a referee or stage manager controlling the video game's world; it must be an active opponent that competes with the human player. By assigning an identity to the computer player and creating a "one-on-one" situation within the game, competition becomes possible and emotional stakes are raised, just as they might be in a two-player game in which human beings compete against one another.

The programs mentioned above, however, are all marketed as games, and would be included in the broader definition of the term found in popular culture. Almost all programs designated as "games" by their makers contain the criteria mentioned above (conflict, rules, player ability, and valued outcomes), albeit to varying degrees. For example, in *SimCity* (1989) and the other "Sim" programs from Maxis Software, outcomes are ongoing as conditions of the simulated world improve or worsen depending on the player's decisions. Conflict occurs between the player (who is trying to provide order to the city) and circumstances or situations (such as natural disasters, taxpaying citizens, crime, pollution, and occasional wandering monsters). The "rules" are built into the game's responses; tax the citizens too much and they will move away, cut funding to the police station and the crime rate will rise, and so on. In puzzle-based games like *Myst* or *Riven*, conflict may arise from the difficulty of puzzle solving, pitting the player's mind against the game designer's mind. Outcomes are also valued in these games; in each, several different endings or outcomes are possible, one of which is more desirable than the others.

A still broader definition of the term "video games" might include educational or utility cartridges made for dedicated game consoles. Some of these, like *Mario Teaches Typing*, incorporate gameplay into learning, although many do not. Still, educational cartridges (like Atari 2600 cartridges *Basic Programming* and *Fun with Numbers*) and utility cartridges (such as diagnostic and test cartridges) often appear in lists of game cartridges, are sought by collectors, and are included within popular usages of the term "video games" found in stores and many Internet discussion groups. Even though these programs are technically not games (according to the above criteria), the read-only memory (ROM) cartridges containing them are the same as those used for games; they are also given identification numbers, similar to the games; and they receive much the same treatment as game cartridges in the marketplace. Thus, the criteria used to group educational and some utility programs together with games reflect their status as commercial and cultural artifacts more than they reflect actual considerations of the program's content or the player's experience of that content.

While the degree to which a program can be considered a game depends on varying criteria, its status as "video" is only slightly less problematic. By the strictest definition, "video" refers to the use of an analog intensity/brightness signal displayed on a cathode-ray tube (CRT), the kind of picture tube used in a television set or computer monitor, to produce raster-based imagery. A slightly looser and more common definition of "video games," closer to the popular usage of the term, would also include games that do not have raster graphics, like vector graphic games, and games that do not use a CRT, such as Nintendo Game Boy games, which use a liquid-crystal display. By these definitions, most arcade video games and home video games using a television, as well as games played on a home computer, would qualify technically as video games. Video games using CRTs also vary in resolution, including standard resolution (640 pixels by 200 lines); medium resolution (640 pixels by 400 lines); and VGA resolution (640 pixels by 480 lines), which is similar to full-resolution television imagery.

Some video game purists, however, might argue that the playing of home computer games constitutes a different experience from arcade and home video game systems, despite the interactive image and CRT used in the home computer games. Since arcade video games and home video games contain computers within them, the argument concerns the idea of the "dedicated processor" or "dedicated system" whose main—and only—function is the playing of video games. Some dedicated systems, like the Nintendo 64 or PlayStation 2, are designed with the connectivity needed for graphically complex games, unlike their home computer counterparts. Yet even early dedicated systems like the Fairchild/Zircon Channel F and the Atari 2600 had educational cartridges teaching math and programming, so they were not used for games only, but had other possible functions.

"Computer games," then, are most usefully seen as a subset of video games, due to shared technologies such as the microprocessor and the cathode-ray tube. Furthermore, many games are now released across multiple platforms at once; for example, *Myst* was released for Macintosh computers, IBM-compatible computers, and Philips CD-I, as well as for dedicated game-console systems like the 3DO Interactive Multiplayer, Atari Jaguar, and the Sony PlayStation. As dedicated systems grow in power and home computers grow in speed and connectivity, the two technologies may converge until only functional differences remain, as well as the degree to which a particular system can be said to be "dedicated" to game playing.

For a game to be considered a video game, one would expect the action of the game to take place interactively on-screen. Thus certain games, like the *Clue VCR Game*, a version of the board game *Clue* which uses video clips on videotape, would not qualify since the video image is not interactive; nor does the action of the game—such as the moving of a player's pieces—occur on-screen. Some games walk the line between board game and video game, involving elements of both. Three games for the Philips Videopac video game system, *Conquest of the World* (1982), *Quest for the Rings* (1982), and *The Great Wall Street Fortune Hunt* (1982), all involved on-screen video gameplay as well as a game board with movers, combining video game and board game play. As the other cartridges available for the Videopac system were all on-screen games, the three video/board games are usually listed along with them, although they are really hybrid games. There are also games which used plastic overlays placed on the screen, such as the early games for the Magnavox Odyssey 100 system or the GCE/Milton Bradley Vectrex system. These overlays contained background images and provided color to black-and-white screen graphics, while the screen provided the moving elements of the player-characters. A number of early arcade games also added nonvideo elements to their game screens, such as *Warrior* (1979), which featured two vector-graphics knights in top view moving through scenery on the screen's overlay. As long as the action itself takes place on-screen, such games can be considered as "video" games.

An even broader popular definition of "video games" includes games and systems whose "video" displays do not use a cathode-ray tube and whose screens have less resolution than a television screen. Nintendo's Virtual Boy system, for example, uses twin monochrome screens (one for each eye), which are high resolution light-emitting diode (LED) displays of 384 by 224 pixels. Sega's Game Gear, a hand-held system, has a liquid-crystal display (LCD) screen of 160 by 144 pixels. Nintendo's Game Boy system uses a reflective LCD screen of 160 by 144 pixels, but with the Super Game Boy, a converter that plugs into the Super Nintendo Entertainment System (SNES), Game Boy games can be played on a television screen through the SNES. And with even lower resolution screens, there is the Atari Lynx, with an LCD screen of 160 by 102 pixels, and the Milton Bradley Microvision system, with an LCD screen of only 16 by 16 pixels.

As we move beyond games using CRTs and screen resolution decreases, the question arises as to how much resolution is needed to call a game a "video" game. The hand-held game systems mentioned above are included in many lists of video games because they are produced by the same companies (Atari, Nintendo, Sega, etc.) that produce video game systems that use television screens, and because they are all cartridge-based systems (as opposed to hand-held electronic games which are hardwired to play one game only).

One of the most important questions regarding the game's visual display is whether or not the game's screen is pixel-based and capable of imaging. Many hand-held electronic games use LED and LCD displays, but are not based on a grid of pixels. Games such as Parker Brothers' *Merlin* (1978) or *Mattel Electronics Basketball* (1978) have banks of lights which can be turned on or off, and while in some cases the lights may be said to represent "players" (as in *Mattel Electronics Basketball*), the lights are not used together as imaging elements. Similarly, in games with LCD displays, like Bandai's *Invaders of the Mummy's Tomb* (1982) and *Escape from the Devil's Doom* (1982) or Mega Corp's *Fireman Fireman* (1980) or *The Exterminator* (1980), the LCD elements or cells that are turned on and off are often shaped like the game's characters in different poses and positions. These poses are laid out across the screen in such a way that they do not overlap, since the cells must be discrete to function independently. Thus the positions that characters can occupy are limited to a few nonoverlapping poses, which are turned on and off in sequence to suggest motion through a marquee-like effect. Whole images of characters are turned on or off, as opposed to pixels arranged in a grid which work together to create imagery.

The concept of a grid of pixels used for imaging, then, can be one criterion dividing the video game display from those used in other forms of electronic games. Pixels, as abstract picture elements (usually squares, rectangles, or dots), are all identical in shape and size and can be used in any part of an image. Only collectively do they produce a design which is recognizable as a character or object. (Pixels, of course, must also turn on and off and use the same marquee effect to suggest movement, but the Gestalt of movement they produce is a much more subtle one and improves with resolution.)

The screen which is a grid of pixels is a useful way to draw the line between the video game and many hand-held electronic games. Yet some hand-held games are occasionally included in a very broad definition of "video game" because they contain versions of arcade video games, for example Nintendo's LCD hand-held versions of *Donkey Kong Jr.* (1982), or Nelsonic's *Q*bert* wristwatch game of 1983. In both cases the game appears on a screen and play is analogous to the arcade game of which it is a version, even though it is highly simplified and the imaging technology is quite different.

The technology used in an electronic game or a video game often is a factor in determining what kind of form, content, and interaction the game can offer. In order to categorize video games and delineate the boundaries of the medium, then, it is useful to consider the different imaging technologies and modes of exhibition of the video game.

Imaging Technologies

Video games require displays whose images can be changed quickly. A variety of imaging technologies are used to produce video game imagery, resulting in different kinds of images. The vast majority of video games use either light-emitting diodes, liquid-crystal displays, vector graphics, raster graphics, or prerecorded video imagery on laserdisc, compact disc, or DVD-ROM.

As noted, certain game systems use light-emitting diode (LED) or liquid-crystal display (LCD) technologies to create their images. LED displays use diodes made with gallium arsenide phosphide, which produces light when a current is applied to the diode. LEDs can come in red, yellow, or green, although red LEDs are the most common. Although there are many hand-held electronic games that use LED displays, Nintendo's Virtual Boy is the only pixel-based imaging system to use an LED display.

The LCD contains a thin layer of long crystalline molecules that polarize light, sandwiched between grids of fine wires and polarizers. The polarizers are lined up in such a way that light passing through the crystals is polarized and reflected back to the viewer, resulting in a bright, clear square. When a current is applied to the grids, the molecules line up together in the same direction and have no polarizing effect, and light is absorbed, resulting in a darkened square. Early LCD screens were black and white, and can be found in many hand-held electronic games from the early 1980s, as well as game systems such as Milton Bradley's Microvision or Nintendo's Game Boy. Color LCD screens are now common, appearing in game systems like the Atari Lynx or Game Boy Color, as well as in most laptop computers.

Vector graphics and raster graphics both use a cathode-ray tube (CRT). The CRT, used in televisions and computer monitors, contains an electron gun at the narrow end of a funnel-shaped glass tube. The electron gun (a thermionic cathode) generates a very narrow, focused beam of electrons which is fired at the screen, located at the wide end of the tube. En route to the screen, the electron beam is deflected by electromagnetic means (such as coils or electrodes), which are controlled by an external signal. The deflected electron beam hits the inside of the screen, which is coated with phosphorescent (light-emitting) material. The electrons cause the material to fluoresce, or glow, producing the pixels of the image on the face of the screen.

Vector and raster graphics differ in the way they use the electron gun to produce the image on-screen. Vector graphics are made up of points and straight line segments, which are stored as coordinates in a set of display commands. The display commands are sent to a *vector generator*, which converts the commands into a signal that is sent to the monitor's beam-deflection circuits. Using this signal, the electron beam is deflected from one line segment endpoint to another, causing the beam to draw the vector lines onto the screen one by one. In vector graphics, all images are made up of line segments and points, and text characters are made up of collections of line segments. Because the path of the electron beam follows the command list instead of a preset scanning pattern, this process is also referred to as "random scan." Vector graphics were the earliest CRT-based computer graphics and were widespread by the late 1960s. Vector graphics appeared in a number of arcade video games in the late 1970s and early 1980s, and in one home game system, the GCE/Milton Bradley Vectrex, which appeared in 1982. The best-known arcade games using vector graphics include *Lunar Lander* (1979), *Asteroids* (1979), *Battlezone* (1980), *Tempest* (1981), *Star Wars* (1983), and *The Empire Strikes Back* (1985).

Raster graphics use the electron gun to draw an image onto the screen in much the same way that a television set does. The raster image is made up of a series of horizontal raster lines, each of which is a row of individual pixels. The raster image, then, is stored as a grid of pixels large enough to fill the screen. The electron gun is then deflected to draw the image onto the screen, one horizontal line after another, from top to bottom. Unlike the random scanning used for vector graphics, raster scanning uses the same electron beam deflection path for every image, allowing the preset path to be hardwired into the hardware. Filled shapes, text, and complex images are also easier to produce with raster scanning, and it is the method used in almost all computer graphics today.

Besides the use of graphics for text, there are different kinds of computer-generated raster graphics used in video games. They may be generated as two-dimensional, two-and-a-half-dimensional, or three-dimensional graphics. In games using two-dimensional graphics, all the characters, objects, and settings appear on a flat plane of space (as in most early Atari 2600 games). Moving objects are achieved through scaleable player-missile graphics, also known as "sprites," which are small pixel maps of a fixed size which can easily be redrawn at new coordinates. Examples of sprites are the individual space invaders in *Space Invaders* (1978), or the Pac-Man or ghost characters in *Pac-Man* (1980), or the bouncing balls or bullets used in shooting games.

Two-and-a-half-dimensional graphics involve overlapping planes of two-dimensional graphics, which is also referred to as "priority" (referring to the determination of which plane is drawn over the others). Through the use of multiple planes of imagery—one behind the other—which scroll through the screen at different rates, a sense of depth can be achieved. Objects can be made to appear to float over backgrounds and the effect of multiple layers can be achieved. Yet while the image is more than a single two-dimensional plane, it is not really three-dimensional either; thus the "and-a-half" is added to denote something in between. Two-and-a-half-dimensional graphics appear in the arcade games *Moon Patrol* (1982) and *Zaxxon* (1982), and in home video games like *Super Mario Bros. 3* (1990) and *Warioland* (1995).

Three-dimensional graphics are those which have been encoded as three-dimensional objects in the computer's memory, for example, cubes, cylinders, spheres, pyramids, or other polyhedra. These objects can be turned and rotated and appear at different angles, unlike the flat grids of pixels in two-dimensional graphics. Three-dimensional graphics appear in the arcade games *I, Robot* (1983), *Virtua Racing* (1992), and many arcade video games produced in the 1990s, as well as many home video games for the Sony PlayStation, Sega Saturn, and Nintendo 64. Some games use pre-rendered graphics stored as images, such as *Myst* (1993), *Gadget* (1993), or *Riven* (1997), while others like *Doom* (1993), *Daytona USA* (1994), or *Tomb Raider II* (1997) generate both foreground and background imagery in real time, allowing perspectives and viewing angles to be changed by the player during the game.

Although the dimensionality of a game's graphics depends on the way in which the graphics are programmed, it is not always obvious from the visuals alone. Two-dimensional and two-and-a-half-dimensional graphics are sometimes designed to appear three-dimensional, and there are a number of ways of representing a three-dimensional space (see Chapter 3). A variety of graphic styles and strategies are used from game to game, many of which are designed to produce images with depth cues and a dimensionality which lies somewhere between two and three dimensions.

Another imaging technology used in video games involves the use of prerecorded video imagery stored on laserdisc, compact disc, or DVD-ROM. Some games, like *Dragon's Lair* (1983), *Space Ace* (1984), and *Time Traveler* (1991), play video clips of animation during which the player is to make a response. Depending on the player's response and timing, the game cuts to various other clips, representing success or failure. Other games, such as *Astron Belt* (1983) and *Firefox* (1984), overlay traditional computer-generated graphics of planes and spaceships over video clips of moving backgrounds, providing more interactivity. (There was even a home laserdisc game system, Rick Dyer's Halcyon system, but at a retail price of over $2,000 it did not do well commercially.) Today, games for home systems using video clips appear on CD-ROM, often in compressed formats with imagery of reduced quality compared with that found on laserdisc. Games like *Star Trek: Borg* (1996) and *Johnny Mnemonic* (1995) contain branching, interactive narratives, whereas other games like *Myst* (1993), *Zork Nemesis* (1996), and *Riven* (1997) incorporate video imagery within computer-generated graphics.

While newer technologies like DVD-ROMs, networks, Internet video, and computer games actively reshape and extend the video game industry and the video game itself, the way in which a game is delivered to the public—its mode of exhibition—has always been an important consideration.

....

Modes of Exhibition

Over the years video games have appeared in a number of different venues, each with their own technologies, capabilities, market sector, and integration into the cultural production surrounding them. These different modes of exhibition include mainframe games, coin-operated arcade video games, home video game systems, hand-held portable games and game systems, and home computer games.

The games created on the giant mainframe computers of the 1960s were the earliest versions of video games, and were limited to the large, refrigerator-sized mainframe computers found only in laboratories and research centers. These games were experiments and were neither sold commercially nor generally available to the public. Some were quite simple, for example, games that played tic-tac-toe. The most famous mainframe game, however, and the earliest one by many accounts, is *Spacewar!* created in 1962 at the Hingham Institute in Cambridge, Massachusetts.[1] Written by Steve Russell, J. Martin Graetz, and others for the PDP-1 mainframe computer, *Spacewar!* consisted of two spaceships (the "needle" and "wedge") that could fly about the screen and fire missiles at each other. Other additions to the game included a starfield background, a star with gravity that pulled the spaceships into itself, and a "hyperspace" feature allowing ships to disappear and reappear elsewhere on the screen. The game was quite small by today's standards; 4 kilobytes, with 6 bits per byte and 3 bytes per word. *Spacewar!* was copied and adapted to other computers throughout the 1960s, and influenced other programmers. In 1971 it was adapted by Nolan Bushnell into the first arcade game, *Computer Space*, and later a version of it appeared among the first cartridges for the Atari 2600 home video game system.

Coin-operated arcade games are perhaps the best-known variety of video games, and were the first and foremost mode of exhibition which brought video games to the public. There are several different forms of

---

arcade games, each allowing for a different type of interaction: stand-alone consoles, cocktail consoles, sit-inside games, and virtual reality style games.

A stand-alone console, the most common kind, is a tall boxlike cabinet which houses the video screen and the control panel for the game. The game's controls might include joysticks, track-balls, paddles (round, rotating knobs), buttons, guns with triggers, and so forth. Occasionally there are controls for more than one player, although single-player games are the most common.

The "cocktail" console is designed like a small table, with the screen facing upward through a glass tabletop. Often the game is designed for two players, and there are sets of controls on both ends of the table, with the screen between them. This type of console is popular in bars or restaurants where patrons can sit and play a video game while setting their drinks on the tabletop (hence the name "cocktail"). Two-player games in cocktail consoles often are designed so that the screen can be viewed from either side, and usually contain games with an overhead view of a playing field (for example, a football game which is viewed from above) so that neither player has an upside-down view.

Sit-inside or ride-on consoles hold or contain the player's body during play and can even involve physical movement of the player's body, usually to simulate the driving or flying of a vehicle in the game, typically with a first-person perspective point of view. The games range from merely having a seat in front of the screen to enclosing the player in a box or even moving the seated player around during the game. In driving and racing games, foot pedals and stick shifts are sometimes included as well. Other types of interaction are possible; *Prop Cycle* (1993), for example, has the player pedaling a bicycle, while *Alpine Racer* (1995) has the player holding ski pole handles and standing on movable skis that lean from side to side during turns. In Sega's *Top Skater* (1997), the player rides on a skateboard, while in Namco's *Final Furlong* (1997) the player rides a "horse." These games tend to be more expensive than other types of games, sometimes requiring as many as four or five quarters per game.

Although virtual reality–style games are often hyped in movies, they have yet to become popular at the arcade; *Dactyl Nightmare* (1992) was the only one available throughout the 1990s, possibly because of its higher cost and need for an attendant. Each player stands inside a circular railing on a raised platform, wearing headsets with miniature screens for each eye, while holding a gunlike device with a trigger, an image of which also appears on-screen. The game consists of two players wandering around an abstract setting composed of platforms, walls, and stairs, trying to find and shoot each other. Adding to the action is a green pterodactyl that occasionally picks up players and drops them. The players' views are sometimes shown on two monitors so that bystanders can watch the game from both points of view. The game's virtual reality interface is a novel feature, but the cost is high (usually about $4.00 for four minutes), and the setup requires an attendant to be on duty, which raises the cost of exhibition. Besides appearing in arcades, *Dactyl Nightmare* has also traveled as a fairground exhibit, its monitors often successfully drawing a crowd of bystanders.

Contemporaneous with arcade games, home video game systems appeared in 1972 with the release of the Magnavox Odyssey Model ITL-200 system designed by Ralph Baer. Home video game systems typically use a television for their graphic displays, although some systems, such as the GCE/Milton Bradley Vectrex or Nintendo Virtual Boy, are designed to sit on a tabletop and come complete with their own screens. Home game systems which display their graphics on a television can be console-, cartridge-, or laserdisc-based systems.

Console-based systems like *PONG*, Wonder Wizard, or Atari Tank have their games hardwired into them and are ready to go when the console is turned on. Many of the very early home video game systems were console based and had games such as tennis, hockey, and table tennis, most of which were variants of ball-and-paddle games. (Magnavox television model 4305 even had a built-in color *PONG*-like game with controllers that connected to the TV set.)

Cartridge-based game systems have their games hardwired into cartridges or cards which are plugged into the game console, allowing new games to be made for the console and sold separately. The first cartridge-based systems was the Fairchild/Zircon Channel F in 1976, although the 1972 Magnavox Odyssey ITL-200 system was plug-in card programmable and originated the idea of interchangeable games.[2] The Fairchild/Zircon Channel F came preprogrammed with *Hockey* and *Tennis*, in addition to having a cartridge slot for which twenty-six cartridges were made. The best-known early cartridge-based system is, of course, the Atari 2600, released in 1977. Cartridge-based systems could provide more games than purely console-based systems (some systems, like the Atari 2600 and the Nintendo SNES, have hundreds of cartridges available), and soon became the main kind of system produced.

Although most systems used the cards or cartridges with read-only memory (ROM) hardwired into them, Rick Dyer's Halcyon system used laserdiscs, which could store video images. As noted, this system was too high priced for most consumers and did not last long on the market.

Hand-held portable games and game systems give players more flexibility than home video game systems since they run on batteries and can be carried along with the player. Hand-held games are usually small enough to fit in the palm of one's hand, and have small LED or LCD screens with buttons and controls beneath the screen or to the sides of the screen. Some of these games (although perhaps not always technically video games themselves) are simplified versions of video games from other systems, such as Nintendo's LCD hand-held *Donkey Kong Jr.* (1982), or games using the same characters, such as *Mario's Cement Factory* (1983). While most of these games are self-contained, there are hand-held cartridge-based systems as well, including Milton Bradley Microvision, Nintendo Game Boy, Game Boy Color, and Atari Lynx.

Although many arcade games and home video game systems have computers built into them, they are dedicated systems whose only purpose is to deliver video games. Beginning in the late 1970s and throughout the 1980s, home computers became available and their numbers grew quickly. Early video game systems helped to usher them in, as early home game systems like *PONG* and the Atari 2600 were often the first computer products to enter people's homes. And game playing has always been one of the more popular uses of home computers. Game software was available for practically every type of home computer, on floppy disk, tape drive, cartridge, diskette, or CD-ROM. Systems, like the Texas Instruments 99/4a computer, had a built-in slot for game cartridges, and other computers, like Coleco's ADAM and the Atari 400 and 800, were even made by game companies. While cartridges for the Atari 2600 contained 2 or 4 kilobytes and later 8 or 16 kilobytes of ROM, computer games stored on floppy disks could be several times larger in size. Storage media like magnetic disks could also be written on, allowing games in progress to be saved, which in turn meant that more complex games, taking more than an afternoon to play or solve, could be produced.

Today most computer games no longer fit on a single disk or diskette but have moved to CD-ROMs (compact disc, read-only memory). While a typical 5¼-inch floppy held around 164 kilobytes, and today's 3½-inch diskettes hold a little over a megabyte, a CD-ROM holds about 660 megabytes. The great increase in the amount of storage on a CD-ROM allows longer and more detailed games, as well as higher resolution graphics which add to verisimilitude. Many games, such as *Riven* (1997), *Star Trek: Borg* (1996), and *Phantasmagoria* (1995), take up multiple CD-ROMs. Newer technologies such as DVD-ROMs, which hold several gigabytes of data, can contain even larger games, and networked games played on-line can also be enormous.

In networked games, which are typically role-playing games (RPG), multiple participants are connected via modem to a video game world on a server, and can interact with the world and with each other's characters. These games can be run locally, over a LAN (Local Area Network), or on the Internet from anywhere in the world. Because many offices have computers networked together, gameplay has entered the workplace, with games like *Quake 3: Team Arena* (2000), *Unreal Tournament* (2000), and *Half-Life* being played during lunchtime and after hours (and, no doubt, in some cases during the workday as well). Networked games have grown in popularity, and in size, from games like *Sceptre* in the mid-1980s, which could have a maximum of sixteen players on-line at once, to 1997's *Ultima Online*, which has thousands of characters and requires multiple servers. Networked games have the potential for being the largest and most detailed video games (for example, *Ultima Online* is said to have "more than 189 million square feet of virtual surface"[3] in its world), as well as for having the largest numbers of players playing together. Many of these games run twenty-four hours a day, with players logging on and off whenever they want.

Although some people make a distinction between "video games" and "computer games," games are often "ported" (rewritten into different computer languages or systems) from one platform to another, broadening their markets and appearing in multiple modes of exhibition. Many dedicated game systems now have larger memories, faster speeds, and use CD-ROMs instead of cartridges. Computer emulation programs can simulate different game systems on a computer, with varying degrees of success. Even the notion of the "dedicated system" may soon be a thing of the past; Sony's PlayStation 2, for example, is designed primarily as a game system, but it also can play DVDs and audio CDs, go on the Internet, and download and store digital music and video from the World Wide Web.

The wide range of modes of exhibition has contributed to both the size and success of the video game industry. The forms these modes have taken, as well as the content of video games, are the result of the influences, precursors, and historical context in which the video game was born and raised.

Context, Influences, and Precursors

Like the invention of cinema, the invention of the video game was the product of many researchers, experimenters, inventors, and entrepreneurs, and its initial form was influenced by other media and technology already in existence. The various forces that converged to produce the video game tended to gravitate around the two poles of art and technology. The 1960s in general saw a convergence of art and technology, and the spirit of experimentation that existed provided a fertile ground for interest in and acceptance of new media.

Apart from the computer itself, much of the technology used by the video game was already firmly in place by the 1960s. Television was well established in the majority of American homes, and as the size of its cabinet shrank and its screen grew, it became more of an appliance and less of a piece of furniture (except for the sets with the largest screens, which were available in wooden floor-standing cabinets into the late 1970s). All that remained to be added was the microprocessor (in the video game console) to supply the television with image and sound, and it was a company that made televisions, Magnavox, that would purchase and market the first home video game system, the Magnavox Odyssey Model ITL200.

By the 1960s, computer graphics were already into their second decade of development. In 1949, the Whirlwind mainframe computer at the Massachusetts Institute of Technology became the first computer to use a CRT as a graphic display. The Whirlwind was shown to the general public on a 1951 episode of Edward R. Murrow's *See It Now*, and demonstrated a bouncing ball program and calculation of a rocket trajectory. Mainframes continued to be produced during the 1950s and became more accessible outside the military establishment. In 1962, around the same time *Spacewar!* was being written, Ivan Sutherland completed his Sketchpad system as a doctoral thesis at the Massachusetts Institute of Technology. The program allowed a user to create graphics on-screen interactively, using a light pen to draw directly on the CRT screen. By 1963, the trade periodical *Computers and Automation* was already sponsoring a competition for computer art, and the late 1960s saw a number of museum exhibitions displaying computer graphics.

Once interactive display graphics were wed to the cathode ray tube, the only remaining barriers to the commercial production of video games were public access and affordability. During the 1960s, minicomputers were starting to replace mainframes in some areas, but they were still neither small enough nor cheap enough for efficient mass production. These problems were solved in 1971 with the microprocessor, invented by Marcian E. Hoff, an engineer at the Intel Corporation. The microprocessor is a central processor placed on a chip, and it allows computer components to be produced more cheaply and in greater quantity. The microprocessor made possible the development of the home video game and the personal computer, as well as cheaper and smaller electronic calculators. Using the new technology, Nolan Bushnell translated *Spacewar!* into a smaller unit containing the electronic circuitry necessary to deliver interactive graphics, which he set, along with a monitor and control panel, into a tall, floor-standing plastic cabinet. The game was renamed *Computer Space*, and appeared in 1971. The following year he used his profits to produce a second game *PONG*, which was more successful and widespread, and became many people's first experience of a video game.

One of Bushnell's most important contributions to the video game was the addition of a coin slot, making the video game a profitable venture and soon a commercial industry. The video game joined a long line of coin-operated machines reaching back into the 1880s, when saloon owners began installing coin-operated machines for bar patrons to compete on, or place bets on, as well as vending machines. Due to their success, there were soon a wide variety of coin-operated machines—strength testers, slot machines, card machines, racing games, and other "trade stimulators," as well as the coin-operated mutoscopes and kinetoscopes that paved the way for the cinema.[4]

Free-standing and countertop coin-operated machines could be found in saloons, parlors, and shop-lined arcades, and continued to flourish into the 1930s and early 1940s. The pinball machine developed out of these machines during the 1930s, and was produced by companies that produced other games, like the Bally Corporation or the Bingo Novelty Company. Through a series of innovations, the pinball machine gradually evolved into the form players are familiar with today. In 1933 electricity was added, and lights and backglasses were added in 1934. The pinball bumper was added in 1937, and the flipper in 1947.[5] After World War II, the pinball game saw its golden age, from 1948 to 1958.

Although pinball games flourished as a source of cheap entertainment during the Depression and war years, they were popular enough that their prices did increase. Originally pinball games cost a nickel per play, but later cost a quarter (today some even charge fifty cents or more). During the

---

early 1970s, the video game was able to achieve commercial success through its integration into the same market venues as the pinball game (at a similar price, a quarter a play). In the years that followed, video games quickly grew into an industry. Besides new companies like Nutting Associates, Kee Games, and Atari, companies producing pinball games such as Bally and Gottlieb also became producers of video games. For players in the arcade, the video game could be seen as one of the newest technological developments in arcade coin-operated gaming.

The early games' content was also influenced by technology. The explosion of technological developments in the United States following World War II, and particularly the space program, renewed the public's interest in science and science fiction. J. Martin Graetz acknowledges that science fiction novels by authors such as E. E. Smith and the science fiction films of Japan's Toho Films Studios (best known for Godzilla movies) were the main influences on the writing of *Spacewar!*[6] Throughout their entire history, video games have maintained a solid tradition of spaceships, shooting, and monsters, and science fiction themes have dominated the market. Computer graphics of the late 1960s and early 1970s, however, were not sophisticated enough to easily and cheaply produce detailed, representational moving imagery in real time, so simple iconography (dots, squares, rectangles) had to suffice. Detail and complexity were sacrificed for fast, immediate, and interactive action; a player could imagine the details, but action had to be depicted as a *visual* display.

Although their simplicity was due to technological limitations and not the result of deliberate artistic choices, the minimal, often abstract graphics of early video games fit in rather well with trends in the art world during the 1960s. During the 1950s, abstract art came to dominate the New York City art scene, and many strands of it developed into the 1960s. There were color-field painters like Barnett Newman and Mark Rothko, and the "hard-edge" painting style of painters like Ellsworth Kelly and Alexander Liberman, emphasizing simple forms and geometric simplicity. Influenced by these and other abstract movements, minimalist art developed in the mid-to-late 1960s. Artists such as Donald Judd, Sol Lewitt, Tony Smith, and others worked with squares, cubes, stripes, geometric shapes, and other minimal forms to create abstractions. Early video game graphics, with their points, lines, and blocks of color, often on a black background, coincided with minimalist, abstract styles of art. Likewise, electronic music developed during the 1960s and came to be known for its new computer-generated sounds and sometimes repetitious compositions. Electronic sounds could be generated and repeated by a computer, and soon synthesized beeps and boops became the computer-generated soundtracks for video games.

The time-based and interactive nature of the video game also fit in with trends in 1960s art. The "happenings" of artists like John Cage and Allan Kaprow emphasized experience and process over product (sometimes including the audience's participation), and Sol Lewitt's famous essay of 1967, "Paragraphs on Conceptual Art," placed more importance on concept than on a tangible art object. There were also performances known as "light shows," like Jordan Belson's Vortex Concerts, or the light works of The Single Wing Turquoise Bird, a Los Angeles group that created abstract projections of light and color for rock concerts in the late 1960s. These shows were huge projections of shifting, moving light and color patterns which were designed primarily as experiences that could never be repeated exactly; chance often played a part in their making. Art installations using video cameras and monitors also appeared around this time. In 1970, Gene Youngblood's book *Expanded Cinema* explored the merger of art and technology of the time and included sections entitled "Television as a Creative Medium" and "Cybernetic Cinema and Computer Films," acknowledging the growing role of television and computer graphics in the visual arts.[7]

The video game, with its abstract, minimalist graphics, represented a new use for television and video; its experiential elements—the real-time interaction with an on-screen image—allowed players to feel as if they were communing with a machine that responded instantly to their actions. Besides coinciding with trends in art and a growing public interest in computer technology, the video game fit in popular culture as well, finding a place in the arcade next to pinball machines, and at home on the television. The video game, then, was perhaps the most commercially successful combination of art and technology to emerge in the early 1970s, and in many cases, the first computer technology widely available to the public and the first to enter their homes. As entertainment, it would soon come to compete with film and television, providing another source of diegetic or on-screen "worlds" of sight and sound—but one in which a player could directly interact.

During the first three decades of the video game's existence, the diegetic worlds of the games steadily improved and grew, and their form was heavily influenced by cinematic visual grammar. Throughout the 1970s and into the 1980s, computer processing power and memory grew, and the somewhat sparse look and feel of the early games gradually gave way to more detailed and representational graphics. As the games' visuals developed, games began using different styles of lighting, different points of view, continuity editing, and other techniques from film and television. Games became more character centered. Visually, backgrounds had more scenery and became locations, and there was often more narrative context surrounding the action of the game. By the 1990s, video games had title screens, end credits, cutting between different sequences, multiple points of view, multiple locations, and increasingly detailed storylines. Many films and television shows were adapted into video games, and during the 1990s, a number of video games became theatrical motion pictures.

The video game medium has matured and continues to develop. While it may borrow or imitate forms from other media such as film and television, the video game as a medium includes new elements such as interactivity, collaboration and competition between players, and labyrinthine narrative structures, as well as new ways of structuring space, time, and narrative (see Chapters 3, 4, and 5). Video games have become a major force, commercially and culturally, and continue to carve out their niche among other media.

....

Notes

1. The information on the development of *Spacewar!* is taken from J. Martin Graetz, "The Origin of *Spacewar!*" *Creative Computing* (August 1981). Although its graphics were displayed on a CRT, *Spacewar!* did not video encode its imagery, so by narrower, more technical definitions, it would not be a "video" game. Also, see Ralph Baer's preface in this book concerning *Spacewar!* and the PDP-1 mainframe computer.

2. According to Ralph Baer,

The first Odyssey (ITL-200) game was plug-in card programmable. The plug-in cards were printed circuit boards that interconnected the circuitry internal to the console in different ways to change the "game." These changes were showing or not showing a vertical bar at the left or at center, or making the bar half height (for volleyball) etc. The first appearance of a cartridge which contains a Read-Only-Memory chip . . . that was indeed introduced by the Fairchild machine which was among the first video game console to have a programmable micro-processor chip in it, something not even a gleam in anyone's eye in 1967–68 when we designed the original circuitry form our Brown Box (which became the Odyssey game).

Therefore, the concept of changing games by plugging a specific cart (or Card) into a videogame console was definitely pioneered by the Magnavox Odyssey. It is hard to believe that the Odyssey choice of plugging in a card didn't ring bells with the Fairchild engineers who were designing their machine around a micro-processor and ROM, a combination well known by the mid-seventies.

From an e-mail from Ralph Baer, October 18, 2000.

3. Cindy Yars, "*Ultima Online*: Playing in the Garden of Eden," *Computer Games Strategy Plus* (July 1997), p. 45.

4. Richard M. Bueschel, *Guide to Vintage Trade Simulators and Countertop Games* (Atglen, Pa.: Schiffer, 1997).

5. Ken Durham, "History of Pinball Machines," GameRoom Antiques website, http://www.olg.com/gameroomantiques/historyPin.htm, as seen on February 13, 1998.

6. J. Martin Graetz, "The Origin of *Spacewar!*" *Creative Computing* (August 1981).

7. Gene Youngblood, *Expanded Cinema* (New York: E. P. Dutton, 1970).

Super Mario Nation

S t e v e n   L .   K e n t

In 1962 an MIT student named Steven Russell pulled off the ultimate hack. Russell was the kind of kid people make jokes about: short, full of nervous energy, passionately devoted to B-grade science fiction, shy, and brilliant. He worked with the Tech Model Railroad Club, a campus organization that had recently begun turning its focus from toy trains to computers. TMRC members had their own vocabulary. Rolling chairs were "bunkies," for instance, and broken equipment was "munged." Impressive feats and practical jokes were "hacks."

Russell's hack was creating the first interactive computer game.

Today, when the ubiquitous Mario brothers are as deeply ingrained in the national consciousness as the Disney menagerie, when arcade games of late Roman brutality are vivid enough to have prompted a Senate investigation, when the voracious M&Ms that made *Pac-Man* the most popular arcade game of all time have become the furniture of a shared past, it is strange to think how brief the history is that has propelled this fixture into our lives: just a quarter-century this year since the first video game went on the market, and thirty-five years since Steven Russell's masterstroke.

Russell created his game on a Digital Equipment Company PDP-1, one of the first computers to display data on a screen instead of printing it out. Given his deep immersion in science fiction, it took the form of something he called *Spacewar!*

"I started out with a little prototype that just flew the spaceships around," he says, "Pete Sampson added a program called Expensive Planetarium that displayed stars as a background. Dan Edwards did some very clever stuff to get enough time so that we could compute the influence of gravity on the spaceships. The final version of that was done in the spring of '62."

In *Spacewar!* the players controlled either a curvy Buck Rogers-style spaceship nicknamed the Wedge or a cigar-shaped rocket called the Needle. It was an accurate portrayal of the physics of space: the ships floated in their frictionless battlefield, and if they strayed too close to the sun in the middle of the screen, they got caught in its gravity and were destroyed.

It was a two-player game. The PDP-1, which was larger than many automobiles but tiny in comparison with many of the computers of the time, did not have enough processing power to create the artificial intelligence required to pilot one of the rockets.

Spacewar! was originally controlled by toggle switches built into a panel on the computer. But the awkwardly placed switches gave the players sore elbows, and after a while some TMRC members cobbled together another set of switches and ran wires between them and the PDP-1—the world's first controllers for the world's first video game.

Russell never copyrighted his game. There was no reason to: he could not market it. PDP-1 computers sold for $120,000, and very few people had access to them. In the end *Spacewar!* became shareware that Digital Equipment technicians used to test their machines.

One person who enjoyed it was Nolan Bushnell. Bushnell liked computers and he liked games. He was working his way through the University of Utah by running midway games at an amusement park—but otherwise it is hard to imagine someone less like Steven Russell than the tall, gregarious, charismatic Bushnell.

He was fortunate in his choice of school. "In the late 1960s," he recalls, "if you wanted to connect a computer up to a telephone or a video screen, you did it only in three places in the world or known universe: the University of Utah, MIT, or Stanford. And it was just serendipity that I went to school at Utah." Bushnell spent hour upon hour playing games in the university's computer lab. His favorite game was *Spacewar!*

In 1968 he graduated and took a job at Ampex, an engineering firm in Northern California. By 1970 he'd decided to merge his formal education with the lessons he'd learned on the midway. He converted his two-year-old daughter's bedroom into a workshop and began looking for an inexpensive way to turn *Spacewar!* into a coin-operated novelty that could be marketed like a pinball game.

The cost of computers had come down in the ten years since Russell created *Spacewar!* but they were still far too expensive to be used as arcade machines. Bushnell came up with a solution. Rather than put the game on a computer, a processor capable of handling several kinds of tasks, he set about designing a single-function machine that could perform just one task: game playing.

He did it on the cheap. "Ampex had a policy that for hobbies they'd give you the parts. Everybody called them 'G-jobs'. As long as it wasn't excessive . . . I mean, they were just fifteen- or twenty-cent items."

Bushnell's first game, *Computer Space*, was a stripped-down version of *Spacewar!* its monitor a black-and-white television he had bought at a Goodwill store.

With his prototype, Bushnell set about using his vigorous powers of persuasion to get someone to manufacture the game. When Bill Nutting, founder of a small electronics company called Nutting Associates, agreed, Bushnell quit Ampex and joined his firm. Nutting manufactured 1,500 copies of *Computer Space* by 1972, but for all Bushnell's eloquent zeal, the company had trouble marketing its creation in the bars and bowling alleys where coin-operated games were mostly found in those days. The people who saw *Computer Space* were confused by its five-button control scheme and lacked the patience to read the two solid pages of instructions that accompanied it.

Nutting wanted to continue manufacturing "television games," but Bushnell blamed him for the failure of *Computer Space*, claiming the company had mismarketed the game and failed to give it adequate support. He turned instead to a friend named Ted Dabney. Dabney chipped in $250, and the two started their own company. They wanted to call it Syzygy, a word referring to the alignment of three celestial bodies, but found (to their considerable surprise) that the name was already spoken for. Finally they lit on a word in the Japanese strategy game *Go* that was the equivalent of "check" in chess. The word was *Atari*.

A man named Al Alcorn was Atari's first full-time engineer, and he was an exceptionally clever one. One day Bushnell told Alcorn that no less a client than General Electric had ordered from Atari a tennislike computer game that would feature two paddles swatting a ball back and forth across a television screen.

It was a total lie. Bushnell had not spoken with General Electric; he simply wanted to acquaint Alcorn with the mechanics of creating computer games and thought the engineer might not be motivated if he knew that the task was merely an exercise. When Alcorn finished the game, Bushnell and Dabney knew it was marketable. They tested the prototype of *PONG* in a rustic Sunnyvale, California, bar named Andy Capp's Tavern, in September 1972.

Nolan Bushnell was not the first person to conceive a computerized tennis game. In 1966 Ralph Baer, the manager of the equipment design division of a military contracting firm called Sanders Associates, had begun seeking a new use for television sets. Baer, a German-born Jew who had emigrated to America as a teenager shortly before World War II, was a precise, austere man who documented every step of his invention process.

He put together a small team of engineers to create games that could be played on a television. In June 1967 the team began work on a game in which players used paddles to catch a dot as it flew across a television screen. When a team member suggested hitting the dot instead of catching it, the game evolved into computerized Ping-Pong. Baer documented his work at each stage.

As a military contractor, Sanders Associates could not market the toy. Baer tried to sell his idea to other companies, and although RCA and a couple of smaller competitors came close to purchasing the technology, they ultimately backed away. It took Baer three years to find a licensee; in 1971 Magnavox purchased Baer's license and used it to create the Odyssey, the world's first home video game console. Within a year Magnavox began presenting its new toy to dealers around the country in private showings. In May 1972, four months before *PONG* made its debut at Andy Capp's, the Odyssey was demonstrated at a trade show in Burlingame, California. Nolan Bushnell attended that show—a fact that would soon lead to litigation.

In the beginning Bushnell had envisioned Atari as a company that designed games and sold them to established manufacturers. Shortly after setting up *PONG* in the tavern, Bushnell went to Chicago to try to sell the game to Bally or Midway, two leading pinball manufacturers. While he was away, Al Alcorn received a late-night telephone call that changed everything.

It was the manager of Andy Capp's, calling to say that the *PONG* machine had just stopped working. He went on to tell about something curious that had happened. "Al, this is the weirdest thing." Alcorn remembered his saying, "When I opened the bar this morning, there were two or three people at the door wanting to get in. They walked in and played that machine. They didn't buy anything. I've never seen anything like this before."

Alcorn went over to fix the machine. Not knowing what to expect, he sprang the coin box to give himself a free game, and a torrent of silver gushed out. The game wasn't broken, just choked; players had fed so many quarters into the coin slot that it had simply jammed. Alcorn scooped up handfuls of change, stuffed them in his pockets, walked jingling over to the

THE EMERGENCE OF THE VIDEO GAME

manager, and handed him a business card. "Next time this happens," he said, "you call me at home right away. I can always fix this one."

The excited engineer called Bushnell in Chicago to tell him the news. Surprised by *PONG*'s instant success, Bushnell changed his plans: instead of selling the game to a manufacturer, Atari would build it. Unfortunately he had already had an initial round of meetings in which he discussed the game with executives at Bally and Midway. Now he had to find a way to convince them that *PONG* was a bad idea without arousing their suspicions.

So the next time Bushnell met with Bally executives he led them to believe that Midway had already passed on the game. This made Bally's people so nervous that they backed off, and so he was telling no more than the truth by the time he sat down with Midway and announced that Bally had pulled out. Freed of entanglements by his shrewd piece of antisalesmanship, Bushnell hurried back to California and secured a $50,000 line of credit, which he used to set up a 2,000-square-foot manufacturing plant.

PONG was an immediate hit. By the end of 1973 Atari had sold 2,500 machines; by the end of 1974, 8,000. The similarities between *PONG* and the tennis game on the Odyssey did not escape Magnavox's attention, and the larger company soon brought suit, charging that Bushnell had blatantly copied its game. Bushnell maintained, as he does to this day, that he invented *PONG* on his own. In later cases against other video game companies, Magnavox's lawyers claimed that Bushnell had actually played tennis on the Odyssey for half an hour; Bushnell has always denied this. Nevertheless, Bushnell could not afford a court battle with a massive company like Magnavox, and he agreed to pay a $700,000 licensing fee; all future competitors would have to pay Magnavox even steeper amounts.

Over the next few years Atari put out several games, many of them highly derivative: *Pin PONG, Dr. PONG, PONG Doubles,* and *Quadra PONG.* During this time Bushnell bought out Ted Dabney. He thought his partner "still had small company ideas."

While Atari was busy releasing its own *PONG* imitations, other companies were too. Atari's success had, Bushnell declared, surrounded him with "jackals," and through the 1970s and early 1980s the most fiercely competitive jackal was Midway Manufacturing. Unlike Atari, Midway did not develop all its own products. Its earliest successes came from Taito, a Japanese company.

Gun Fight (1975), Midway's first video game hit, was a Western shootout in which players used pistol grip joysticks to move cowboys up and down the screen as they squeezed off shots at one another.

When Midway's engineers first tested *Gun Fight*, they were dismayed: the graphics were crude and blocky, the movement of the gunfighters very limited. In hopes of salvaging the game, Midway went to an outside designer named David Nutting, the brother of Bill Nutting, the man who had hired Nolan Bushnell to build *Computer Space*. By this time Nutting Associates had gone out of business, and Bill Nutting was in a very different field of endeavor, flying relief supplies and missionaries into impoverished African nations. Dave Nutting, however, went on to create several classic games—and to revolutionize the industry.

The prototypical *Gun Fight* that Midway's people handed Nutting simply featured two cowboys shooting at each other. Nutting sharpened the graphics, then looked for a way to put obstacles between the fighters. His proposed changes would drink up an inordinate amount of power, but Nutting saw a way around this. His improved—and highly successful—*Gun Fight* was one of the first games built with a microprocessor.

At about the same time, a different jackal introduced another durable component to the video game industry: social alarm. In 1976 the Exidy company released a game called *Death Race 98* that had players drive a car along a haunted road beside a cemetery. Gremlins and skeletons would materialize in the road, and players earned points by hitting them with their cars. Despite Exidy's nicety in calling them "gremlins," they were in fact stick figures—people—and their advent caused the first national outcry against video game violence.

A woman in Babylon, New York, was so offended that she launched a very effective one-person campaign against video game violence, alerting *Donahue* and *60 Minutes* viewers to the potential spiritual carnage. "It's very tame by today's standards," says Eddie Adlum, publisher of *RePlay* magazine, who is all but omniscient about video game history, looking back on *Death Race 98*. "Every time you made a hit, a little cross would appear on the monitor signifying a grave. Nice game. Fun. Bottom line, the game really took off when TV stations started to get some complaints from irate parents that this was a terrible example to set for children. The industry got a lot of coast-to-coast coverage during news programs. The end result was that Exidy sales jumped."

Communities passed zoning laws that discouraged arcade companies from building new locations. But by now the games were beginning to come into homes themselves.

Despite *PONG*'s success, the Magnavox Odyssey never sold very well. Baer had originally seen his invention as an inexpensive novelty, something that could be manufactured cheaply and sold for $20 or $30. Magnavox executives had other plans. They built twelve games into its circuits and sold the system with cards, poker chips, and plastic overlays to create suitable backgrounds for whatever was being played. The final package sold for $100—too much for a simple novelty—and then the people who were marketing the Odyssey made an even bigger mistake: they hinted that it worked only on Magnavox television sets. Predictably, this dim ploy did not sell more Magnavoxes; it frightened away would-be Odyssey purchasers. In 1972, the game's first year of life, only slightly more than 100,000 Odysseys were sold.

In 1975 Nolan Bushnell took Atari into the home market. One of Al Alcorn's engineers had proposed a home console version of *PONG*, and the team designed a working prototype based on the same digital technology used in the arcade game. The big dilemma lay not in building the product but in selling it. Toy stores rejected it because it cost too much; like the Odyssey, it carried a suggested retail price of $100, and one toy buyer told Bushnell that the only product his store carried that cost more than $29 was a bicycle.

Nor were electronics buyers enthusiastic. They saw home *Pong* as a toy, and a mere novelty at that. The public no longer cared about digital watches; why would television games be different? They were all too aware of the Odyssey's sorry sales record.

One person who was interested, however, was Tom Quinn, the sports department buyer at the Sears, Roebuck headquarters in Chicago. As Bushnell tells it, "The guy had done really well the year before on Ping-Pong tables. In winter the sporting goods section would sell some hockey equipment and a few basketballs, and that was about it. To make his Christmas numbers, the Sears buyer was focusing on Ping-Pong tables and pool tables, and he thought consumer *PONG* might be just the thing for the family rec room."

Quinn said he'd visit Atari the next time he was in California. Three days later he dropped in at the offices at 8:00 A.M., before any of the company's executive team arrived. He wanted to arrange an exclusive deal between Atari and Sears. His enthusiasm prompted Bushnell to take one final stab at selling home *PONG* himself, but finally he accepted Quinn's terms.

The next step was persuading other Sears executives to support the product. Quinn arranged for a demonstration in a conference room on the twenty-seventh floor of the Sears Tower in Chicago. A daunting group of executives in business suits filled the room and watched as Alcorn hooked a home *PONG* prototype to a television set and turned the game on. Nothing happened.

Thinking as fast as he ever had in his life, Alcorn figured out the problem. The Sears Tower has an antenna on the roof that broadcasts a signal on Channel 3; the home *PONG* prototype was set for Channel 3, and the broadcast blocked out its signal. Alcorn told a colleague to cover for him and grabbed the prototype. "I turned it upside-down and opened the bottom up. I got it to work in about ten minutes. I was sweating now and ready to jump out the window. This was too much pressure for the kid.

"So I finally played the game and it all worked and they were OK, but I could see that something was bothering them. They had seen inside the prototype while I was adjusting it.

"I said, 'We'll replace the wires with a silicon chip that's the size of a fingernail.'

"Carl Lind, the head of the department, says, 'Mr. Alcorn, you're telling me that you're going to reduce that rat's nest of wire to a little piece of silicon the size of your fingernail?'

"'Yes, sir.'

"He looked at me, leaned over the table, and said, 'How are you going to solder the wires to it?'"

Home *PONG* received more than enough support. Quinn asked how many units Atari could manufacture. When Bushnell told him 75,000 in time for Christmas, Quinn insisted that he double that output. Bushnell agreed.

Sears executives calculated the success of the products in their catalogue by comparing dollars with inches: they measured the amount of space given to each product and matched it to the amount of dollars they grossed. Through 1975 the reigning champion was an Adidas sneaker. By the beginning of 1976, home *PONG* had emerged as the new dollars-to-inches champion.

That year was a tumultuous one for the young industry, with several companies wrestling for leadership in the home market. There was a shortage of microchips, and because Coleco, a name derived from the Connecticut Leather Company, was the only outfit that received a full shipment of chips in 1976, it became the biggest home console manufacturer that spring. By August, however, Fairchild Camera and Instrument had released the Channel F, the first game console that used interchangeable cartridges. The consoles made by Atari, Coleco, and other competitors were like calculators and could play only games that were built into their circuits; the Channel F, on the other hand, was like a minicomputer that could be programmed to play a library of games.

Atari also had a cartridge system under development—-the Video Computer System (VCS). Compared with the VCS, which used the same 8-bit microprocessor as the Apple II computer, the Channel F was as primitive as *PONG*. But Atari didn't have enough money to produce the VCS in the quantities necessary to dominate the market. Seeking more capital, Bushnell took the first steps toward selling Atari stock on the New York Stock Exchange, but a slump in the market scared him. The only other option was to sell the company. Bushnell found a willing customer in Warner Communications. Atari, a company founded just four years earlier with $500, sold for $28 million.

Warner Communications took over Atari during one of the video game industry's bleakest years. The national protests against video game violence had taken their toll on the arcade business; so too had the lack of innovative games. The home business was also slow; consumers had wearied of home *PONG* and its myriad imitators.

Atari manufactured 400,000 units of the VCS for Christmas 1977, but sales were low, and although they remained steadier than expected after the holidays, Steve Ross, the president of Warner Communications, was furious. He had by then invested $100 million buying and building Atari, and so far he had seen very little return.

The tension between Bushnell and the new owners of his company increased. They saw him as no longer caring about his company. This may well have been true; at a budget meeting Bushnell claimed that the market was saturated with VCS systems and that Atari needed a new console. After the grim Christmas of 1977, Ross fired Bushnell. He replaced him with Ray Kassar, a flamboyant man who had risen through the ranks of Burlington Industries. Ross first sent Kassar to decide whether he should liquidate Atari or continue its operations after the disappointing Christmas. Kassar knew nothing about high tech industries, but he liked the VCS and suggested giving the company another year.

Though he knew little about computers, Kassar was a man who understood the public's taste. In 1978 Atari enjoyed a record-setting Christmas, and the year marked the beginning of a new era of home video game technology, as the industry, still less than a decade old, enjoyed its first real boom.

In 1978 Midway distributed a new arcade game from Taito. When the game was launched in Japan, it barely received any notice, and Taito executives dismissed it. A few months after its release, however, the game had become so popular that Japan was suffering a national coin shortage. The cause of this frenzy was called *Space Invaders*. Prior to its advent a top-selling arcade game meant about 15,000 units sold. Taito sold 300,000 *Space Invaders*, 60,000 of them in the United States.

Space Invaders helped everybody in the industry. Its popularity opened new outlets to coin-operated games. Soon they could be found in movie theaters and restaurants. It even helped Nolan Bushnell, whose new venture was Pizza Time Theaters, a company that opened Chuck E. Cheese's restaurants—pizza parlors with video game arcades.

Ripples of *Space Invaders'* success also reached Atari's consumer division. Kassar purchased home rights to the game and translated it into a major bestseller for the VCS. In 1979 an Atari coin-op engineer created a game in which players cleared asteroid fields with a small free-floating spaceship. Atari would sell 70,000 copies of *Asteroids* in the United States.

Meanwhile, Midway was busy placing 100,000 units of its new *Pac-Man* game in North America alone. Other companies followed suit. Atari released *Missile Command*, *Tempest*, *BattleZone*, and *Centipede*. Williams Electronics, a leading pinball manufacturer, had its biggest hit with *Defender*. Taito of America, the new U.S. arm of Taito, released *Qix*, *Front Line*, and *Jungle Hunt*. Stern Electronics released *Scramble*. Nintendo released *Donkey Kong*, *Donkey Kong Junior*, and *Popeye*. The most successful game in U.S. history was an updated version of *Pac-Man* called *Ms. Pac-Man*—with more than 115,000 sold.

Video game arcades became more plentiful than convenience stores. "*Pac-Man* and *Space Invaders* were going into virtually every location in the country with the exception of funeral parlors," says Eddie Adlum of *RePlay*. "And even a few funeral parlors had video games in the basements. Absolutely true. I believe churches and synagogues were about the only types of locations to escape video games."

Suddenly video games had become a major force in popular culture. In 1981 Americans spent 20 billion quarters playing 75,000 man-hours on them. The games out-grossed movies and the recording industry. A hit song was written about Pac-Man, and the characters that inhabited the electronic landscapes of *Pac-Man*, *Donkey Kong*, and other games appeared on their own television shows in Saturday morning cartoons.

In his 1983 State of the Union address, President Ronald Reagan defended aid to the Nicaraguan contras by comparing it with the money spent on video games. "The total amount requested for aid to all of Central America in 1984 is about $600 million; that is less than one-tenth of what Americans will spend this year on coin-operated video games."

For President Reagan to have been correct, every American man, woman, and child would have had to spend almost $30 a year in a video game arcade. But he missed more than the numbers; the feverish trend itself was winding down at the time he spoke. By June 1982 what the industry still remembers as the golden age had already dimmed. Business softened alarmingly, and by year's end arcades had begun closing. This downward trend has continued, with only a few positive spikes, for nearly fifteen years.

The home console market took a brutal beating the next year. VCS sales had been strong for four years despite new competition. In 1979 Mattel, one of the world's leading toy manufacturers, had entered the market with the Intellivision, a system that offered better graphics and more complex games than the VCS. Mattel sold an impressive 200,000 units in its first full year but barely dented Atari's market. In 1982 Coleco unveiled the ColecoVision, a sophisticated home console that ran excellent versions of top arcade games. All three companies made enormous profits.

Atari had the largest profits, but they were not enough. In 1982 Atari released two VCS cartridges that cost the company dearly. The first was *Pac-Man*, the long-awaited but poorly programmed home version of the arcade smash. Atari made 12 million copies of the game, many of which came back from disgruntled customers.

The second cartridge was based on the phenomenally successful movie *E.T.* According to several sources, Ross forced the game on Kassar after promising the film's director, Steven Spielberg, a whopping $25 million royalty for the exclusive video game rights to the movie. The game was dull and hard to play. In the end Atari created a landfill in a New Mexico desert, dumped in it millions of *E.T.*, *Pac-Man*, and other cartridges, crushed them with a steamroller, and buried the fragments under cement.

Atari's profits dropped for the first time in eight years. When, on December 7, 1982, Atari executives revealed that the company had not reached its projections, Warner Communications stock tumbled from 51 points per share to 35, and Ray Kassar was fired.

Over the next two years Mattel pulled out of the video game market. Coleco imploded after investing all its resources in a highly flawed home computer, and Warner Communications sold Atari Home Computers. Under its new ownership Atari managed to limp out of the wreck of the home console market and even showed a $450 million profit in 1988. However, it never reemerged as a force in the video game industry, and in 1995 the company was purchased by a disk drive manufacturer.

Now it was Japan's turn. In 1985 Nintendo announced that it would restart the American video game market by releasing a game console called the Nintendo Entertainment System (NES). Though the system was very popular in Japan, American software developers, many of whom were nearly bankrupted by the collapse of Atari, scoffed at the idea. Retailers refused to carry it.

In October 1985, Nintendo of America's president, Minoru Arakawa, proved his product's viability by releasing it in New York, a city generally considered one of the toughest markets in America. To persuade retailers to carry the NES, he promised to buy back any unsold items and set up his own elaborate displays in stores. The system sold out at almost every location.

Nintendo's impressive graphics, speed, and game control quickly developed an avid following. The NES came with *Super Mario Bros.*, an arcade game based on a popular character named Mario, a plumber who had first appeared in *Donkey Kong* and then gone on to star in several hit games. Mario got his own Saturday-morning cartoon and indeed became a cultural fixture. According to the 1990 Q ratings, a series of surveys that grade the recognizability of real and fictitious public figures, more American children recognized Mario than they did Mickey Mouse.

Under Nintendo's leadership, the home video game industry became more profitable than ever before. By 1991 more than 33 million homes had NES consoles. Though Nintendo charged steep fees for allowing others to publish games on their hardware, many companies became rich doing just that.

In 1989 Sega, another Japanese video game company, entered the market with a 16-bit game system called Sega Genesis. The console received little attention in 1990, but when Sega of America hired a new president, Tom Kalinske, the console took off. Kalinske, a former head of Mattel, began an aggressive attack on Nintendo's 92 percent market share. He dropped the price of the Genesis nearly to cost; then he set up a large software development division in the United States to create games that would appeal to American audiences. His strategy was Gillette's old one: give away razors in order to sell the blades.

Under Kalinske, Sega adopted a new mascot—a hyperactive blue rodent named Sonic the Hedgehog—and adopted an advertising campaign that ridiculed the weaknesses of Nintendo's six-year-old console.

Nintendo unveiled the 16-bit Super NES in time for Christmas 1991. While Nintendo sold every piece of hardware it could bring to the United States, the big surprise was Sega, which sold almost equally well. For the first time, Nintendo faced real competition. Within a year it had become apparent that Sega had established itself as a much "cooler" company in the minds of the fifteen- to eighteen-year-old boys who made up the bulk of the video game buying public. Older players preferred the Genesis because it had better sports games; young players were actually embarrassed to be seen playing games on a Super NES. When Sony ran a focus group, some kids refused to admit that they owned one.

Over the next three years Nintendo and Sega slugged it out while shutting out other competitors. Sega enjoyed a slight lead in the market through most of this period, and nothing Nintendo tried could close the gap. When the extremely brutal game *Mortal Kombat* (which ends with such impressive fillips as the victor yanking the vanquished's skeleton bloodily out through his throat) appeared, Nintendo insisted that the publisher take out much of the violence. The uncensored Genesis version outsold the Nintendo version three to one. Incensed by this new and far gaudier spate of video game violence, Sen. Joseph Lieberman of Connecticut and Sen. Herbert Kohl of Wisconsin launched an investigation in December 1993. Though they gave grudging praise to Nintendo for editing *Mortal Kombat,* they condemned the entire industry for recklessly allowing children access to acts of extreme violence. The hearings resulted in the video game industry's adopting a rating code to alert parents. When Acclaim released *Mortal Kombat II* the following year, it carried a warning label.

In 1994 home video game sales started to soften. By this time executives had learned that the market was cyclical, and rather than abandon it, as Mattel had done in the eighties, Nintendo and Sega began developing newer and more powerful systems. Despite the weakening market, Nintendo sold more than 7 million copies of *Donkey Kong Country,* which featured superb computer-modeled graphics.

By 1995 Sega released the heavily promoted 32-bit Saturn system. Overpriced and sent out into the world with very little software, the Saturn did poorly. In September Sony released a new 32-bit system called the PlayStation®, which cost $100 less than the Saturn and did a better job handling three-dimensional games and digitized video. The PlayStation® outsold the Saturn in the United States by nearly three to one.

By the time Nintendo finally released its latest system, the Nintendo 64

(N64) in America, Sony had shipped more than 3 million units here and more than 8 million. By November 1995 Sony had more than a $1 billion in PlayStation® sales in North America alone. Thus, as the industry marked its twenty-fifth anniversary in 1996, it was clearly well out of the most recent down cycle.

Perhaps as significant as any of the inroads the video game industry has made into our lives is its role in helping drive the computer market. Recent surveys discovered that after word processing, the most common use for home computers is playing games, and games are one of the leading forces that push consumers to upgrade their computers. After all, you can still run most word processors on a 486, but today's top computer games require a Pentium processor. Such leading computer companies as NEC and Gateway 2000 have launched computers specifically designed to play games, and Microsoft has vowed to make computers a competitive gaming platform.

And it is on computers that video games—the most frenetic and immediate of creatures—can clearly be seen to have become a part of history. They are now the objects of a small nostalgia boom, with collections of older games being reissued for computer play.

As for the founders of the industry, it is a young enough enterprise that some are still active in it. Ralph Baer consults and invents toys and games. Steven Russell worked for Digital Pictures, which created a highly controversial game called *Night Trap*, until the company declared bankruptcy in 1995. And Nolan Bushnell has unveiled a new line of coin-operated Internet machines.

What these men and their colleagues have made is, of course, all around us. The plunk and boing and sizzle, those postnuclear landscapes, the waterfront gunfights with casualty rates on the scale of the Battle of Shiloh, the gladiators pulling off one another's limbs—this is all familiar stuff now. It was a strange, extemporized, intuitive birth, but the child is healthier than its parents could have dreamed a quarter-century ago, and it will likely outlive us all.

II

Formal Aspects of the Video Game

3

Space in the Video Game

Mark J. P. Wolf

One of the many elements shared by film, television, and video games is the use of on-screen and off-screen space in the creation of a diegetic world. While the video game's use of space relied on precedents set in other media, such as the conventions of stage space, cinematic space, and the use of space on television and video, the video game's added elements of navigation and interaction lend an importance to diegetic space which is unlike that of other media. Technical as well as aesthetic factors influence the design and use of space in the video game, and the individual game's worldview also determines how the game's diegetic world is constructed and represented on screen, and what it means.

The following sections examine the creation of space in the video game, eleven different types of spatial structures or configurations, and ways of representing a three-dimensional space on-screen. These descriptions of spaces in the video game serve to demonstrate the uniqueness of the video game's use of space, and suggest new ways of thinking of the space represented in other media.

The Creation of Space in the Video Game

Just as cinematic off-screen space differed from theatrical off-*stage* space that preceded it (for example, characters could walk off-screen into the space behind the camera), the off-screen space of the video game differs from that of film. First, unlike off-screen space in film, off-screen space in a video game does not need to have a pro-filmic referent, existing prior to the film itself, the way a filmed space does. When a film camera is set up and pointed at something, there is always space outside the frame, off-screen, whether it is actively used or acknowledged by the filmmaker or not. In a video game, not only the representation of space, but even its implication, depend on being programmed and actively created. Second, because the video game has no default structure for its off-screen space, that space can be shaped and structured in new ways that did not develop in film or television. And finally, the video game, as an interactive medium, often gives the player some control over the point of view, allowing one to choose which spaces appear on-screen or off. Rather than wait for the film camera to show it, off-screen space can often be actively investigated and explored by the player, and in some cases, like *Doom* (1993), *Dark Forces* (1994), *Descent* (1995), *Stonekeep* (1995), and later mazelike games, it can constitute a large part of game play itself.

The design of the spaces depicted in video games can be attributed to both technical limitations and aesthetic influences. As video game technology developed, factors like hardware, software, processing speed, and memory limited what was technically and graphically possible; breakthroughs like the invention of the microprocessor in 1971 and development of the inexpensive AY 3-8500 chip in 1975 made smaller and faster games more common, as well as a flood of dozens of *PONG* (1972) imitations. Graphically, improvements in computer technology have helped games evolve from the simple blocky graphics of *PONG* and the Atari 2600 to the high-resolution, shaded, photorealistic images in CD-ROM games like *Myst III: Exile* (2001), or like the games in the *Doom, Quake,* or *Tomb Raider* series featuring detailed three-dimensional graphics that can change in perspective during real-time interaction. These graphical advances, along with greater storage capacity, allowed the diegetic worlds of video games to enlarge beyond a few screens, requiring methods of representation which could link different spaces together, and link on-screen and off-screen spaces.

Technical limitations, however, were not the only factors. The video game had a wide range of aesthetic influences; for example, commercially, it followed precedents set by pinball and other arcade games, and early cabinets and controls were designed accordingly. Graphically, it was limited by what computer graphics could reproduce: vectors (lines) and raster graphics (pixels). In the areas of representational characters, narratives, and spaces, there were the enormous precedents set by film and television imagery. It is perhaps due to the desire to measure up to the standards of visual realism set by film and television that video game graphics have evolved as they have; today there are far fewer of the abstract game designs that were once so common in the days of *Qix* (1981) and *Tempest* (1980). Likewise, as computer technology allows faster and more affordable rendering and three-dimensional graphic environments, the structuring of off-screen space within video games increasingly follows the examples set by film, which in turn paved the way and set precedents regarding the representation of complex, connected spaces on-screen. Today, the navigation of on-screen space has become more important than ever with the expansion of the World Wide Web, as well as with the nascent virtual reality spaces which are gradually finding their way to the Internet. Video game worlds, then, can be seen as a precursor of cyberspace.

En route to their present state, video games have explored a wide range of spatial structures, most of which can still be found in some form or another, or linked with other forms within a game. In order to compare the diegetic worlds of video games to those of film, some description of their possible spatial geometries is needed, and a sense of how terms like "on-screen" and "off-screen" might function within them, as well as some description of how space is configured within them.

Spatial Structures in Video Games

While there are a large range of spatial structures or "spaces" possible in video games, these can be broken down into more elementary structures, some of which have similar counterparts in film. All of these spaces have appeared in video games individually, and different combinations of them occur together in a variety of games. Each has found its niche, as some kinds of games are more appropriate in one type of space than another, or because some require less computing power than others. These types of spaces apply not only to arcade and home video games, but also to computer games and hand-held games, and some of these will be included as examples. They are presented here in order of visual and conceptual complexity, each requiring varying amounts of concentration from the player; unlike the film viewer, who is led (visually) through the film's diegetic world by the film's characters, the video game player has a stake in the navigation of space, as knowledge of the video game's space is often crucial to a good performance.

1. No visual space; all text-based

A genre of home computer games, known collectively as "text adventures" or sometimes "interactive fiction," includes *Planetfall* (1983), *The Hitchhiker's Guide to the Galaxy* (1984), and the early games in the *Zork* series.

These games are completely text based; the scenery, other characters, and the player's surroundings are presented as verbal descriptions delivered as text on-screen, and the player's replies and requests are typed commands, such as "north" or "open door." In this sense, there is no on-screen space to speak of; everything has to be imagined on the basis of the descriptions. One could argue that *everything* takes place off-screen, as on a radio program; or, if the concept of on-screen space is necessary for the concept of off-screen space to make sense, one could argue that neither is present at all. Or, in still another sense, one could consider "on-screen" to mean "that which is currently being described by the text on-screen"; the use of descriptive text, then, raises the question of what it means to be "on-screen."

Part of the reason for the use of all text, at least initially, was the difficulty of doing graphics. Nor did the computer keyboard have a control like a joystick (although many games now use arrow keys or some other configuration of keys to indicate directions of movement). However, instead of seeing this as a liability, these games took advantage of the lack of graphics to leave the images to the player's imagination, much as a novel or as TSR Hobbies' tabletop game *Dungeons & Dragons* did (*D&D* used graph paper, dice rolls, and verbal description to build fantasy worlds). Although early computer graphics would have been fairly limited in what they could depict, any amount of subtle detail could be verbally described; the player could even be told what he or she was feeling in certain situations, if needed.

Today, text continues to be used in some of the MUDs (Multi-User Dimensions) or MOOs (MUD, Object-Oriented) on the Internet, the gaming "rooms" visited by multiple players simultaneously, where all description, interaction, and dialogue are composed of text (although some MUDs and MOOs now use avatars and other graphics to represent players). When a player is inside a "room," he or she can hear all the dialogue occurring in that room, as well as descriptions of occupants' actions. After leaving the "room," the player will no longer know what is going on "inside" of it; instead, there will be descriptions of the current "location" being visited. In this way, notions of "on-screen" and "off-screen" can reappear, even in a text-based environment.

The text-based environment differs from that of a book in that it can be time based, especially when there are multiple players. Even though the descriptions may provide more detail than low-resolution graphics would, players must imagine the spaces on the basis of descriptions, and react verbally as well; to some degree, both brain hemispheres are required to match up verbal and spatial processing, if the scenes described are to be visualized and connected. Because the action taking place is indirect, the pace of these games is slower, and reaction time much less of a factor, making these games something of an exception—and today a rarity—in the world of video games. Although some games may incorporate text-based informational screens (as in *Stellar Track* [1981]), only a few games, like *Myst* (1993), come close to being a graphic equivalent of these kinds of games; *Myst*, in fact, makes frequent use of on-screen text in a series of books and letters the player reads on-screen.

A few games, such as *Rogue* (1980), used text characters as graphic elements, using rows of characters to form walls and rooms. These games, while not text adventures, do bridge the gap between text adventures and graphical games, and are among the first attempts to graphically display the game's diegetic world on-screen.

2. One screen, contained

Text-based games represent only a tiny minority in the video game world compared to graphic-based video games, in which space is graphically depicted instead of just verbally described. Even the simplest graphics in a game such as *Spacewar!* or *PONG* can convey action with an immediacy that text cannot; it is not merely described, but *seen*. Since its beginnings on mainframe computers, then, the video game has been primarily graphics oriented.

Many early video games were designed so that the entire game was contained on a single screen of graphics; the player did not leave the screen, nor did the screen scroll to reveal off-screen space. *Space Invaders* (1978), *PONG* (1972), *Breakout* (1976), and other games had all their action contained on one screen and there were no other levels; the destroyed characters or objects simply were replaced and the action was faster. Cinematically, these games resembled the early films of Lumiére and Méliès, in which the camera was pointed at the action and remained static for the duration of the action, without any editing to link it to other locations. Even the instantaneous disappearance of game objects or characters (like the destroyed space invaders) is similar to Méliès' stop-action effects in films like *A Trip to the Moon* (1902) and *The Black Imp* (1907), in which objects or people suddenly vanish.

Both the early films and the early games also acknowledged that there was a space outside the frame, even if it was never shown; for example, in

PONG, missed balls fly off-screen, scoring a point, and in *Space Invaders*, bullets missing the invaders fly up and off-screen. Likewise, Lumiére's *Workers Leaving the Lumiére Factory* (1895) showed people moving through the frame who disappeared off the edge of the screen in a manner similar to the bullets and balls. Although this off-screen space was not actively used (objects leaving the screen were not seen again), its presence was implied in both cases.

3. One screen, contained, with wraparound

A variation on the single screen video game is one in which space is finite but unbounded; objects leaving one side of the screen immediately reappear on the opposite side, maintaining their same speed and trajectory. This is referred to as "wraparound," since the top and bottom of the screen wrap around to meet, as do the left and right sides of the screen (in mathematics, such a spatial structure is referred to as a Euclidean 2-torus). The first commercial arcade video game, *Computer Space* (1971), featured wraparound space. *Asteroids* (1979), a more popular game, also used this kind of space, and so did certain games in *Combat* (1977), the cartridge shipped along with all Atari 2600 systems. The asteroids (or fighter planes in *Combat*) move in straight lines, exiting the frame and reentering on the other side until destroyed by the player. In this sense, there is really no off-screen space to speak of; everything in each of these tiny universes is represented on-screen, a structuring of space that had never arisen anywhere in film (although it could have, in animation).

A slight variation on this ordering of space occurs in *Pac-Man*; the game has a space similar to that of type 2 (one screen, contained), except for a tunnel allowing Pac-Man to exit the screen on the right or left side of the frame and reappear on the opposite side. When passing through the tunnel, though, Pac-Man does not immediately appear on the other side; there is a slight pause between the moment he leaves the screen and the moment he reemerges. This implies that the tunnel is slightly longer than what is shown on-screen and suggests a tiny bit of off-screen space that is never seen which the character can pass through. For the most part, though, games using "wraparound" depict a self-enclosed space, finite but unbounded, in which all the game's action occurs.

In both type 2 and type 3 (one screen, contained, with wraparound) spaces, the player can see everything there is to see on-screen and will probably concentrate most on the character represented there which he or she is controlling. However, the reactions to the two spaces differ somewhat; in type 2 the edges of the screen are walls, and thus it is safe to turn one's back to them; the focus then, becomes mainly the center of the screen, where threats are more likely to come from. In type 3, targets or attackers can disappear off one side of the screen and reappear on the far side, and so edges must be paid more attention, since it is often harder to keep track of these off-and-on movements. Although in both cases the action is wholly contained on-screen, different parts of the screen become important and require attention depending on how the space is configured.

4. Scrolling on one axis

Certain genres of video games require more than a single screen's worth of graphics for their action; racing games like Atari's *Street Racer* (1978) and Activision's *Skiing* (1980) need a long strip of space for players to travel through. Games involving the shooting or catching of moving objects while moving through a space, like *Defender* (1980) or Activision's *Stampede* (1981), also use a long, tracklike space. By moving the game's "set pieces" across the screen, often synchronized with the player's movements, the game designer can create a "scrolling" space in which objects come on and off the screen.

Scrolling games vary in their emphasis on the importance of off-screen space. In some games, the configurations of objects found in this space are always the same, allowing a player to anticipate what lies ahead in the game, off-screen but approaching. These games make active use of off-screen space, using it to build a player's anticipation and sometimes creating the illusion of an endless track of space which players could continue moving through, provided they were good enough at the game to keep going. Seeing more and more of this "track" can itself be a kind of reward, just as moving to higher levels is in other games.

Spatial scrolling usually occurs horizontally, as it does in games like *Defender*, *Stampede*, *Space Jockey* (1982), and others, or vertically, as in *Skiing* and *Street Racer*. It can also be used to reveal spaces which the player has to return to later, as in Activision's *Keystone Kapers* (1983), which depicts three levels of a department store; the screen scrolls horizontally, and the upper levels of the store can only be reached by elevators or escalators at the far right and left ends of the scrolling space. Cinematically, the revealing of off-screen space by "scrolling" or reframing the image is accomplished by tracking shots and crane shots (or by panning and tilting, if one ignores the changes in perspective in each). This movement can be traced back to panning used in early films like Porter's *The Life of an American Fireman* (1903), the tracking shots used in Queribet and Hepworth's *A Day with the Gypsies* (1906), or even further back to the scrolling images of the dioramas of the late 1800s. In both the games and often in film, space scrolls through the frame in order to keep the moving character visible on-screen, to follow the action, and to build anticipation in the viewer. In the video game, however, it is the space which is being moved instead of the camera/viewer.

The first game to make use of scrolling was Atari's arcade game *Football*, in 1978. Atari patented the scrolling technique and has won a number of lawsuits due to this patent, which has provided the company with more income than *Football* could ever have provided. The patent is possible only because space in video games does not exist prior to appearing on-screen the way pro-filmic space does in the cinema; it is difficult to imagine what the cinema would be like today if early filmmakers could have patented panning or tracking shots and collected royalties on their usage by others!

Whether or not a player must be able to recall the spaces passing on and off screen depends on the game. Some, like *Stampede* and *Street Racer*, do not allow the player to stop or change direction, nor is the space passed through ever returned to (except in repeated playings, where a player may be able to anticipate what is coming). Games like *Keystone Kapers* and *Defender* allow a player to navigate and revisit spaces, putting more emphasis on spatial orientation and navigation as well as making the experience more interactive.

5. Scrolling on two axes

Some games, like *Gauntlet* (1985), *Ultima III: Exodus* (1983), *Dark Chambers* (1988), *Sid Meier's Civilization* (1991), or *SimCity* (1989), have screens that can scroll both side to side and up and down. This results in more than just a combination of the two types of scrolling, because it implies a large plane of space, of which only a small rectangle is seen at any given time. Most of these games involve a bird's-eye view of some terrain, although the objects within that terrain are typically shown in side view (resulting in scenes with perspectives similar to those found in medieval paintings before the Renaissance). Cinematically, this kind of sideways tracking movement is found mainly in cel animation, and occasionally in live action, such as the cut-away office set of Godard and Gorin's *Tout Va Bien*

(1972), which the camera tracks side to side and up and down.[1] The amount of scrolling possible can vary from one axis to the other (up-and-down movement may be limited to only certain spaces), as will the importance placed on spatial navigation. As with the wraparound screen, players often must monitor the edges of the screen for incoming characters, but there is more uncertainty as to when and where these characters will appear. Just as few films are long, unbroken tracking shots, most games do not use two-axis scrolling for displaying all of their spaces; instead, both media usually employ "cuts" between adjacent spaces.

6. Adjacent spaces displayed one at a time

In the cinema, the joining of contiguous spaces through cutting signaled the arrival of editing. Likewise in video games like the arcade game *Berzerk* (1980), or *Adventure* (1978) and *Superman* (1979), both for the Atari 2600, adjacent spaces or rooms are displayed as a series of nonoverlapping static screens which cut directly one to the next without scrolling, not only following the precedent set by film but also relying on it to allow the player to make sense of the geography of the game. As the player's on-screen character moves off-screen in one direction, the screen changes instantly and the character reenters on the opposite side of the screen; the direction of screen movement is conserved, and the screens are seen as being immediately adjacent to one another, an assumption that relies on one's knowledge of continuity editing in film.[2] In both *Adventure* and *Superman*, the games' spaces can be mapped out as a series of screens joined side by side (although the *Superman* screens join together in a wraparound pattern; in some places, if you fly in one direction long enough, you will eventually return to the same screen).

As film editing developed, some films were structured into a similar pattern of nonoverlapping adjacent spaces. For example, in both *The Lonely Villa* (1909) and *A Corner in Wheat* (1909), D. W. Griffith divides certain spaces into a series of static camera setups. The spatial representation of the villa in *The Lonely Villa* is remarkably like that of a video game in both editing and graphics. As Rick Altman describes it,

> The film's space is divided up into a dozen mutually exclusive shots; that is, there is no overlapping between the fields of one shot and another. This method produces a fragmented view of space in which we never see an object or stationary character from more than one

point of view. This fragmentation is compounded by the fact that the camera always remains immobile and level (except for a single low-angle shot of the burglar who climbs a pole to cut the wires).[3]

The movement of characters within the film is also graphically similar to the video game; "Each edge of the frame represents an entrance or exit; the dominant motion is thus across the frame, either horizontally or diago-nally."[4] Robert Adams describes Griffith's *A Corner in Wheat* as having a similar setup of adjacent nonoverlapping spaces, and this time including vertical spaces as well; for example, when the Wheat King falls through a trapdoor into a grain bin, the two spaces are shown separately.[5] As Altman points out, these films also use static camera setups, at right angles to the scenes, depicting them from a single point of view, which is a visual style similar to that found in many video games, visually simplifying the diegetic world and the action taking place there.

Adjacent spaces displayed using "cuts" between them can in some ways provide more suspense than a scrolling space, since the player does not see the space until it is entered. In *Adventure*, for example, a dragon would occasionally be hovering near the edge of the screen, and an unsus-pecting player could be attacked immediately upon entering the screen. While similar "shock" cuts can be used in the cinema, in video games it is the player who decides when to cut to the next scene, and so there is an ele-ment of responsibility, control, and decision making that one does not find in the cinema, which is often used to add an element of suspense to the design of a game.

While *Rogue* (1980) was the first mainframe game to use multiple screens (using text characters for graphics), *Adventure (1978),* created for the Atari 2600, was the first home video game to make use of multiple con-necting screens as well as nonplayer characters (three dragons and a bat) who can come on-screen and off-screen or even be followed from one screen to another. The game contains more than two dozen interconnected screens, most of them spatially adjacent to one another. The way in which these spaces connect, however, need not be limited to those which can be mapped out on a flat surface. The interiors of the castles, which are entered through the on-screen castle gates rather than sides of the screen, are an exception. The interiors of the castles in *Adventure* were among the early instances of off-screen space occurring *behind* or *inside* an object pictured on-screen, a space like that used for interiors in film.

In *Theory of Film Practice*, Noël Burch divides off-screen space into six "segments" and describes the first four of these as the areas beyond the four borders of the frame. He then adds,

> A fifth segment cannot be defined with the same seeming geometric precision, yet no one will deny that there is an off-screen space "behind the camera" that is quite distinct from the four segments of space bordering the frame lines although the characters in the film generally reach this space by passing just to the right or left of the camera. There is a sixth segment, finally, encompassing the space existing behind the set or some object in it: A character reaches it by going out a door, going around a street corner, disappearing behind a pillar or behind another person, or performing some similar act.[6]

The castle interiors are clearly an example of Burch's sixth "segment" of space; entering the castle gate (located in the middle of the screen) immediately takes the player to a screen depicting the castle interior. *Adventure* was also the first video game with a non-Euclidean structure for its space. The Blue Labyrinth and the Black Castle, for example, feature configurations of screens which cannot be mapped onto an unbroken flat surface. While non-Euclidean space has appeared in other media (for example, the Tardis on the TV show *Dr. Who*, Lady Elaine Fairchilde's Museum-Go-Round on the television show *Mr. Rogers' Neighborhood*, and the house on Ash Tree Lane in Mark Z. Danielewski's novel *House of Leaves*, all of which are spatially larger on the inside than the outside), it is surprisingly infrequent in video games and suggests a possible future direction of development for the medium.

Besides the player's character, *Adventure* also features three dragons and a bat that can freely pass over the terrain and the objects on-screen; thus Burch's sixth type is also evoked as these characters pass in front of scenery. Although this was a step toward the idea of z-axis depth on-screen (depth toward and away from the viewer), it was only indicated by the momentary replacing the pixels of the background with those of the character as it passed over (a concept in computer graphics known as "priority"). In *Adventure*, then, overlapping planes are indirectly suggested but not graphically depicted with the illusion of depth.[7]

7. Layers of independently moving planes (multiple scrolling backgrounds)
A number of games, such as *Zaxxon* (1982) and *Super Mario Bros.*, depict a

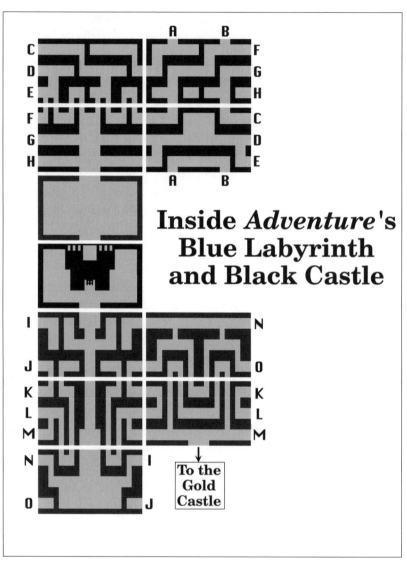

Inside *Adventure*'s Blue Labyrinth and Black Castle

Adventure *for the Atari 2600 displays adjacent spaces one at a time, cutting between screens as characters leave or enter the frame. The player enters the Black Castle through the gate in the middle of the screen and reappears in an empty room which leads into the rest of the castle. The screens containing the maze in the Black Castle connect in wraparound fashion, top to bottom and side to side as shown above. Notice how the paths connect on the sides of the screens, resulting in a space which loops around itself and contains connections that cannot be mapped onto a flat surface. The Blue Labyrinth, below the Blue Castle, likewise is connected in wraparound fashion. Although non-Euclidean spatial structures are possible in video games, they are surprisingly rare, but their great potential suggests a future direction for the development of spatial structures in video games.*

space made up of layers of overlapping and independently moving planes of graphics, with the front layer containing the player-character (and often the scenery the character stands on), while the back layer contains background graphics and scrolls at a slower rate than the foreground, creating an illusion of depth. In some games, like the arcade games *Streets of Rage* and *Double Dragon* (1986) or home games like *Warioland* (1995) for Nintendo's Virtual Boy system, the player-character can even jump from one plane to the other at places indicated in the game. In these games, figu-ground relationships can become more complex, as graphic planes can function as either, depending on what is "behind" or "in front of" them, requiring a more sophisticated degree of spatial orientation than was needed for the flat, single-plane scenes of earlier games (the Virtual Boy system uses stereo three-dimensional graphics to help separate out its planes of action, though most games are wholly dependent on other depth cues).

The use of layers of planes creates a three-dimensional effect without being truly three-dimensional; each layer is still a flat two-dimensional plane. The effect is similar to that created by the theatrical flats used on-stage as scenery, with several layers of them providing depth as well as places for actors to enter and exit. In video games, characters are present within these layers (as opposed to between them) along with the scenery, although the layers themselves pass in front of other layers. This is similar to layers of cels in animation, or compositing in film and video; for example, a television weatherman placed over a weather map, combining two layers of imagery. Thus, in these games, Burch's sixth segment of off-screen space came into maturity, bringing the graphical depiction of z-axis depth to the games, even if it was in a somewhat limited fashion, as a series of two-dimensional overlapping and independently moving planes.

8. Spaces allowing z-axis movement into and out of the frame

Burch's fifth segment of space, extending behind the camera (or the viewer's point of view), was the slowest to emerge in video games due to the difficulty of depicting the dimensional movement it required (objects growing larger until they move out of frame). Early appearances of objects moving toward the viewer and out of the frame can be found in the arcade game *Tempest* (1980), *Star Ship* (arcade game, 1976; Atari 2600 version, 1977), and *Night Driver* (arcade game, 1976; Atari 2600 version, 1980). *Tempest*, a color vector game, depicts objects coming up the inside surfaces of a tunnel, growing larger until they reach full size at the edges of it. In a sequence at the end of each level, the tunnel grows in size, and the player's point of view is made to appear to be flying down through it to the next level; the tunnel, then, is passing into the space located behind the camera/viewer.

In *Night Driver*, the screen is black and contains two series of white rectangles, or posts, which come down the screen, growing in size (and moving sideways, as one "steers") to produce the illusion of driving on a road. In the Atari 2600 home version, a house, tree, and oncoming car that grow in size as they move down the screen provide additional depth cues. Although the space behind the camera/viewer is acknowledged, it is not actively used; the posts passing into it are not used or seen again (like the *PONG* balls or *Space Invaders* bullets that leave the screen); in this sense, the z-axis movement is one-way, as it is in the early scrolling games, which do not allow players to back up or return to spaces passed through. Likewise in *Tempest*, the z-axis movement is one-way and does not affect play; the player's point of view moves through the tunnel only between levels (thus no steering is even required), and the only other z-axis movement is that of objects growing in size as they move up the tunnel to its edge, where the player's character is; the three-dimensional effect employed is just for show. Active use of the space behind the camera/viewer only later appeared in games representing an interactive three-dimensional environment (see type 10 space below), such as Atari's *Battlezone* (1980).

9. Multiple, nonadjacent spaces displayed on-screen simultaneously

One of the more rare types of spatial structures found in video games involves two different points of view—each belonging to one of the players—displayed on-screen on a single screen at the same time. While each of the viewpoints can contain any of the types spaces mentioned here, the combination of multiples viewpoints can make for a very different game, since attention can be split between two points of view. One such game is Atlus' *High Velocity* (1995), a racing game for the Sega Saturn. Players can see both their own and their opponents' point of view on-screen and can use this information to monitor each other's progress and in some cases even slow each other down. One of the more interesting uses of this type of space, and one of the earliest examples of it, appears in *Spy Vs Spy*, a game released by First Star Software in 1984, for the Commodore 64, Apple II, and Atari home computers. In the game, two players (the White Spy and the Black Spy) travel through rooms looking for certain objects (passport, money, key, and secret plans) that a player must get in order to win. While doing so, each player can set traps for the other player or get caught in the other player's traps. The screen is divided into two smaller screens, showing the rooms where each player's Spy currently is, and both players play simultaneously and can see what the other player is doing at all times, even if they are in different rooms.[8] In order to play the game well, a player must find the required objects as well as watch what the other Spy is doing elsewhere. Since multiple, nonadjacent spaces are depicted on-screen simultaneously, each Spy is in his own space and screen; "off-screen" could then apply to the rest of the rooms of the maze not on-screen, or, if we take "off-screen" to mean the *player's screen* within the game, we could say that the opposing Spy's off-screen actions are depicted on the other player's screen. The meaning of "off-screen" varies, then, depending on the screen to which we are referring.

A number of arcade video games, such as *Final Lap* (1988), *Virtua Racing* (1992), *Dactyl Nightmare* (1992), and *Daytona U.S.A.* (1994), use two separate screens, one for each player. The overall effect is different from that in a split-screen game, where two points of view compete for the player's attention. Whereas split screens are found only occasionally in video games, the representation of multiple nonadjacent spaces on-screen is more common in film. Split screens have been used in a wide variety of films (*Carrie* [1976], *Pillow Talk* [1959], Abel Gance's *Napoleon* [1927], and most notably in *Timecode* [1999], which was shot in real time by four cameras), often to show simultaneous events or actions of characters. The use of the split screen in the video game, then, serves a similar purpose (the depiction of simultaneous actions) but differs from the film because of the interaction possible in the video game and the control the players have over which spaces are depicted or remain off-screen. In video games, a player also has more reason to identify with one screen (with the player-character), giving it the majority of his or her attention, rather than dividing it equally among the images in a split-screen sequence of a film. Games like *Spy Vs Spy*, in which watching the other player's actions is an important part of the strategy, create an interesting tension between passive watching and active playing, and between thought and action, that can make the player much more aware of the difference between the two modes of activity.

10. Interactive three-dimensional environment
Although *Spy Vs Spy* represents movement through a three-dimensional interactive environment, it still depicts each of its spaces—the rooms—from a single point of view, much like a Griffith film of the action would

(although Griffith, of course, would have used cross-cutting instead of a split screen to depict the simultaneous actions). Most games representing their diegetic space as an interactive three-dimensional environment follow, to some degree, the precedent set by the space represented in the classical Hollywood film.[9] Spaces and the objects in them can be viewed from multiple angles and viewpoints which are all linked together in such a way as to make the diegetic world appear to have at least enough spatial consistency so as to be navigable by the player. The extent to which the player is allowed to freely navigate the space varies widely. A few games, like *Dragon's Lair* (1983) or *Space Ace* (1984), which use film clips stored on a laserdisc, give the player some control over a character's actions, but spatially are not much more navigable than a film, which gives the viewer no control over which spaces are seen when. Others, like *Myst*, allow for more navigation of space but limit the player to a selection of rendered views of the space, limiting the viewing angles and standpoints available. Still other games, like *Doom* (1993), *Dark Forces* (1996), *Descent* (1996), and *Stonekeep* (1995), as well as various virtual reality games, provide players with an unbroken exploration of space, allowing them to pan, tilt, track, and dolly through the space, which is usually presented in a first-person perspective view and is navigable in real time.

The first commercial game to offer a first-person perspective of an interactive three-dimensional environment was the arcade game *Battlezone* (1980).[10] The player's point of view was that of a tank which roamed a sparsely decorated landscape and fired upon other tanks (which were, in turn, trying to shoot at the player's tank). The other tanks could sneak up from behind, so a player had to be vigilant in watching and turning in order to locate the other tanks first; off-screen action could be as important as on-screen action. *Battlezone* was also the first game to feature off-screen sound and events; sounds of the player's tank getting hit indicated an off-screen tank's attack, alerting the player to turn and fight. The first-person perspective increased the importance of off-screen space because it positioned the player within the space, subjectively, as opposed to the third-person objective view in earlier games.[11] This shift also allowed a more mature usage of off-screen space and one closer to that of cinematic off-screen space.

In cinema, the understanding of a narrative may depend on a detailed understanding of the space it unfolds in, but this is not always the case. Indeed, some cinematic spaces—such as Rick's diner in *Casablanca*

(1942)—function adequately within the narrative but physically are not consistent enough to be reconstructed into a coherent space. Most video games, however, require players to know their way around the diegetic world in order to be successful in the game, and multiple playings are almost always necessary. For example in *Myst*, knowledge of what areas have not been seen may lead to the discovery of unseen areas or views (for example, the tree elevator behind the cabin); spatial orientation is useful in solving a puzzle in the Selentic Age and is crucial to puzzles in *Riven*.

With the development of 32-bit and 64-bit home video game systems, games involving three-dimensional interactive environments have become quite common, and computer games on CD-ROM feature increasingly detailed graphics in their three-dimensional environments (one need only compare *Doom* [1993], *Dark Forces* [1996], *Stonekeep* [1996], and *Tomb Raider 2* [1997] to see how much this technology developed over a five-year period in the mid-1990s). Navigation through a maze is a large part of these games, and books are often sold for these games which provide maps of the different levels. Often, however, maps of the spaces are built into the games themselves which depict the off-screen space in highly simplified schematic form.

11. Represented or "mapped" spaces

As the size of the video game's diegetic world grew from one screen to several screens to intricate multi-leveled three-dimensional mazes, providing the player with some visual representation of a conceptual map became more important. These represented or "mapped" spaces became an on-screen representation of off-screen space; they were not spaces in and of themselves, but rather simplified schematic versions of spaces designed to orient a player or indicate important events occurring in off-screen space. For example, *Battlezone*'s visuals included a small radar screen which used a series of dots to represent enemy tanks in an overhead view, giving a player a 360-degree sense of the immediate surroundings. *Defender* (1980) likewise has a small map on the edge of the screen in which on-screen and off-screen spaceships are represented as dots. Some games use a map only to indicate a player's progress from level to level, as in the interlevel screens of *Warioland* (1995), but these provide little information for the actual play of the game. Games in which figuring out the maze is part of the objective do not provide maps, and those that do can discourage their use (*Spy Vs Spy*, for example, subtracts 70 points from a player's score for calling up the "help map"). But quite often these maps are designed to provide warnings of off-screen foes or to provide just enough information to keep a player interested, without giving too much away.

Typically, these orientation maps are iconic and contain very little detail. Some of these maps are even worked into the diegesis of the game; in *Myst*, there is a map of the island in the library which lights up various portions of the island as their marker switches are flipped. This map indicates that there is something behind the cabin which a player might have missed—the tall tree with the elevator in it (the angles of the views of the island that a player sees while moving about it are designed so that the tall tree can be seen only from certain vantage points on the island).[12] Books in the *Myst* library also include maps of various ages which are useful in finding the secret rooms in the Mechanical Age as well as finding one's way around the Channelwood Age. In *Riven*, the sequel to *Myst*, geography becomes even more integrated into the puzzles in the game.

Other games, such as *Stellar Track* (1980), *SimCity* (1989), *SimCity2000* (1994), and *Caesar II* (1996), are based entirely on maps, using maps as their graphics as well as for informational purposes. Here, too, off-screen sounds are used to indicate events; in *SimCity*, for example, off-screen sounds of disasters can occur, and the game can be set to immediately bring these locations on-screen right after the disasters occur. Video games, then, have come full circle; whereas once their spaces were simple and iconic fields with little detail, today they can be so complex that low-detail maps of their spaces are far more complex graphically than any of the early games were.

Finally, off-screen spaces can be represented as unseen on-screen space. In games in which exploration is important, such as *Sid Meier's Civilization* (1991), unexplored areas of the screen remain blacked out until a player has moved into the area. In this sense, off-screen space could be in the middle of the screen; the player could circle around an area, not venturing into it, leaving it black. Once this area is ventured into, its contents are revealed and appear on-screen, the black area having represented the unexplored space without revealing what was in it. Here, too, the notion off-screen space can be interpreted in two ways: it could refer to the land areas which lie outside the frame at any given moment while not including the black areas (which are still "spaces" even though their content is not shown); or, the blacked-out spaces on-screen could be included in the term because their contents are not displayed on-screen, just like the areas

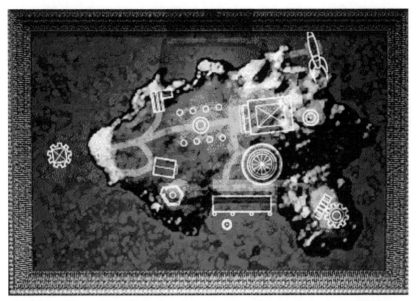

The map on the wall of the library in Myst®. *The white outlines on the map only light up once the locations have been visited and their marker switches have been placed in the "on" position. The space of the map is both conceptual, orienting the player on the island, and physical, since it takes up space on the library wall. All* Myst®, Riven®, *and* D'ni® *images and text* © Cyan, Inc. All rights reserved.

lying outside the frame. It all depends on whether the space, or what is in the space, must be depicted in order to be considered "on-screen."

Other games indicate events occurring behind on-screen objects; in the arcade game *Crystal Castles* (1982), some screens feature tunnels that pass through castles and emerge behind them on the far side of the screen. When the player's bear enters these tunnels, the bear disappears, but an outline of the bear's hat and feet remain on-screen, laid over the other graphics in a position indicating where the bear is inside the castle. In *I, Robot* (1983), the first arcade game to feature polygonal graphics, the player's robot occasionally moves behind rises in the playing field, and when it does, the graphic of the hill becomes wireframe, allowing the robot to be seen through it. *I, Robot* also allows the player to alter the viewing angle of the scenery during the game, and rewards greater points for actions completed in a shallower angle (as opposed to the overhead view, which gives a more clear idea of how the space is laid out). The way in which space in used and seen in the video game's diegetic world becomes an important part of the experience of the game, and an understanding of how that space is constructed can be as crucial to gameplay in the same way as the understanding of space is often crucial in the following of the narrative in film.

Ways of Representing Three-Dimensional Space

In film, images depicting a three-dimensional space usually result from the photographing of actual three-dimensional objects and settings. This need not always be the case, however. Since the resulting images are two-dimensional planes and the camera recording them is (in most cases) monocular, a number of optical tricks are possible which create images with misleading depth cues designed to change the way the space is perceived by an audience. Forced-perspective sets, built along exaggerated lines of perspective, appear to be deeper than they actually are, and foreground miniatures placed near the camera can be photographed in such a way that they appear to be larger and farther away. Front and rear screen projection systems combine projected imagery with actors and sets to make the setting appear to continue behind them, for example, to make a car filmed on-stage appear to be driving through a city. The three-dimensional spaces depicted in film, then, can be constructed in different ways.

Likewise in most animated films, images depicting three-dimensional spaces are wholly the result of depth cues derived from lines of perspective and the relative sizes and positions of the elements in a scene. Through compositing, hand-drawn animation, computer animation, and live-action elements can all appear to inhabit the same space believably, provided the perspective, depth cues, and relative positions of each of the elements are consistent with one another.

The z-axis is the axis of motion that points out of the image toward the viewer and inward toward the vanishing point within the image where lines of perspective meet. Objects moving along the z-axis create an illusion of depth through gradual changes in size; as objects grow larger they appear to be moving toward the viewer, and as they grow smaller they appear to be moving away from the viewer. High-resolution images like those found in 35mm film allow this enlarging and shrinking movement to appear very smooth and result in a strong illusion of depth. The smaller the units by which the height and width of an object change, the more smooth the z-axis movement appears; thus the smoothness of movement along the

z-axis depends on the resolution along the x-axis (width) and the y-axis (height) of the image.

In lower resolution imagery such as that found in early video game systems like the Atari 2600, graphics were typically low resolution and looked very blocky. This made smooth z-axis movement difficult or impossible; objects like the spaceships in *Star Ship* (1977) appear first as small objects, pause briefly, appear momentarily as medium-sized objects with only slightly more detail, and then appear as large objects. While an astute observer can surmise that the object is flying toward the viewer, the gestalt of the movement is almost entirely lost, and it is only with a great leap of imagination that the illusion is conveyed at all. It comes as no surprise, then, that most early video games remained limited to a single, flat plane of action with little or no z-axis movement.

Lack of sufficient resolution is not the only reason for a tendency toward flat two-dimensional graphics. True three-dimensional computation requires objects to be modeled in three dimensions within the computer's memory, so that such things as object overlap, foreshortening and apparent size, and changes in perspective occurring in moving imagery can all be calculated and then rendered from a particular point of view before the images can be displayed on screen. The entire process must also be done for every image displayed on screen, and be done at the rate the images are displayed (for NTSC video, roughly thirty images per second).

The computation of true three-dimensional moving imagery done in real time as the game is played, at resolutions high enough for the illusion of depth to be successful, takes an enormous amount of computing power and speed. Only in the mid- to late 1990s did arcade games and home computers become powerful enough to attempt these sorts of games, although as anyone who has played these CD-ROM games knows, they still can often be either a bit blocky in their imagery or slow and halting in their movement. Still, the desire to put three-dimensional graphics on the screen and give depth to the imagery of the games led to attempts at three-dimensional imagery long before the computational power for true three-dimensional computation was commonly available. Many games today, and most of the games in the past, avoid the difficulties of true three-dimensional computation through a variety of strategies, just as the methods described above saved filmmakers from having to create sets and three-dimensional environments that would have been too big, too expensive, or too difficult to build.

As noted, the simplest way of evoking a third dimension is by changing the relative size of the object; smaller objects are supposed to be in the distance, while larger ones are assumed to be closer to the viewer. This occurs in games such as *Star Ship* (1977), *Night Driver* (1976), *Starmaster* (1982), and *Tempest* (1980). Position and movement also play a role; in *Night Driver* objects near the top of the screen are farther away and grow larger as they descend the screen toward the player's car. White posts in *Night Driver*, pointlike "stars" moving along diagonal lines out from the center of the screen in *Starmaster*, and vector lines of perspective in *Tempest* also provide depth cues. *Battlezone* (1980) also effectively used the line weights or varying brightness of its vector graphics for depth cueing; objects that were farther away were not only smaller but also fainter on the black background of the screen. Since the pictorial detail of the imagery in these games is low and the games rely mainly on size changes and movement to produce the illusion of depth, temporality becomes an important factor in establishing the *z*-axis.

Additional depth cues are provided in the Atari 2600 versions of *Pole Position*, *Battlezone*, and *Zaxxon*. Adapted from arcade games containing more detailed graphics, the graphics of these games had to be greatly simplified for the 2600. *Pole Position*'s moving scenery was limited to the alternating red- and white-striped strips on the edges of the road, and an occasional car on the road. The red and white stripes on the roadsides are thinner toward the horizon and thicker toward the bottom of the screen, creating a texture gradient which acts as a depth cue. In the adaptation to the Atari 2600, *Battlezone*'s vector graphics became low-resolution raster imagery, and a first-person perspective became an over-the-shoulder view. Likewise, the land area between the player's tank and the horizon employs a texture gradient as well as a color gradient, which mixes green and brown horizontal lines to create a darkening effect as the land stretches away to the mountains on the horizon. *Battlezone* also indicates depth through the use of a small radar display of an overhead view, with enemy vehicles represented as white dots on a field of black. And finally, *Zaxxon* features a plane which flies up and down over an aircraft carrier that scrolls down vertically, enlarging as it approaches so as to appear to be moving toward the viewer in perspective. Here, both diegetic and nondiegetic depth cues are provided; on the side of the screen is a blue line indicating the plane's height, and within the image the plane has a shadow. The vertical distance between the plane and its shadow is intended to indicate the plane's height, although the aircraft carrier is so lacking in detail that the height of it and the objects on it relative to the plane are not always easy to determine. These games reach the limits of what detail and depth are possible with lower resolution graphics, and quite often success in one of these early games can depend on how well a viewer/player can read the crude gestalt of implied positions and movement. A number of arcade games and later home video games use similar strategies of growing and shrinking flat-plane graphics, but do so with greater resolution and detail, thus creating a greater illusion of depth and space.

Another more successful strategy of creating a three-dimensional look without doing any three-dimensional computation while the game is being played is the use of background images drawn so as to appear to have depth. This is similar to the use of theatrical backdrops and painted flats on-stage, or the use of rearscreen projection or composited matte paintings in live-action film, or the background drawings in animation over which cels are placed. An example of this is the pyramid of cubes used in Q*bert (1982); the cubes appear to add depth to the scene, but the characters are simply placed over them as they move. The characters may overlap one another occasionally, but they do not foreshorten or have any other signs of moving along a z-axis as they traverse the pyramid; they appear the same size no matter where they are on-screen. Likewise in *Spy Vs Spy* (1984), the rooms that the spies are in foreshorten, but the spies move around on top of the image without changing size or appearance, and no three-dimensional computation is necessary. Some games, like *Dragon's Lair* (1983) and *Star Trek: Borg* (1996), use all animated or live-action video clips; here the characters are contained in the background images.

Myst (1993), *Riven* (1997), and *Gadget* (1993) are also made up of still images used as backgrounds and video clips, but the images they use are all rendered views of three-dimensional objects that were modeled on a computer. The images in these games differ from those in Q*bert (1982) and *Spy Vs Spy* in that they did require three-dimensional computation, although that computation occurs at the time the game is created and not during gameplay. Video clips of moving three-dimensional computer-generated imagery are also used as backdrop imagery, for example in *Rebel Assault* (1993), where the player-character's spaceship is placed over clips of computer-animated backgrounds and must steer the ship to match the preset flight paths, which are always the same. The ability to steer the ship within the path, and occasionally choose between two paths, gives a strong impression of an interactive three-dimensional environment, even though no three-dimensional computation is occurring as the game is played. One way a viewer can test a game to see if a prerecorded flight path is being used is to try to steer off the path to get a different view; in an environment where true three-dimensional calculation is occurring this will be possible, but not otherwise.

Finally, there are games which do three-dimensional computation in real time as the game is being played (most of which present their worlds in a first-person perspective). They range in graphic detail from the sparse monochromatic vector world of the arcade version of *Battlezone* (1980), to the multiple-player fighting and racing worlds of *Daytona U.S.A.* (1994), *Super GT* (1996), *Battletech* (1992), and *Red Planet* (1992), to the claustrophobic interiors of the CD-ROM games *Doom, Descent, Quake,* and *Dark Forces,* to the virtual reality game *Dactyl Nightmare* (1992).

In one sense, the space in *Dactyl Nightmare* is no more real than the space in *Star Ship* (1977), despite great improvements in detail, depth cues, and interactivity; one is more convincing as an illusion than the other, but they both remain illusions. Computationally, the difference is great, since *Dactyl Nightmare* involves the manipulation of actual three-dimensional computer-generated models. Thus games can be considered more "real" than others to the extent that three-dimensional models can be said to be more real than two-dimensional images of those models.

Three-dimensional video game worlds continue to grow more convincing and photorealistic, but they will likely also continue to experiment with different configurations of space that have not been seen in other media. As Michael Benedikt demonstrates in his book *Cyberspace: First Steps*, computer-generated representations of spatial structures are completely fluid, leaving the video game plenty of room to explore the representation of space.[13] Tools for home computer games and game systems have been developed and improved, like Apple's *QuickTime VR*, a scrolling (type 5) kind of space mapped onto the inside of a sphere as it rotates, to give the illusion of being an interactive (type 10) kind of space.[14] The use of space—on-screen and off—in video games is certainly linked and owes a great deal to cinematic space, which was an important influence on its development. However, through combinations of the spatial structures discussed above, video game space goes beyond cinematic space and shows the various possibilities for organizing space within a diegetic world, as well as broadening the sense of what a diegetic world can be through added elements like navigation and interaction. The cinema offered a window and positioned the spectator within the world it depicted; the video game goes further, allowing the spectator to explore that world through the surrogate of the player-character and take an active role in its events. As games continue developing and film moves into the realm of computer graphics, film may, in some ways, look to and follow precedents set by video games.

Notes

1. *Tout Va Bien* also has a number of long tracking shots which are visually very similar to scrolling video game graphics.

2. As far as the player-character's movement off the edge of the screen and back on-screen on the opposite side is exactly like the on-and-off movement in spaces of type 3, except for the change of background, which indicates the new space.

3. Rick Altman, "*The Lonely Villa* and Griffith's Paradigmatic Style," *Quarterly Review of Film Studies* 6.2 (Spring 1981), pp. 123–124.

4. Ibid., p. 129.

5. See Robert L. Adams, "D. W. Griffith and the Use of Off-Screen Space," *Cinema Journal* 15.2, pp. 53–57.

6. Noël Burch, *Theory of Film Practice*, trans. Helen Lane (New York: Praeger, 1973), p. 17.

7. The asteroids in Atari's arcade game *Asteroids* were superimposed vector graphics that passed over each other and so could not be considered to be an example of Burch's sixth segment of off-screen space.

8. If one player's Spy enters the room where the other one is, the action appears on one of the screens, and the other goes blank, until the Spies are in separate rooms again; thus there can be times in the game where off-screen space (from either player's point of view) is not depicted on-screen. Likewise, *High Velocity* also merges its views when players are close together.

9. David Bordwell, "Space in the Classical Film," in *The Classical Hollywood Cinema: Film Style and Mode of Production to 1960*, ed. David Bordwell, Janet Staiger, and Kristin Thompson (New York: Columbia University Press, 1985), pp. 50–59. Sometimes video games do break with conventional cinematic continuity; for example, during the fight scenes in *Tekken 2* the 180-degree rule is occasionally broken.

10. Prior to video games, flight simulators using computer animation offered first-person perspectives of interactive three-dimensional environments, but these were not commercially available for public use.

11. Text adventures created a first-person perspective verbally by describing what a player was seeing, hearing, feeling, etc. (although grammatically employing "you" in the text instead of "I"); but this is, of course, much different than a game with graphics.

12. When the elevator in the tall tree is running, it produces a periodic, metallic "ka-chunk" sound that can be heard even on other parts of the island; likewise, when the right plaques by the fountain are activated, there is an off-screen sound of water indicating that something is happening. Games, then, that have similar spatial structures as those seen in films can use off-screen sounds in a fashion similar to film.

13. Michael Benedikt, "Cyberspace: Some Proposals," in *Cyberspace: First Steps*, ed. Michael Benedikt (Cambridge, Mass., and London, England: MIT Press, 1991).

14. For an overview of the technology and how it works, see Dominic Milano, "QuickTime VR: An Overview of Apple's Virtual Reality Tools," *Interactivity* (March 1996), pp. 34–43.

4

Time in the Video Game

Mark J. P. Wolf

C inema rendered time more malleable than it had been on the live theater stage, but the video game presents even more possibilities for temporal structuring. And, quite often, more time is spent with a video game than with individual works in other media; most films are less than three hours, but some video games, like *Tomb Raider* (1996), *Morpheus* (1998), or *Twinsen's Odyssey* (1997), may take a player dozens of hours to see everything there is to see in the game. The interactive and conditional nature of what the player sees means that some degree of nonlinearity is often present in the experience as well.

To examine the use of time in the video game, we might first begin with a look at the ideas of stillness and movement, which give the player the experience of time passing (or not passing). Next we will look at repetition and cyclical or looped structures of time, which in some ways combine notions of movement and stasis. Finally, we will compare time within the game's diegetic on-screen world to interludes and title sequences, and how both of these in turn relate to the "real" time passing as the game is played. Throughout, we will see how the use of time is integral to the design and experience of the video game.

Stillness and Movement

In the world around us, movement is always occurring, and by "stillness" we usually mean that there is no *perceptible* movement (or, perhaps, that there is very little noticeable movement). If we limit our perception to media, we can find stillness in a painting (a "still life"), in a stone sculpture, or in a photograph. Of course, any kind of "moving" imagery, whether film, television, or video game, is made of a series of still images, but the overall effect experienced when one is watching them is often that of perceived motion. Yet this need not always be the case either.

We might say, then, that in media imagery, there are several distinct kinds of stillness. First, there is that of photographic slides. A single image is projected and remains on screen, and there is no movement of any kind. This stillness is the same as we might find in a painting or photograph.

Second, there is the freeze frame found in film; the same image is seen, frame after frame, but through a series of images being projected, all of which are photographs rephotographed from the same image, instead of the continuous projection of one single photograph, as in a slide. In a freeze frame in film, the *image* does not move, but the *grain* of the image does, as opposed to the slide, where neither the image nor the grain moves. This gives a certain "liveness" to the image, since we know the film is moving through the projector, even though the same image is being repeated (thus a freeze frame involves repetition, whereas a slide does not).

Third, there are "still" shots in film in which nothing (or very little) happens, even though the camera is continuously recording the scene. Although visually such a shot may be nearly indistinguishable from a freeze frame, one can usually tell the difference through minute changes occurring in the image (effects of wind, slight changes in lighting, etc.), or because there does not appear to be any noticeable degradation due to rephotography. This kind of "still shot" is a series of images photographed on location, whereas the freeze frame is a single image taken on location and rephotographed repeatedly. The "still shot" differs experientially from the freeze frame in that there seems to be a *potential* for movement present (and often, very small or subtle movements). In other words, the image and the grain both "move" (as opposed to simply holding or repeating), but there is no movement or very little movement *within* the image, or of a subject in the image.

Movement, then, can occur at the level of the medium (slides vs. literally "moving" imagery like film), at the level of the image (freeze frames vs. still shots), or within the content of the image (still shots vs. shots of people or things moving around). Since video imagery is limited to the same grid of pixels for every image, changes in the grain of the imagery are far less noticeable than in film, making freeze frames and still shots harder to distinguish from each other. Only slight variations in the colors of the pixels, rather than their sizes and positions, can indicate that a sequence of images is being seen instead of a repeated single image. This variation or grain effect is visible when films are transferred to video, and partially accounts for the "film look" that is often desired for projects appearing on video.

Except for when they play video clips, computer displays and video games also differ from both film and video in that they do not have a linear series of prerecorded images to display on-screen; the computer displays the current image in its screen buffer repeatedly until changes occur due to the program's algorithm or the input of the user. Unlike video, the computer controls the color of the individual pixels precisely, so that there is usually no change in grain occurring from frame to frame (unless changes in grain appear in the clips played, as in many *QuickTime* clips). Because a cathode ray tube needs constant refreshing to retain an image, an unchanging image is similar to a freeze frame, although without a visibly changing grain its stillness is visually closer to that of a slide. At the same time, the interactive nature of the computer and video game means that the potential for movement always exists (unless the computer locks up, but even this becomes noticeable only when one tries to move the cursor and finds the machine unresponsive). Because the grain pattern that makes up the screen is unchanging, many video games visually alter the screen to allow the player to distinguish between a "paused" game and one which is running with no action on screen (for example, some darken the screen, or display a "paused" sign). Likewise at the end of a game, movement often continues, either in the form of end credits, through changes in screen color (for example, in Atari 2600 games), or in the continuation of on-screen action; for example, most arcade video games return to a demonstration mode when not in use.

In the medium of film, grain, hiss, and flicker are nondiegetic indicators of time passing. Such sonic and visual ambience—very slight, almost imperceptible changes in sound and picture—give the audience a sense of time passing and indicate that neither the image nor the sound track has stopped running. While ambience may be more limited in the video display, the fact that an image is visible indicates that the machine is running. With the added potential for interaction, in which the movement or statis of the on-screen imagery is often partly a player's choice (unlike film), time is experienced more actively than in the viewing of film, which runs independently of the viewer. Even when a player does not do anything in a game, the computer continues to check for input, and events in the world of the game continue, often with something happening to the player-character if it stays in one place too long. In *Adventure* (1978) for the Atari 2600, for example, the bat might enter the screen and pick up what the player-character is carrying, or a dragon might enter and attack. As in film, diegetic events continue despite the player's inactivity, but in video games, inactivity is usually a choice on the part of the player.

In film, movement occurs when either the subject being photographed moves, or the camera moves. Although no camera is involved in nonphotographic video game imagery, camera moves are simulated through movement of the backgrounds of scenes. Character movement and background movement are typically what set the pace in video games, and in many games, both of these speeds increase as a player advances into more difficult levels of play. Just as in physics, where time and motion are relative and depend on one another, accelerating action and accelerating time can be seen as different aspects of the same experience. For example, in *Myst* (1993) and *Riven* (1997), there is a "zip mode" available to players which allows them to jump to places seen in the distance without having to see the intervening screens; one could see this as speeding up the player's movement, or condensing his or her travel time.

Since video games usually do not have the same nondiegetic indicators of passing time mentioned above (moving grain, flicker, hiss, and so forth), other forms of ambience are sometimes added to scenes to emphasize the potential for movement and keep the image feeling "live." In *Myst* and *Riven* for example, there is usually an ambient sound of some kind (wind, water, insects, and so on), and ambient motion in the background of many of the scenes, such as moving water, insects or birds flying about, and turning or rotating objects like the windmill, fan blades, antennae, and so on. This kind of movement, which repeatedly returns to the same position, combines stillness and movement in a form of cyclical or "looped" time.

Repetition and Cyclical or Looped Time

Although cycles of repeated time occasionally appear in film and television—such as in the film *Groundhog Day* (1993), the episode "Cause and Effect" of *Star Trek: The Next Generation*, music videos, or experimental films in which shots are repeated—they are not very common to live-action media. Animation commonly uses cycles of images for repeated actions like walking or running, although usually with the character or background in motion. Cycles of repeated time and repeated series of images are both prevalent in video games, and are a major strategy for keeping the game's imagery in motion without great demands on image storage or creation. Some image cycles, like those of *Myst* or *Riven*, mentioned in the last section, are a form of visual ambience, while others are actively encountered in the games in which they appear. Often, rows or columns of cycling elements are used as obstacles or hazards (like the rows of cars in *Frogger* [1981] or the cars in *Dodge 'Em* [1980]), or as targets (as in *Circus Atari* [1980], Coleco's *Carnival* [1980], or other shooting gallery games). Cycles of action also occur, such as bouncing ball cycles in *PONG* (1972) and *Breakout* (1976) when conditions are right. Repeating cycles of actions or scenes are also displayed on many arcade games when they are not in use, in an attempt to lure players into trying them.

Whereas films are often viewed only once by an audience member, video games are designed to be played multiple times by a player, and unless the game's algorithms are programmed to be entirely random, actions and behaviors of the game's computer-controlled characters often recur. Learning the patterns of behavior and working around them is usually itself part of the game, allowing a player to advance to higher levels once the pattern is recognized and mastered. Cycled action builds player expectation and anticipation, and knowledge of a pattern is often crucial to the timing of the player-character's actions, such as the dodging of bullets, pursuers, or falling objects, or in running, jumping, and using elevators, escalators, swinging doors, and so forth. Often a game's levels will be almost impossible to complete the first time through, since they may require a player to know in advance an exact series of actions that will get him or her through a level. Repetition, then, becomes a form of training, and each time through the level becomes a slightly (or even substantially) different experience for the player.

Even in narrative or puzzle-oriented games, time loops like the one found in the film *Groundhog Day* occur, in which players finds themselves returning to the same situation repeatedly until they give the correct response or perform the correct action. In text adventures and graphical adventures, players can often return to the same location, reading the same text descriptions or watching the same video clips several times over until the right choice or response is made. In interactive movie games like *Dragon's Lair* (1983) or *Star Trek: Borg* (1996), players can find themselves in the same narrative branch more than once if the wrong decision is made, and after a certain number of unsuccessful tries, the game may even be terminated. Just as players must often have some idea of a game's spatial structures in order to navigate through them, a sense of the temporal loops and their timing, linkages, and other structures is often also important and may even be navigable.

Repetitions, cycled images, consistent and repeating behaviors, revisited narrative branches, and the replayability of many of the games themselves create a sense of expectation, anticipation, and familiarity for the player. They encourage the player to find underlying patterns which allow him or her to take control of the situations encountered, and this assured orderliness may well be an important factor in the allure that video games have for many people. On the other hand, complete predictability can hurt the replayability of a game. This balance of predictability with randomness, of theme and variation, is necessary to most video games, just as the games must be easy enough to play so as not to be discouraging, yet challenging enough to invite more playing. Also important to the overall experience of a game are the beginnings and endings of action sequences, the opening and closing sequences that surround them, and the interludes, or "cut scenes," that often occur between levels or scenarios in a game.

Interludes and Title Sequences

As graphics become increasingly complex, detailed, and photorealistic, a greater number of cinematic elements are being incorporated into video games. Camera angles, lighting, music, and editing often follow cinematic conventions, and opening title sequences and end credits are common in CD-ROM-based games. Public service announcements even appear before title sequences in some arcade games. There are even composers, like George Alistair Sanger and Tommy Tallarico, who specialize in writing the soundtracks for video games.[1] Tallarico even has his music available in an album from Capitol Records, entitled *Tommy Tallarico: Virgin Games, Greatest Hits Volume One.* As the presentation of the video game grows more cinematic through the use of some of the same conventions and devices, audience expectations also become more like those of film viewers. Unlike many of their earlier predecessors, newer video games often present their action in a more detailed context, and title sequences, opening and closing credits, and interludes throughout the game-playing experience break up action scenes and provide a sense of structure and pacing.

Title sequences in video games function in a similar manner to their counterparts in film. Although opening sequences appeared in such early games as *E.T.* (1982) and *Raiders of the Lost Ark* (1982) for the Atari 2600, they are much more common, and almost obligatory, in CD-ROM-based games. Like commercial feature films, they often begin with a logo of the distribution company and production company, after which are opening titles and credits, usually set in motion and shown with a soundtrack. Title sequences often contain narrative material (scenes, voiceover, etc.) which sets up the action of the game, as in *Myst* (1993) or *Star Wars: Rebel Assault* (1993), or sometimes are more abstract, introducing various themes and images from the game's narrative, as in *Gadget* (1993). Thus, as in film title sequences, it is often a mixture of diegetic (inside the world of the game) and nondiegetic (outside the world of the game) material which introduces the game. End credits are now also common on CD-ROM games; they typically appear like film credits (light lettering on a dark background) and are accompanied by a soundtrack. Sometimes a Quit button may also appear, allowing a player to skip the credits and end the running of the program.

Interludes, or moments in which the game's interactive potential is briefly suspended, either by a short scene or a screen informing the player of the change of level, occur in many video games, and for a variety of reasons. Sometimes the reason for an interlude is purely mechanical; early home computer games needed time to load various parts or levels of the game from disk, and even today some CD-ROM games require brief pauses to search and load parts of the game. To make these breaks less intrusive on gameplay, these pauses can be worked into the game itself, as in *Myst* (1993), where the linking from one age to another is accompanied by sound effects and a fade-out and fade-in. More often, however, a dialog box will ask the player to wait while game data loads, or in games using multiple CD-ROMs, the dialog box may ask the player to change compact discs. Usually such interludes appear only between scenes or during breaks in the action so as to disrupt the narrative as little as possible.

Other interludes are used within the game's narrative as a means of pacing. An action film which is well paced will typically have "breathers" or "slow" scenes which appear between action sequences to vary the pacing. These scenes allow the audience a moment of relaxation and recuperation, creating a contrast; scenes of fast action appear more intense when placed between slower paced scenes that allow tension to be released so that it can be built up again. For example, a chase in *Raiders of the Lost Ark* (1981) ends with the explosion of a truck in which Indiana Jones believes Marion Ravenwood is being held captive, and the next scene is a slower, quieter scene in which he mourns her death. In video games, the player is physically involved in the action through the controlling of the player-character, who is often chased or in danger, and breaks in the action are even more useful in providing a moment of rest for the player. Just as slower scenes are often preceded by character's deaths in movies, there are typically breaks in the action between a player-character's "lives." These breaks are typically filled with short animated death sequences, such as Pac-Man shriveling up to an electronic musical flourish, Q*bert falling off the pyramid of cubes with a shrill scream, or the great variety of death throes and victory dances found in the *Soul Edge* (1995), *Tekken* (1995), or *Mortal Kombat* (1992) fighting games. These sequences provide a brief moment's rest while holding the player's attention and keeping the player involved in the game.

Players usually need not die, however, in order to gain a moment's respite. The player is often given brief pauses in the action after successfully completing a certain objective or before advancing to a new area or "level" of the game. In CD-ROM games like *Tomb Raider* (1996), these pauses usually contain short animated scenes. Many earlier games featured musical flourishes or short animations between levels. In *Tempest* (1980), for example, once a level is complete, there is a fly-through sequence to the next level of the game. In some games, such as *Star Wars: Rebel Assault* (1993), after the completion of a level, passwords are given which allow a player to start future games at a higher level once lower levels are mastered. Other game information may be displayed between levels as well; scores or time remaining can be shown, or bonus lives may be given for the completion of a level. While most interludes allow a player to sit back and watch, some allow interaction; for example, in *Warioland* (1995) for Nintendo's Virtual Boy, the player-character Wario rides an elevator between levels and is given time to choose between several doors. When a choice is made and a door is entered, the next level begins. In such an interlude, where interaction is possible, there is often no time pressure, so that the player can wait before advancing to the next level. Most interlevel interludes, however, allow no interaction and are of a set duration (and short), keeping players on the ready and concentrating their attention.

In many cases, interludes or "cut scenes" between levels or areas of a game will advance the game's narrative (particularly in CD-ROM games). There are a few exceptions, for example, the cut scenes between certain levels in *Pac-Man* (1980) which feature simple animated sequences of the game's characters chasing each other across the screen. Most of the time, however, the narrative is kept moving along through animated clips joining events or locations in the storyline. In *Gadget* (1993), for example, animations of the trains or plane travel (and in one case, stairs and halls) take a player from one location to the next, and no interaction is available during these sequences. *Star Wars: Rebel Assault* (1993) and *Tomb Raider* (1996) feature short narrative clips of story sequences connecting the scenes and player-character's tasks from one level to another; these allow no interaction either.

Since advancement of a game's narrative can occur during interludes and interaction is also possible during them, interludes and action sequences can take on a reversible figure-ground relationship. Games which are sometimes called "interactive movies" are made up of branching video clips or images, the branching of which is decided by a player's actions. Players are often called to make a decision at points in the game where the action stalls or loops, or during action sequences that allow player input which can stop or change the course of action while the video clip is running. For example, *Star Trek: Borg* (1996) features a storyline which the player can steer into a few directions at points where choices are required between two or more alternatives (pausing too long or not making any choice also has consequences). Thus, this sort of game (or "interactive narrative") becomes a series of long narrative sequences punctuated by moments of decision, quite the opposite of games with constant decisions and player-controlled action punctuated by noninteractive interludes. As the number of different narrative paths and moments of decision decrease, the temporal experience of these narratives becomes less like that of a game and more like that of watching a film or video, in which a viewer has no direct control over the duration of the experience.

Game Time vs. Real Time

The experience of passing time is always a subjective one, dependent on what a person is doing; an hour in the dentist's chair during a root canal may seem subjectively much longer than an hour spent with a loved one on a holiday. Cinematic techniques attempt to simulate these effects by changing the pacing of scenes and by what they choose to show or leave out. Although films can contain slowly moving scenes, overall, most films compress time and their stories take place over a much longer period than that which the film itself actually runs.[2] The compression of time comes from the use of ellipses, in which durations of time are left out of the story between cuts or scenes. Apart from the use of cuts with overlapping action, and varied camera speeds used in slow-motion and time-lapse photography, most individual shots unfold at a rate not unlike that by which we normally experience time, often referred to as "real time."³ Because of all the ellipses between shots and scenes, however, cinematic time is very malleable and flexible.

To the degree to which video games are similar to films, they can also feature ellipses between shots and scenes, as well as compress time. But the more interactive a video game is, the more control the player may have in the game's duration (which may also depend on the player's skill). In games like *Myst* (1993) and *Adventure* (1978), the player can control when the game "cuts" from one view or location to another, in addition to the duration of time spent in each location. Games with first-person perspectives and fluid, three-dimensional movement through a space (such as is found in *Doom, Dark Forces, Quake,* or *Tomb Raider,* and their sequels), however, show continuous points of view as a player moves; instead of a series of cuts, the effect is the creation of one long take until the level ends or the player-character is killed (or if the player pauses the action to take a break). In such cases, game time and real time are more closely correlated, since the time experienced by the player and player-character in the game must be fairly congruous for the sake of the interactive experience; in a film, by contrast, a character might react much more quickly (or slowly) than we ourselves would.⁴

The pacing of a video game, then, becomes a combination of the preset pacing of the computer-controlled events and characters in the game, along with the pacing determined by the player, where the player is given that option. Often these two paces come into conflict; if the player is not quick enough, the player-character can get killed. The temporal experience of the game can be a mixture of prerecorded sequences or animated clips taking a certain amount of time, computer-controlled characters and events whose speeds can be varied by the game, and the speed of the player's own decisions, reactions, and movement through the game's world. The balance of these factors differs from one type of game to the next, and sometimes even between different playings of the same game. The early stages of an adventure game may concentrate mainly on exploration and navigation, while later stages may consist of action and the solving of puzzles. Obstacle course, driving, and racing games may be moved through faster once players are able to increase their speed without encountering difficulty. Multiple-player games add competing player-characters, controlled by other people, who can alter the course of events and timing.

Different modes of exhibition can also add restrictions to the experience of time in a game. Some Internet-based games involve a time lag due to the sending and receiving of information over phone lines and remote servers, making play less instantaneous, but at the same time resulting in complex, long-running role-playing scenarios lasting several weeks or more, with hundreds of players involved. Games networked over local area networks (LANs) are faster paced, and arcade games, in which players pay for each game play individually, tend to have games with very fast action that are typically over in a few minutes, allowing for more play and thus more income. The better players are, the longer they last, and the more value they get for their money; however, getting better may require practice and many games (and quarters) to begin with. In contrast, home game systems and computer games, which are purchased rather than paid for game by game, can afford to have slower puzzle-based or adventure games lasting hours on end, and games more involving and contemplative in nature. It is no surprise that text adventures and games like *Myst* never appeared in the arcade.

Home video game players also have other means of controlling game time which are usually not available to arcade game players. Many games have speed settings, which allow a player to play the same game with the same action at different speeds (in simpler games, speed is often the only difference between easy and difficult levels). Because home games could be more involved and take a longer time to play or solve, Pause and Save functions were often included in computer systems and more recently, in console-based game systems with the ability to write game data onto a computer card. Both Pause and Save functions allow the playing of a game to extend beyond a single sitting, allowing players to become more invested in a game without the fear of losing all their efforts due to disruptions or a lack of time. With the Save function, players could also save a game at a point where a decision was required, and then play the game out multiple times from the saved game, making a different choice each time. This allowed adventure games to become more complex, as the Save function made difficult tasks or complex game structures less frustrating since a player-character's "death" would only make the player start over from the last saved game position, rather than from the very beginning of the game. The Pause function can also be used to interrupt game play to allow players to perform some action faster than they normally could (for example, in *Tomb Raider* (1996), to change weapons, or use a medi-pack to heal an injury during a fight). Use of the Pause function differs from the interludes described above in that pauses are initiated by the player rather than built into the structure of the game's narrative. These pauses last for an indefinite duration, just as hitting the Pause button on a VCR differs from an intermission of set length built into a long film like *Dr. Zhivago* (1962).

For the most part, video games are meant to be experienced without much, or any, use of the Pause function, since, as in many films, time pressure is often necessary for the creation of narrative suspense—particularly so when you, as the player, are racing against the clock and the outcome is yet to be determined, as opposed to when a character in a film you are watching is racing against the clock in a prerecorded sequence whose outcome is already determined at the end of the reel.

Time Pressure and Ticking Clocks

Clearly the participatory nature of the video game adds to the player's involvement in the gaming experience (physically at least, if not emotionally as well). While during a film we have the leisure to sit back and think about what we might do in a given situation while watching characters work out their troubles on-screen, most games require a player to react rather than reflect.[5] Although time is always passing as a video game is running, and fast action and careful timing are often relied upon to some degree, many games (dating back to early developmental models in 1967) also have ticking clocks or time counters of some kind to further accentuate the feeling of time pressure. These timers may move at the same rate as real time, or at vastly different rates, ranging anywhere from the timers used in *SimCity* (1989) and *Sid Meier's Civilization* (1991), which measure time in months and years, with one month taking only a few minutes of real time, to the timer in Activision's *Skiing* (1980) for the Atari 2600, in which one minute of the game timer's clock takes over two minutes of real time to elapse. Thus the diegetic time within the world of the game can vary a good deal from the real time the player experiences; the cinematic equivalent would be film sequences in time lapse or slow motion.

Time pressure due to a ticking clock differs somewhat from time pressure due to pursuers during a chase. In a chase scenario, for example, in *Pac-Man* (1980), where the ghosts are in constant pursuit of Pac-Man, quick decisions are required as to which routes to take to avoid the ghosts while eating up all the dots; however, quick action is more important than economical movement or choosing the shortest route, since the player has an unlimited amount of time to maneuver as long as the ghosts are carefully eluded. On the other hand, in a scenario in which a player is completing task in as little time as possible (such as in *Superman* [1979] for the Atari 2600) or trying to beat the clock (as in *Skiing* or other racing, obstacle course, and sports-related games), the amount of time spent is crucial and an economy of movement and precision maneuvering is important. Time is an important element in both games, but it is experienced differently.

Ticking clocks can also be running up, adding to an ever increasing amount, like a stopwatch, or down to zero, like an hourglass. In games with a "stopwatch" timer, the "high score" is typically based on the shortest amount of time used, whereas in games with an "hourglass" timer, the object is to see how high a score can be reached in a fixed period of time before it all runs out. In the former type, the task is fixed and the amount of time taken to complete it varies, while in the latter, the amount of time is fixed and how much the player accomplishes varies; games with an hourglass timer, then, typically feature repeatable tasks such as scoring points or making accurate shots, as opposed to games with a stopwatch timer, in which the player usually has larger tasks to accomplish. Games in which multiple players try to beat each other's performances rather than beat the clock usually fall somewhere in between the two timers, since time is typically limited only by the speed of the opposing players, rather than an objective timer.

Games can also mix unlimited time with situations in which time is limited. In *Myst* (1993), for example, the tree elevator and the battery in the Stoneship Age require a player to perform some action within a limited timeframe, even though the rest of the game has no time constraints. Likewise, games with swinging doors or ropes, walkways or elevators that run continuously, moving targets or obstacles, and so on, all require precise timing even though the game overall may allow unlimited time for the completion of the game's main objective.

Another way that limited and unlimited time can be combined in a game is an action-based clock, which depends on actions instead of on the passing of real time alone. In *Spy Vs Spy* (1984), each player has a separate clock running, and the time each shows can vary; when one spy gets knocked out by another, extra time is subtracted. In *Stellar Track* (1980), the "stardates" are used up only when a player travels from one quadrant to another; the passing of time within the game has no correlation at all to the passing of real time, since staying in the same quadrant does not use up time. Stardates, although they measure time, are treated like any other limited resource in the game such as photon torpedoes or units of energy, the only difference being that they cannot be replenished. The opposite can also occur; resources can be linked to time passing and run down as time goes on, such as battery power, fuel, or air (for example, when the player-character is underwater in *Tomb Raider* [1996]).

In the cinema, time pressure is felt (by both the characters and the audience) through the use of some kind of indicators of passing time, which are present on-screen. They can take on a variety of forms, including clocks of various sizes, watches, digital readouts (such as those which are always very visible on bombs in James Bond films), hourglasses (like the one in *The Adventures of Baron Munchausen* [1989]), or even the setting sun, which provides the time pressure in the chase to the castle in *Bram Stoker's Dracula* (1992). Indicators of passing time can be nondiegetic, as they are in a television sports broadcast; a digital clock, number counter, or lengthening or shortening colored bar appears in a box or at the edge of the screen, separated from the action. Or a warning that time is running out may be indicated by some other formal means; for example, in *Combat* (1977) for the Atari 2600, the on-screen scores begin flashing when the time allotted for the game is almost up, providing players with last-minute suspense as they try to score a few final shots.

As video games are made with higher resolution imagery, more and more diegetic clocks and indicators of passing time appear within the games' worlds, in forms similar to those one finds in film. Even in earlier games, one can find diegetic indicators of passing time; in *Krull* (1983), *Raiders of the Lost Ark* (1982), and *Robot Tank* (1983), all for the Atari 2600, the rising sun is used to indicate passing time. *Raiders of the Lost Ark* incorporates the rising sun into its storyline, which is based on the film of the same name, and also features a stopwatch to let the player know when the sun is about to rise, which is crucial to finding the lost Ark. In *Robot Tank*, hours and days are displayed and correspond with the rising and setting of the sun in the background, which also affects gameplay, since visibility conditions are different during daytime and nighttime in the game.

As in the cinema, temporal structures are a central element of a video game's experience. Whether time is used for action or contemplation, is limited, unlimited, or some combination of both, or flows at different or even controllable rates of speed, it is often closely tied in to gameplay. While the same malleability of time available in film is available in video games, the video game often involves the player more in the temporal structure of the video game experience, and thus can vary greatly depending on the player. While films have a fixed length or running time, video games do not, and it is not uncommon for some games, like *Myst III: Exile* (2001), *Oddworld: Abe's Exoddus* (1998), *The 7th Guest* (1995), or *Final Fantasy IX* (2000), to take dozens of hours or more to complete—far more time than most films, including the fifteen-hour-plus length of Rainer Werner Fassbinder's film *Berlin Alexanderplatz* (1980). Video games and other forms of interactive narrative open up a variety of possibilities and questions concerning the temporal structures of audiovisual entertainment which film and television have only begun to explore; the development of these possibilities seems only a matter of time.

Notes

1. Zach Meston, "Rock 'n' Roll 'n' Video Games," *Wired* (May 1995), p. 47.

2. Besides Lumiére one-shot actualities, there are a few feature-length films that take place in the same amount of time as their running time, including *Rope* (1948), *My Dinner with Andre* (1981), *Nick of Time* (1995), and *Timecode* (1999).

3. The term "real time" is used in computer graphics to denote rendering or interactive graphics which are created as they are seen, and without any lag between images, in much the same way as we visually experience the world around us.

4. Although game and real time are usually correlated, they need not flow at the same rates. *SimCity* (1989), for example, in which the player makes decisions which affect a developing city, measures its game time in months and years. A month of time within the game may pass by in only a few minutes of the player's time, but the pace is still consistent and predictable.

5. Even largely contemplative games like *Myst* have moments in which gameplay involves a limited response time, for example, if one wishes to catch the tree elevator before it descends underground. Simulation games like *SimCity* likewise are generally calm but have moments of crisis calling for quick decisions.

5

Narrative in the Video Game

Mark J. P. Wolf

As the video game's use of space and time grew more complex and graphics grew more representational, the medium became increasingly narrative based. Although certain genres exist which are typically nonnarrative (for example, most puzzle, quiz, card games, and abstract games), the majority of games consist of characters in conflict within an on-screen or "diegetic" world. The audiovisual and spatiotemporal nature of the video game places it alongside other such media like film and television, which also contain narratives played out in an audiovisual diegetic space. At present, the often simple narratives found in many video games are a far cry from the complex and detailed ones found in other media (although the video game, as a medium, is still relatively new and far from reaching its potential). The video game's simple narratives, however, involve the audience in a uniquely direct manner, making the *viewer* into a participant or *player*, by allowing the player to control (to some degree) a character in the game's diegetic world. Rather than merely watching the actions of the main character, as we would in a film, with every outcome of events predetermined when we enter the theater, we are given a surrogate character (the player-character) through which we can participate in and alter the events in the game's diegetic world. It is still, in the end, a vicarious experience, but a more interactive one.

Although most video games still have a very narrow emotional range and rarely move players to deep emotions or tears,[1] they nonetheless can bring about an emotional response, ranging from the primal reflex reactions required in fast-paced action games to the more subtle melancholy and contemplative moods arising in *Myst* (1993) and *Riven* (1997). As the video game matures, so, too, its emotional range and articulation will likely broaden and deepen, just as early cinema took time to develop storytelling with pathos. At the same time, however, as much as the video game borrows from and imitates the conventions of film or other media, it will remain a separate and distinct form of experience, and will be successful only insofar as the formation of its conventions exploits the medium's unique peculiarities and manner of involving the audience. And there will always be games with narratives that are little more than simple kill-or-be-killed shooting scenarios.

In the brief examination of the video game's first thirty years of development that follows, we will trace the growth of the diegetic world of the video game, and how outside or extradiegetic factors also shaped their narratives. Narrational orientation and point of view will be discussed, and finally, the combination of narrative with player interactivity. Although heavily influenced by other media, video games are slowly developing their own conventions and styles, resulting in a different and unique kind of narrative experience.

The Diegetic World of the Video Game

One of the concepts shared by film, television, and the video games is the diegetic world. This is the "world" seen on-screen, where the characters exist and where the story's events occur. By the time the video game appeared, the concept of the diegetic world was already familiar to most audiences through film and television. The video game used much of the visual grammar from these media in the construction of its worlds, and was able to build upon established conventions (such as conservation of screen direction when cutting from one space to another) through added participatory elements. Some of these elements, such as navigation and interaction, place certain limitations on to the diegetic world that are unlike those found in film or television. And as with film, the development of the diegetic world did not occur in a smooth, straightforward fashion.

Initially, video games had simple graphics and simple goals; moving a "paddle" to bounce and return a ball, shooting at moving targets, and avoiding projectiles. Early games featured spaceships, tanks, or other vehicles, or rectangular paddles in the case of sports games, to represent the player on-screen; these on-screen player-character icons were defined strictly by what their functions were. The on-screen player-character was generally not anthropomorphic and had no identity apart from that of the human player controlling it.

One of the first important shifts, then, was the move to character-based games.[2] Chapter 3 has already described the various ways in which the diegetic world grew spatially, from single screens of graphics to multiple or scrolling screens, to detailed three-dimensional environments. Concurrent with the graphic development of space was the design of the characters inhabiting that space. In the mid-1970s, anthropomorphic characters began appearing in video games. In some cases, like the arcade game *Death Race* (1976), they were simply "gremlins" that were targets to be run over.[3] Some human figures merely replaced vehicles; *Outlaw* (1978) for the Atari 2600, was similar to *Combat* (1977) except that figures of cowboys shoot at each other instead tanks. Likewise in sports games, squares and rectangles representing players were gradually replaced with blocky human figures, as can be seen in a number of early Atari 2600 sports games such as *Basketball* (1978) or *Football* (1978). *Space Invaders* (1978) featured a group of abstract characters (the invaders) that appeared high on the screen and fired bullets at the moving player-character below, a game design later used in games such as *Galaga* (1981), *Demons to Diamonds* (1982), and a host of other games. Occasionally a facial detail like an eye or mouth might even appear on a character (e.g., the bat and the dragons in *Adventure* [1978]); character designs improved as graphics were capable of displaying more detail. Yet whether characters are represented by high-resolution photographic images or a few colored squares, certain basic narrative roles and functions (protagonist, antagonist, obstacles, etc.) are always present, and there are always limitations or "rules" as to what goal-oriented characters may do or not do while engaging in conflicts or pursuing their quests.

While graphics were slowly developing in the late 1970s and early 1980s, text adventures played on home computers contained the most detailed narratives. In these games, graphics were limited or nonexistent, and everything was described verbally in on-screen text. Each room or area had a description that appeared when the place was entered, and areas were often connected by the use of north, south, east, west, up, or down commands. Characters' entrances and exits and other events would also be noted by descriptions. Likewise, a player made choices and performed actions by typing in text such as "open door," "take sword," or "drink potion." The memory available in the home computer allowed the diegetic worlds of video games to grow beyond the limits of the cartridges of console-based games. Since the amount of memory needed depended on how much text was used and the way the interactions were programmed, diegetic worlds of text adventures could be quite large. Some, like *Planet-fall* (1983), *The Hitchhiker's Guide to the Galaxy* (1984), and the first few games in the *Zork* series, could take many hours to solve, and were usually not likely to be completed in a single sitting.[4]

The lure of graphics, and players' preferences of depiction over description and immediate action over typed commands and responses, meant that graphic adventure games would eventually eclipse text adventures. In 1979, the first all-graphics adventure game appeared: the home game *Adventure* for the Atari 2600, which featured advances in mise-en-scène and character development. The game had a range of locations (the blue labyrinth, the catacombs, three castles of different colors and their interiors), with a grand total of thirty-one interconnecting screens. *Adventure* also had a number of props that the player used during the game, including a sword, magnet, bridge, chalice, and three keys, all of which increased the interactivity of the player-character. Often several of these items would have to be used in conjunction with one another in order to complete an objective. Three dragons and a bat also appeared in the game. Like the ghosts in *Pac-Man* (and preceding them by two years), the dragons were identical in design but were different colors, and each had a different name (Yorgle, Grundle, and Rhindle). But whereas the ghosts' behaviors were nearly identical, *Adventure*'s dragons each had distinct duties (for example, the guarding of different objects), and were also distinguishable from each other by their behavior. Even the bat, which flew through the screens picking up and dropping objects, had two different possible "states" it could be in; one normal, and one agitated. Other games for the Atari 2600 from the next few years featured multiple, interconnected screens and more detailed diegetic worlds, including *Haunted House* (1981), *Superman* (1979), *Raiders of the Lost Ark* (1982), and *E.T. The Extraterrestrial* (1982), the last three of which were adaptations of films of the same names. These games featured some visual advances as well; for example, *E.T.* and *Raiders of the Lost Ark* mixed top views of scenery with side views (for example, mesas or pits seen from above and from the side). Several of these games also allowed the characters to carry multiple objects and had on-screen inventories in the form of information bars with icons that appeared above or below the main screen image. Games like *Superman* and *E.T.* even had human characters whose detail featured clothing, including discernible hats, shirts, pants, and shoes, although such details were each composed of only a few colored pixels.

Besides developing graphically, characters had to develop personalities if they were to establish an identity. Games such as *Superman, E.T.*, and *Raiders of the Lost Ark* relied on characters established in other media rather than creating original characters for their scenarios. Apart from adaptations, most video game characters were either nondescript player-characters or duplicates of simple moving targets, like the space invaders or "gremlins" in *Death Race* (1976). Whereas *Adventure* represented a step forward for home video games, a major turning point in the development of character-based arcade games was the appearance of Namco's *Pac-Man* in 1980. The game moved away from the macho themes of earlier games, attracting both male and female players. It also was the first game with massive crossover appeal in the area of marketing, appearing on a wide range of products and toys, including lunch boxes, glasses, clothing, and even spawning a board game version. Much of the appeal came from the characters: Pac-Man, who was little more than a yellow ball with a mouth, and the colored ghosts, who were given both names and nicknames.[5] *Pac-Man* was a step forward in character development, naming all its characters (including the player-character, unlike *Adventure*) and displaying more detailed and anthropomorphic drawings of them on the game's cabinet. Within the game itself, there were also short narrative interludes between levels during which the game's maze would disappear and brief scenes with the ghosts chasing Pac-Man would be shown along with a musical theme. These interludes were among the first instances of video game characters appearing in animated form outside of the game's usual diegetic world. Also, when Pac-Man died, he did not merely vanish, as other characters did, but instead shriveled up with an accompanying sad musical flourish as if soliciting sympathy from players and bystanders.

Throughout the 1980s, after the phenomenal success of *Pac-Man*, more video game characters endowed with simple personalities appeared. There was the hand-animated Dirk, of the laserdisc game *Dragon's Lair* (1983); Q*bert, his archenemy Coily, and others in *Q*bert* (1983); Mario Mario, the hero of *Donkey Kong* (1981), as well as the ape himself; and Mr. Do of *Mr. Do* (1982). Characters became the link to sequels and spin-offs— *Donkey Kong Jr.* (1982), *Mr. Do's Castle* (1983), *Ms. Pac-Man* (1981), *Jr. Pac-Man* (1983), *Pac-Land* (1984), *Pac-Mania* (1987), and so on. The characters even began to appear in product lines outside of video games, on toys, lunch boxes, board games, and clothing. Characters provided such a sense of identity that some of them, like Nintendo's Mario or Sega's Sonic the Hedgehog, soon came to metonymically represent the corporations that made the games.

Characters in video games can be categorized by the function they perform. First, there are "player-characters," who are the main, goal-oriented agents in the game, and who are said to "win," "lose," or score points. The player-character is the human player's surrogate character in the game's diegetic world; games with multiple human players have multiple player-characters. In some multiple-player games, there are settings that allow the computer to control player-characters when human players are not present; these, then, are computer-controlled player-characters. They are still player-characters because they have abilities and restrictions similar to those of the human-controlled player-character and a similar status within the game's diegetic world.

Apart from these characters, there are also computer-controlled incidental characters which move the game along but are not "players" in the same sense; they perform narrative functions that help to move the story along, but they are not goal-oriented in the same way as the player-characters; they cannot win or lose. The computer-controlled incidental characters can be helpers, hinderers, beneficiaries, neutral characters, or narrators. Helpers aid player-characters in the completion of their goal; they are clue givers, informants, assistants, or sidekicks. The hinderers work against the player-characters; they might be monsters, villains, pursuants, or obstacles. Beneficiaries are characters that you help—characters who are rescued, customers, or even citizens (as in *SimCity* [1989]). Neutral characters neither help nor hinder; they may be present merely for atmosphere, like background extras. And finally, narrators set up the story, and may or may not take part in it (for example, Atrus in *Myst* and *Riven*). Of course, it is not always obvious what role a character might play; whether a character is helpful or misleading may not be known until later in the game. And some characters, like the bat in *Adventure*, may provide both help and hindrance depending on what they do at any given moment. Finding out which characters are helpful and which are not can even be a central element of the game.

The mid-1980s also saw growth in the area of character interaction, which had previously only appeared in dialogue form in text adventures (apart from characters shooting at each other). A number of games combined graphics and text to create a diegetic world, enabling characters to be seen and heard (or rather, read). The best example of these games is the *Ultima* series, which began in 1980 and includes around a dozen sequels. Throughout the run of the series, there are noticeable technical and aesthetic advances from one game to the next, including increases in the size of the diegetic world, the visual complexity of its representation, and the range of interactivity of the player-character. *Ultima I* (1980) was the first game (in video game history) to feature both horizontal and vertical scrolling scenery, a trait shared by most of the *Ultima* series. The second game, *Ultima II: Revenge of the Enchantress* (1982), allowed interaction with the characters of the game's world, albeit in a very limited fashion. *Ultima III: Exodus* (1983) included a musical soundtrack, and *Ultima IV: Quest of the Avatar* (1990) featured a much more detailed conversation system for interacting with computer-controlled characters as well as more emphasis on story development. *Ultima IV* also added the dimension of ethics; the following of certain ethical principles became crucial to solving the game. *Ultima V: Warriors of Destiny* (1988) included character motivations for the game's incidental characters, as well as introducing a new, more three-dimensional style of graphics. Although the game's graphics were still primarily grid-based, characters and scenery were represented obliquely instead of being merely standardized icons on a grid.[6] Graphics engines of the games continued to improve, as did character and story depth, and as the games increased in size and complexity, their diegetic worlds became more detailed and involving. And finally, there is the Internet game *Ultima Online* (1997), available twenty-four hours a day, with several hundred thousand players, a vast map of millions of square feet, and a variety of economic and social structures in which players take part, building their characters' abilities, wealth, and connections. The rise of networked games meant that many players could be playing at one time, and games could last weeks or months. Likewise, the diegetic world had to be big enough and active enough to warrant the subscription fees many such games charged. Because of the modular and gridlike nature of these worlds, however, their graphics were limited to mainly overhead or oblique views rather than first-person views.

Although first-person points of views had been around as early as *Battlezone* (1980), creating them in real time represented a computational challenge because they required the game's diegetic world to be represented as a three-dimensional model which could be rendered from changing points of view. Due to the limitations of earlier graphics engines, three-dimensional worlds would have to be fairly limited, like *Battlezone*'s; or small, like the screen of polyhedron structures in *I, Robot* (1983); or stored in prerecorded sequences, as in all laserdisc games.

During the 1990s, however, advancements in computer hardware and software brought about games, for both the arcade and home, which featured complex three-dimensional environments rendered in a first-person perspective. Some games, like *Doom* (1993), *Dark Forces* (1994), and *Tomb Raider II* (1997), have a moving point of view, controlled by the player, while others, such as *Myst* (1993), *Gadget* (1993), and *Riven* (1997), have mainly static viewpoints with only a few prerendered sequences of moving imagery. The diegetic worlds of these games are highly detailed and complex, and may even require the player to have a keen sense of the three-dimensional structure of the world to successfully navigate it and solve puzzles based on its geography.

Another turning point in the development of the video game's diegetic world came in 1993, with the release of *Myst*. *Myst*, the best-selling CD-ROM of all time, had a variety of environmental ambiences and over 2,500 beautifully rendered screens of images from various angles and standpoints. The images in *Myst* made use of painterly light and shadow effects unlike any game before it, and placed an emphasis on creating mood and atmosphere in the game's settings. Everything is rendered in first-person perspective, and players are encouraged to explore on their own, without time pressures or the possibility of getting killed. Cuts, dissolves, and fast wipes are used as transitions between views. Like the later *Ultima* games, the worlds of *Myst* and its sequel, *Riven* (1997), have detailed backstories that the player unravels during the game, and an intricate diegetic world which even includes maps of itself within the game's world, as well as books and diaries providing backstory and a sense of history.

And finally, there are "interactive movies" like *Johnny Mnemonic* (1995) and *Star Trek: Borg* (1996), which are made sometimes entirely from film and video clips, carrying on the tradition of laserdisc games and continuing to close the gap between the diegetic worlds of film and video games. These games weave interact moments into narrative which play out in prerecorded video clips, with a player's decisions determining which clips are seen. The fewer the decisions left to the player, the more the CD-ROM becomes like a film and less like a game. In most cases, these moments of interactivity and the second-person address of the on-screen characters are some of the only differences between the diegetic worlds of the game and film. Some games, like *Tomb Raider II* (1997), even letterbox some of their action sequences in an attempt to give them a more cinematic feel through the use of a similar aspect ratio.

The role of the video game's diegetic world has become increasingly important in the gaming experience. While early games consisted of simple goals, repetitive action, and high scoring, games of the late 1970s and early 1980s began using multiple goals and sometimes required knowledge of the game's world in the solving of a quest. In many of today's CD-ROM-based games, a detailed knowledge of the game's world is necessary simply to navigate about within it, as well as to solve the game or complete its objective. Branching narratives with multiple endings might require several playings to see all of the story that there is to see. And in many cases, much of the narration may occur outside of the game itself.

Before the Game Begins: Extradiegetic Narration

Games adapted from movies, television shows, novels, comic books, or other sources have the advantage of referring to a diegetic world in another medium that may already be familiar to the player. By placing the video game's action within a detailed narrative context, the game's diegetic world is given a greater illusion of depth, and the player, as the story's main character, is given motivation so that there is more at stake than if the game's action were merely some random, meaningless exercise. Playing the game means participating in the story, fighting for a cause, searching for an answer, beating a foe, and so on, rather than just the honing of an eye-hand coordination skill or the solving of a puzzle. Narrative unifies the action of the game and helps to create the feeling that the player is participating instead of merely interacting.

Narratization of the game's action, then, usually begins before the player even starts the game. Some arcade games, when not in use, loop through video segments of backstory, shown in imagery and on-screen text (for example, the story of *Mortal Kombat 4* [1997] gives the history behind the central character, as he stands in the rain while the viewer's point of view circles around him). Games in which the action is fairly simple are most in need of additional narration outside of game. Games in the *Mortal Kombat, Tekken,* and *Soul Edge* series are basically fighting games in which one fighter confronts another in hand-to-hand single combat. Players can choose between a number of different characters to use as their player-character, and each character has different attributes, weaponry, and moves. Books, manuals, and magazines which focus on these games often contain detailed backstories of the characters, giving them brief histories, as well as the motivation behind why they fight. By carefully writing and marketing these characters, the games are able to differentiate themselves from their competitors, even though the games are graphically and conceptually very similar. Since CD-ROMs are able to hold around 660 megabytes, game makers can also put extradiegetic material in the title and credit sequences and interludes between levels which adds information about the game's characters or storyline. *Tekken 3* (1998), for example, has brief scenes introducing each of its fighter characters; the scenes are set in various locales (urban, rustic, industrial, etc.) and the set, props, lighting, music, and compositions are all designed to create a particular mood or feeling for each character the clip is showcasing, giving a particular impression of the character. Between the levels of *Tomb Raider II* (1997), there are brief scenes involving the heroine Lara Croft and her various adversaries, connecting the levels into a storyline.

Home video games, particularly the earlier ones, had much less memory to use for extradiegetic scenes and backstory, but they still had ways of putting their action within a narrative context. Many cartridges were adaptations of movies or television shows, so the game's characters and situations would likely be already familiar to the player. The fact that they would be taken from the larger and more detailed diegetic worlds of a movie or television show also added to the illusion that the games had more depth than they actually had.

For those games that were original material and not adaptations of characters and storylines in other media, the packaging and marketing of the cartridges could provide a narrative context. The manuals that came with cartridges and the boxes in which they were packaged were often adorned with colorful illustrations that suggested an experience far more complex and detailed than the games could offer.

Even for some of the earliest, simplest home video games, the writers of game manuals came up with ways of turning even something as abstract as a screenful of colored blocks into a story, however much of a stretch it took. An example is *Super Breakout* (1981) for the Atari 2600, a game which featured rows of colored blocks across the top of a black screen, with a paddle and "bouncing ball" below. The paddle could be moved back and forth to bounce the ball up where it would hit the blocks, each of which would vanish from the screen with an electronic beep or boop sound. The object was to remove as many blocks as possible before missing the ball. The *Atari Game Program Instructions* gave the following narrative context:

> Imagine you're in a one-man space shuttle travelling [sic] through the heavens at the speed of light. You and your tiny ship are totally

engulfed in darkness, except for the luminance of an occasional passing star.

Suddenly, without warning, there's a brilliant flash straight ahead. You check the radar screen. Nothing. Pretty soon there's another flash, and another. Next thing you know the flashes have turned into one gigantic force field of some kind and it's dead ahead. You check the radar screen again, still nothing.

The colors in this mysterious force field are so bright, they're almost blinding. And they seem to be in layers. But the strangest thing is that nothing shows up on the radar screen. What could that mean? Is it possible to travel through this mysterious force field or will you crash and be destroyed? And what about the layers? If you make it through one, can you make it through the next, and the next? It's decision time and there are only a few seconds to think about it. Turn back or blast ahead and try to make it through the layers of this brightly colored force field. It's up to you.[7]

Apart from the melodramatic language and the unusual premise, one could note that the context of a spaceship trying to fly through a force field doesn't quite match the ball-and-paddle nature of the game; is the spaceship the ball, moving and bouncing off the force field, or is the paddle the spaceship, even though it doesn't move anywhere near the force field?

Most game program instructions included with Atari 2600 cartridges began with a section setting up the game's narrative context, and most of the later, less abstract games fare better in this regard. Some games, like *Centipede* (1983) and *Yar's Revenge* (1982), even came packaged with small comic books whose stories set up the context of the game's action. Today, movies, books, and television shows are sometimes spin-offs of video games and not just sources for them; video games have become just another sector of vast, cross-media marketing schemes.

Whereas extradiegetic narration was especially important for games with limited graphics, memory, and processing speed, the diegetic worlds of most CD-ROM-based games have become detailed enough that a good deal of narration can be embedded in the design of the game itself, and can rely greatly on the player's narrational orientation.

Narrational Orientation and Structure

The development of narrative structures situated within the diegetic worlds of video games were aided by advances in the point of view constructed for the player, and in the narrational orientation and outcomes of the game's plotlines. Early video games, with their simple graphics, toed the line between abstraction and representation, and in some cases the on-screen image could not be said to represent a spectator's point of view any more than an abstract painting might. Games with representational graphics generally displayed a side view, as in *Space Invaders* or a top view, as in *Tank* (1975) or *Football* (1978). Some games were so simple as to leave the question open; *PONG*, for example, could be arguably a top view or a side view, depending on how you interpreted what the gameplay represented.

Text adventures typically had no optical viewpoint and were written from a second-person point of view (i.e., "You stand in the field . . .," "You walk down the stairs . . ."). Little used in literature, the second-person address made sense in an interactive environment like the text adventure. A second-person point of view was also used in many game descriptions found in manuals, like the one from *Super Breakout* given above, in an attempt to more closely involve the player in the game and compensate for the less involving third-person perspective of the game itself.

Developments in point of view often depended on technical advances in graphics. Nearly all the graphical games of the 1970s were from a third-person perspective, when a "perspective" could be construed at all. But there were a few early games that attempted a first-person perspective, or something close to it. As discussed toward the end of Chapter 3, *Star Ship* (1977) and *Night Driver* (1980) for the Atari 2600 made rudimentary attempts at motion along the z-axis, although in *Night Driver*, the player's car is seen at the bottom of the screen, producing more of an over-the-shoulder third-person perspective while remaining optically closer to a first-person perspective than most games. The most effective depth cues which do not require motion along the z-axis are lines of perspective. Vector graphics, which could produce line drawings more easily than filled, solid-color areas, were better equipped for creating images in which lines of perspective reached toward a vanishing point. In 1980, two vector graphics games appeared, *Battlezone* and *Tempest*, which made use of three-dimensional graphics. *Tempest* had a third-person point of view for most of the game, except for the interludes between levels, in which the well or tunnel of the level just completed would enlarge and engulf the screen, as if the player were flying through it. *Battlezone*, however, had a first-person point of view that the player could control and steer in real time. With the development of three-dimensional graphics calculated in real time, first-person perspectives were easier to achieve, and games like *Spectre* (1993), *Daytona U.S.A.* (1994), and *Super GT* (1996) allowed a player to select different views of the action of the game, including overhead, over-the-shoulder, and first-person points of view. In some games with first-person point of view, the player-character is implied but never seen, just as the photographic image often constructs a point of view without showing whose point of view it is. The player-character, then, is often visually situated in the off-screen space.

Whatever the optical point-of-view, the *narrational* point of view is usually one concerning a goal-oriented main character. Although characters in a film or novel may be goal oriented, video games (and games in general) frequently rely more on the attainment of a particular goal and a win/lose distinction rather than on character and thematic development. Thus the main goal in the video game tends to be score oriented, conflict oriented, task oriented, or some combination of these.

Instead of depending on an all-or-nothing win/lose outcome, score-oriented games indicate a player's relative success or failure through the gain and loss of points, which are often indicated numerically on-screen. In games with multiple "levels," the number of levels a player completes is another way a score can be indicated. While most games are "high-scoring," where the object is to get as many points as possible, in some games, like golf, the object is to get as few points as possible. Scoring is often closely related to time; in racing and obstacle course games, the time taken to complete a course is often used as the player's score, with lower scores and shorter times being desirable. Score-oriented games quantify success and allow any two players to compare their abilities, even though most scoring games are single player. The notion of a numerical high (or low) score also means that players can compete against themselves and try to better their performance in subsequent games, resulting in return play, which in the case of arcade games means more money spent by the player.

Conflict-oriented games involve the beating of an opponent through the display of greater skill in some activity like shooting, fighting, racing, or strategic thinking. While players often have the same goals and compete, players can have also different roles and goals to carry out; for example, one player-character may pursue and try to capture the other, who, in turn, is trying to elude and escape. Two-player games are almost always conflict oriented, and many single-player games, like *Tekken* (1995) and *Mortal Kombat* (1992), match computer-controlled player-characters against human-controlled player-characters. Games like these usually have a series of computer-controlled opponents for a player to fight, and while these are similar to the levels in scoring games, they sometimes need not be fought in any particular order, unlike levels, which are typically hierarchical. In the conflict-oriented game, play usually continues until a player has beaten all opponents or is beaten by them. Scoring, when present in a conflict-oriented game, often serves other functions, such as limiting the time of gameplay (players play until one of them reaches a given score), determining differences in changing player abilities (for example, in a fighting game strength may decrease as fatigue or injuries increase), or indicating how close a match is (one player beats the other by only a small margin).

Task-oriented games involve the successful completion of a given task or quest, the solving of a puzzle, or, in educational games, the learning of a lesson. Winning/losing is determined by whether a task has been completed (sometimes partial completion may be taken into account). Since task-oriented games (like *Myst* [1993], *Riven* [1997], and *Gadget* [1993]) often do not involve the development of physical skills or competitive scoring, they are inevitably designed to be single player and are noncompetitive. Once the task has been completed or the puzzle solved, there is little reason for players to play again, so it is not surprising that such games rarely appear as arcade games. Only as games for purchase are they commercially viable to most game companies. Task-oriented games can also involve conflict, like *Spy Vs Spy* (1984), where players compete at collecting the same objects, but the primary goal is completion of the task rather than defeating one's opponent.

The orientation of a game's goals determine much of how a game is experienced (or reexperienced) by the player, and so does a game's narrative outcomes. Winning and losing are similar to the notion of "happy endings" and "sad endings" found in other narrative forms, particularly because of the close connection between the player and player-character. While a win results from the beating of an opponent or completion of a task, a loss can result from running out of time, a player's getting trapped or put in such a situation that the completion of the task is impossible, or the player-character's death (or, as is often the case, the last of a series of several deaths, in games in which a player has multiple lives). As noted, in many score-oriented games, high scoring takes the place of a win/loss distinction. Pac-Man is always caught by the ghosts in the end, and the space invaders always defeat the player-character; in win/loss terms, the player always loses.[8] But even in a game based on scoring there are different levels of achievement for the player—the highest scoring game played that day or week, the best score recorded on a particular machine, the player's personal all-time best score, and the best scores of all time as recorded in the fan culture surrounding the game. Whether a particular score is regarded as good or bad, then, depends on what the player was hoping to achieve.

The changing nature of a game's narrative outcome from one playing of the game to the next is one of the prime reasons for players to return and play again. Interactivity invites players to select narrative directions and outcomes, and is also one of the greatest challenges in the creation of narratives for video games.

Interactivity and Narrative

At first glance it would seem that interactivity and the inclusion of a predetermined story would work against each other. The author, after all, sets up a chain of events linked by cause and effect which leads to a particular outcome, and that outcome and the way in which it is reached will often embody ideas or themes that the author is expressing in the work. If, on a subsequent rereading, Captain Ahab successfully kills the white whale, *Moby Dick* would no longer be the same book or mean the same thing. If Raskolnikov suddenly changed his mind in *Crime and Punishment* and decided not to murder the old woman, it would be quite a different story, and probably a much shorter one. How can a story proceed in orderly fashion from one point to the next and finally reach a conclusion if the reader/player is allowed to step in and make the decisions, acting as the main character?

One solution is to severely limit the amount of narrative contained in the game itself, or have none at all. To what degree can *Space Invaders* (1978) be said to have a narrative? It would have to run something like this: aliens attack, and the player-character tries shooting them down without getting shot (and the aliens eventually win). Some games are narratively simply but have elaborate backstories (like the one from *Super Breakout* quoted above) which limit the action of the game to a single point in a larger storyline. Though some interaction is involved, such stories are essentially linear in form, with one chain of events leading to a single outcome. Such linear stories need not be simple; *Gadget* (1993) has a long series of episodes and locations which takes several hours for a player to move through. In *Gadget*, events and locations in the story must always take place in a particular order (for example, the train will not leave the station until you get on), and there is only one ending. At certain places along the way, the player may wander within the confines of a certain location, but there are no choices to make which can affect the outcome of the game (one hesitates to even refer to it as a "game"). There are things that players may not find if they do not look around enough—for example, people at the station who will give you information if you go up to them (although it has no effect on the outcome). A literary equivalent to this would be to have footnotes in a novel providing additional information which a reader could read or ignore. Such "footnoting" provides room for interaction and a better understanding of the narrative, but does not give a player any control over the narrative. Likewise in *Myst* and *Riven*, players explore empty landscapes and discover clues which together form the backstory of what had previously happened on the islands. Players cannot change the backstory; they can only uncover it and piece it back together.

Myst and *Riven*, however, differ from *Gadget* in that they include moments of decision which influence the outcome of the story. When such points are included, the narrative must branch in multiple directions, leading to difference sets of consequences. No longer is there a single predetermined ending, but several of them, and which one will end the narrative and the game depends on the player's decisions. Under the right circumstances, though, these branches can occasionally reunite, as they do in *Star Trek: Borg* (1996), when different series of decisions make the narrative eventually converge into the same situation or set of conditions. Instead of having to write an exponential number of different endings, some paths rejoin each other at points, requiring fewer endings to be written. However, if too many branches are collapsed into each other, the story becomes linear again.

If, on the other hand, the branches are connected in such a way that a player can return to the exact same situation more than once, the structure starts to become nonlinear. There may be many outcomes or even a single one, but many different paths to arrive at a particular outcome. Yet even the design of a nonlinear structure can still force the user toward a more linear progression, and a certain ending can be designated as the "right" one which the player is directed to attain. In more nonlinear and branching structures, there are multiple narratives lines running concurrently, only one of which can be experienced by the player at any given time. Finally, there are games which have no preset narratives, only narrative structures, such as sports games or simulation games. In baseball games, for example, there are strict rules of play and nine innings, but what happens in those innings is determined by the players themselves. Likewise in *SimCity* (1989), much of what happens is based upon the choices made by the player who designs and runs the city. In these games, complex narratives can occur, through a combination of rules, chance events, and the players' own decisions and actions.

Interactivity, then, does not have to work against narrative or even linearity; it simply requires that multiple lines of narrative be present, or the potential for a variety of narrative possibilities. In novels with multiple storylines, each character performs a different series of actions and suffers the particular consequences for those actions. Some characters are cautionary characters who come to bad ends, while other characters are rewarded for their deeds. In an interactive narrative, different sets of actions and consequences are available to the same player-character and can be experienced on a subsequent playing of the game.

Rather than creating an inherent message or metaphor within a single storyline or multiple lines lived by different characters, the author can imbed a worldview into the structure of the game itself, which is then "lived out" by the player-character. For example, some games involve a "kill or be killed" mentality such that if the player-character does not attack or kill other characters, he is killed and the game ends badly. Other games might be designed to reward pacifist behavior, though relatively few do. So while a player might feel free to move about or interact within a game, as opposed to watching a character in a film or reading about one in a book, the ideas and worldview of the author are still shaping the experience, albeit in a more subtle manner. The very "rules" and cause-and-effect logic that dictate the events of the video game's diegetic world contain an imbedded worldview which matches actions with consequences and determines outcomes, and it is here that an author can best guide a player into a particular way of thinking (and acting). Goals and obstacles, choices and their consequences, and the means and ends with which the player is provided; these become the tools that shape narrative experience, and the real narrative becomes the player's own passage through the narrative maze of branching storylines and events. At the same time, though, it is likely that games with the simplest of narratives (fighting, shooting, racing) will remain popular and, for some, will always be the core experience of video gaming.

Through limited interactivity and its one-on-one nature, the video game opens up new possibilities in narrative construction. As the size, complexity, and graphical capabilities of video games grow, their diegetic worlds grow larger and more detailed, allowing greater potential for storytelling. Although the interactive nature of video games has led many designers to concentrate on goal-oriented narratives, other possibilities remain to be explored. Likewise, the construction of and theorizing of the interactive narrative has only just begun. Interactive narratives are growing more complex and are changing the nature of storytelling, and they are already beginning to shed new light on narratological concerns.

Notes

1. There are cases in which people do cry because of a video game. One such game is *Aquazone* (1994), a "virtual aquarium" program made by 9003, Inc., a Japanese software company. Describing this electronic fish tank, Kim Eastham writes,

> The fish grow, mate, and have offspring over months or years if you choose to draw out the drama (time frames are variable). The fish, water, and environment are so lovingly crafted, an untrained eye would take an Aquazone for the real thing. . . . Make no mistake, the 30,000-plus users of Aquazone are seriously into fish. The software has a library function with illustrated data on fish, plants, and parasites, care, and breeding.
>
> Better read up—and make a printout for the neighbors—'cause those little sparks of light might be lying at the top of the screen if you're called away on a business trip.
>
> "We had a couple who phoned us in tears when their fish died," said Takashi Mineyoshi, sales manager of Lits Compute in Tokyo. "People really become attached to this pet." ("Artifishal Experience," *Wired* [July 1994], p. 122).

For an article on interactive plant simulations, see Mark Fraunfelder, "The Interactive Life of Plants," *Wired* (July 1994), p. 35.

2. The rise of character-based games also meant the decline of abstract games. Today there are far fewer abstract games than there were in the days of *Breakout* (1976), *Tempest* (1980), *Qix* (1981), and other games.

3. Exidy's arcade game *Death Race* (1976) is also sometimes referred to as *Death Race 2000*, after the movie of the same name, on which it was based. This the same game that Steven Kent refers to in Chapter 2 of this book as *Death Race 98*, because, according to Kent, Exidy's Pete Kauffman referred to it by that name.

4. The text adventure also points to an economic reason why narratives were more developed in home computer games and home game systems. While home games were purchased outright, arcade games were "rented" by players for a quarter a game, and so the quicker a game was over, the more often it could be played, and the more money could be made. Players who were better at a game could play longer, and thus got more for their money. Games with extensive narratives requiring an hour or more of play were not financially feasible in the arcade. Even today, arcade games are based on speed and action and have some of the simplest narratives.

5. The ghosts in *Pac-Man* actually have both names descriptive of their behaviors as well as nicknames:

The four ghosts, which your character must avoid, each have a different color, name, nickname and personality. The pink ghost is Speedy, nicknamed "Pinky"; he's fast. The red ghost is Shadow, nicknamed "Blinky"; he's always behind you and it's hard to shake him. The light blue ghost is Bashful, nicknamed "Inky"; he's terribly shy and will actually run away from you. And the orange ghost is Pokey, nicknamed "Clyde"; he'll try his best to get you, but he is slow.

From the "Description" section on the Killer List of Video Games *Pac-Man* page, found at http://www.klov.com/P/Pac-Man.html.

6. The earlier *Ultima* games, and many games of the 1970s in general, featured a top view of the land or playing field being shown, but side views of the individual characters and objects, similar to medieval style of graphical representation used before vanishing-point perspective. Over-the-shoulder views and first-person perspectives soon brought players down into the action, involving them more in the game visually by building a space that appeared to extend around them.

7. Atari, Inc., *Super Breakout Atari Game Program Instructions* (Sunnyvale, Calif.: Atari, Inc., 1981), pp. 2–3.

8. The overall worldview of games like *Pac-Man* (1980) and *Space Invaders* (1978) could perhaps be seen as somewhat pessimistic or depressing; in the end the player is always caught and killed, regardless of his or her efforts.

6

Genre and the Video Game

Mark J. P. Wolf

The idea of categorization by genre, and the notion that certain conventions are present in each genre, has proven to be a useful way of looking at both literature and film. The idea of genre has not been without difficulties, such as defining what exactly constitutes a genre, overlaps between genres, and the fact that genres are always in flux as long as new works are being produced. And genre study differs from one medium to the next. In *Hollywood Genres*, Thomas Schatz outlines some of the distinctions between literary genre study and film genre study, noting that genre study in the past often focused on subject matter and neglected the role of the audience. He writes,

> Genre study may be more "productive" if we complement the narrow critical focus of traditional genre analysis with a broader socio-cultural perspective. Thus, we may consider a genre film not only as some filmmaker's artistic expression, but further as the cooperation between artists and audience in celebrating their collective values and ideals. In fact, many qualities traditionally viewed as artistic shortcomings—the psychologically static hero, for instance, or the predictability of the plot—assume a significantly different value when examined as components of a genre's ritualistic narrative system.[1]

One could easily substitute "video game" for "film" in the above quote; video games' heroes are certainly more static than film heroes, and plots are often even more predictable. And most of all, the interactive experience of playing a video game is even more of a "cooperation between artists and audiences," who go beyond "celebrating collective values" by applying those values to the activity found in the gameplay (the "ritualistic narrative") itself.

Video game genre study differs markedly from literary or film genre study due to the direct and active participation of the audience in the form of the surrogate player-character, who acts within the game's diegetic world, taking part in the central conflict of the game's narrative. In regard to narrative, Schatz describes the general plot structure of the genre film as

establishment (via various narrative and iconographic cues) of the generic community with its inherent dramatic conflicts;

animation of those conflicts through the actions and attitudes of the genre's constellation of characters;

intensification of the conflict by means of conventional situations and dramatic confrontations until the conflict reaches crisis proportions;

resolution of the crisis in a fashion which eliminates the physical and/or ideological threat and thereby celebrates the (temporarily) well-ordered community.[2]

Apart from the fact the video games often do not have happy endings (games usually end with a player-character's death), Schatz's four terms describe the action of most video games. If a film genre represents a "range of experience" for the audience, as Schatz argues, video games fit the description even more closely. In some ways, player participation is arguably the central determinant in describing and classifying video games—even more so than iconography.

Iconography versus Interactivity

In "The Idea of Genre in the American Cinema," Ed Buscombe lists three areas in which genre elements may appear in film: iconography, structure, and theme.[3] While iconography and theme may be applicable to narrative-based video games, games like *Tetris* (1988) and *Ataxx* (1990) are abstract to the point where little or no narrative exists, and some games, like *Video Pinball* (1981) and *Scrabble* (1996), are patterned after relatively nonnarrative activities, and do not contain much in the way of diegetic worlds populated by characters. While the ideas of iconography and theme may be appropriate tools for analyzing Hollywood films as well as many video games, another area, interactivity, is an essential part of every game's structure and a more appropriate way of examining and defining video game genres.

Just as different forms of dance (fox-trot, waltz, ballet, jazz) are defined by how the dancers move rather than how they look, an examination of the variety and range of video games reveals the inadequacy of classification by iconography, even for narrative-based games. While some video games can be classified in a manner similar to that of films (we might say that *Outlaw* [1978] is a Western, *Space Invaders* [1978] science fiction, and *Combat* [1977] a war game), classification by iconography ignores the fundamental differences and similarities which are to be found in the player's experience of the game. *Outlaw* and *Combat*, both early games for the Atari 2600, are very similar in that both simply feature player-characters maneuvering and shooting at each other in a field of obstacles on a single, bounded screen of graphics, with cowboys in one game and tanks in the other. In a similar vein, Activision's *Chopper Command* (1982) for the Atari 2600 is essentially a version of *Defender* (1980) with helicopters replacing the spaceships. Conversely, an iconographic analysis of *Space Invaders* (1978), *Spaceward Ho! IV* (1996) *Defender* (1980), and *Star Wars* (1983), as well as many other games, would consider them all "science fiction" even though they vary widely in player experience. As narrative games grow more complex and cinematic, iconographic and thematic generic classifications from film will be able to be applied more usefully, but interactivity will always be an important factor in the way the games are experienced.

Genres based on interactivity also avoid some of the problems found in literary and film genres. In "Genre and Critical Methodology," Andrew Tudor points out that in relying on theme for the determination of genre, one is confronted with the difficulties in isolating a film's (or rather, film author's) intentions.[4] In a video game, there is almost always a definite objective that the player strives to complete (or find and complete, as in the case of *Myst* [1993]), and in doing so very specific interactions are used. Thus the intention—of the player-character at least—is often clear, and can be analyzed as a part of the game. The game's objective is a motivational force for the player, and this, combined with the various forms of interactivity present in the game, are useful places to start in building a set of video game genres. The object of the game can be multiple or divided into steps, with the result that the game may be placed in more than one genre, just as a film's theme and iconography can place a film in multiple genres (the film *Blade Runner* [1982], for example, fits in both science fiction and hard-boiled detective genres). The main objective in *Pac-Man* (1980), *and the activity* by which a player gains points and advances levels, for example, is the eating of the yellow dots. In order to do so successfully, the player-character must avoid the pursuing ghosts as well as navigating a maze. Thus while *Pac-Man* may be primarily classified (according to the terms below) as a "Collecting" game, we may also classify it as an "Escape" or "Maze" game, albeit secondarily. By beginning with the interaction required by the game's primary objective, we can start to divide the wide variety of video games into a series of interactive genres.

Interactive Genres for Classifying Video Games

The following list of genres based on interactivity can be used in conjunction with the existing taxonomy of iconographically or thematically based genres (like those of film) when one is attempting to categorize video games. The genres listed below take into consideration the dominant characteristics of the interactive experience and the games' goals and objectives as well as the nature of each game's player-character and player controls. Also, certain genres listed here (Diagnostic, Demo, Educational, Puzzle, Simulation, and Utility) contain programs which are arguably not "games," but since they appear as cartridges or discs in a form similar to game cartridges and discs (and are treated as such by many game collectors), and because they sometimes contain gamelike elements (such as *Mario Teaches Typing 2.0* [1997]), they have been included here for the sake of completeness.

In the culture surrounding the video game, certain generic terms such as the "Shoot 'Em Up" are already established and in use among players, and these terms and distinctions are reflected in the proposed list of terms below. Some of these genres overlap commonly used genres of moving imagery (such as Adaptation, Adventure, Chase), while others, such as Escape, Maze, or Shoot 'Em Up, are specific to video games and reflect the interactive nature of the medium. These genre terms regard the nature of interactivity in the game itself rather than ask whether the game is single player, multiple player, or designed to be playable over a network. Due to the different types of action and objectives that can occur in a single game, games can often be cross-listed in two or more genres. Also, some games, like *M*A*S*H* (1983) or *Star Wars: Rebel Assault* (1993), feature different sequences or scenarios, each of which can be categorized into different genres. Video games used as examples here include arcade video games, home video games, home computer games, and networked games. The format of this list is patterned after the Library of Congress Moving Imagery Genre-

Form Guide compiled by Brian Taves (chair), Judi Hoffman, and Karen Lund, whose work was the inspiration and model for this list.

The genres covered in this list are as follows: Abstract, Adaptation, Adventure, Artificial Life, Board Games, Capturing, Card Games, Catching, Chase, Collecting, Combat, Demo, Diagnostic, Dodging, Driving, Educational, Escape, Fighting, Flying, Gambling, Interactive Movie, Management Simulation, Maze, Obstacle Course, Pencil-and-Paper Games, Pinball, Platform, Programming Games, Puzzle, Quiz, Racing, Role Playing, Rhythm and Dance, Shoot 'Em Up, Simulation, Sports, Strategy, Table-Top Games, Target, Text Adventure, Training Simulation, and Utility.

Abstract

Games which have nonrepresentational graphics and often involve an objective which is not oriented or organized as a narrative. Often the objective involves constructing, visiting or filling every part of the screen (as in *Tetris, Qix, Pipe Dream*, or *Q*bert*), or destroying or emptying the screen (as in *Breakout* or *Pac-Man*). Characters appearing in abstract games may be anthropomorphic in design (such as Q*bert), but usually do not attempt to represent real-world animals or people or their behaviors. Abstraction is, of course, a matter of degree, though it is usually possible to discern whether or not the game was intended to be deliberately representational. For example, despite their simple, blocky graphics, early Atari 2600 games such as *Basketball* or *Street Racer* attempted to represent people and race cars, which is reflected not only in their design but in their interaction within the game. Nor should the term be used for games which are adaptations of games existing in different media, such as *Checkers* or *Othello*, which are abstract in design and play, but which are nonetheless adaptations and thus representations of games from other media.

Examples: *Arkanoid; Amidar* (with Collecting); *Ataxx; Block Out* (with Puzzle); *Breakout; Marble Madness; Pac-Man* (with Collecting, Escape, and Maze); *Pipe Dream; Q*bert; Qix* (with Collecting); *Super Breakout; Tempest* (with Shoot 'Em Up); *Tetris* (with Puzzle)

Adaptation

Games based on activities adapted from another medium or gaming activity, such as sports, table-top games, board games, card games, or games whose action closely follows a narrative from a work existing in another medium, such as a film, television show, comic book, graphic novel, or play. This involves such questions as how the original work is changed to allow for interactivity and the completion of an objective, or in the case of adapted games, how the original activity changes as a result of being adapted. This term should not be used for games which use the same characters as existing works in another medium but make no attempt to even loosely follow plots or imitate activities found in those works. Home video games and computer games may also be adaptations of arcade video games, in which case they are usually reduced in graphic detail, complexity, or speed when compared with the original. In a few cases, arcade games, such as *Computer Space* (1971), are adaptations of mainframe computer games. This term should be applied to simulation games only when they are adapted from games or gaming activities in other media.

Note: See Sports, Table-Top Games, Board Games, Card Games, Pencil-and-Paper Games, and Simulation.

Examples: Adapted from card games: *Casino; Eric's Ultimate Solitaire; Ken Uston Blackjack/Poker*. Adapted from cartoons: *Spy Vs Spy; The Simpsons, Teenage Mutant Ninja Turtles*. Adapted from comic books: *Spiderman, X-Men*. Adapted from film: *Tron; Star Wars; Krull; Muppet Treasure Island*. Adapted from pencil-and-paper games: *Hangman; Tic-Tac-Toe*. Adapted from sports: *American Football; Atari Baseball; Hot Shots Tennis*. Adapted from table-top games: *PONG; Sure Shot Pool; Virtual Pool*. Adapted from television game shows: *Family Feud; Jeopardy; Joker's Wild; Password; The Price Is Right; Tic-Tac-Dough; $25,000 Pyramid; Wheel of Fortune*

Adventure

Games which are set in a "world" usually made up of multiple connected rooms, locations, or screens, involving an objective which is more complex than simply catching, shooting, capturing, or escaping, although completion of the objective may involve several or all of these. Objectives usually must be completed in several steps, for example, finding keys and unlocking doors to other areas to retrieve objects needed elsewhere in the game. Characters are usually able to carry objects, such as weapons, keys, tools, and so on. Settings often evoke a particular historical time period and place, such as the Middle Ages or Arthurian England, or are thematically related to content-based genres such as science fiction, fantasy, or espionage. This term should not be used for games in which screens are only encountered in one-way linear fashion, like the "levels" in *Donkey Kong*, or for games like *Pitfall!* which are essentially limited to running, jumping, and avoiding dangers (see Obstacle Course). Nor should the term be used to refer to games like *Dragon's Lair*, *Gadget*, or *Star Trek: Borg*, which do not allow a player to wander and explore its "world" freely, but strictly limit outcomes and possible narrative paths to a series of video sequences and linear progression through a predetermined narrative (see Interactive Movies).

Note: For adventure games which are primarily text based, see Text Adventure. For related games similar in theme to adventure games, see also Obstacle Course and Interactive Movie. Examples: *Adventure* (for the Atari 2600); *E.T. The Extraterrestrial* (with Adaptation); *Haunted House*, *Krull* (with Adaptation); *Myst* (with Puzzle); *Raiders of the Lost Ark* (with Adaptation); *Superman* (with Adaptation); games in the *Tomb Raider* series; *Venture*; games from the *Daggerfall* series; games from the *Ultima* series

Artificial Life

Games which involve the growth and/or maintenance of digital creatures of some sort, which can "die" without the proper care by the player. Often growth and the "happiness" or "contentedness" of the characters are the goals of the game. (Whether or not all such programs constitute "games" is debatable.) The term should not be used for games which deal with the allocation of resources or games which are primarily concerned with management (see Management Simulation).

Examples: *Aquazone*; *Babyz*; *Catz*; *Creatures*; *Dogz*; *The Little Computer People*; *The Sims* (with Management Simulation)

Board Games

Games which are an adaptation of existing board games (see Adaptation) or games which are similar to board games in their design and play even if they did not previously exist as board games, like *Fooblitzky* and *Jones in the Fast Lane*. Games of this genre include either classic board games like Chess, Checkers, or Backgammon, or trademarked games such as Scrabble or Monopoly. This term should not be used for games adapted from games such as pool or table tennis, in which physical skills are involved (see Table-Top Games), for games adapted from games which require only paper and a pencil to play, such as Hangman or Tic-Tac-Toe (see Pencil-and-Paper Games), or for games adapted from games which are primarily card based and do not use a board (see Card Games). Three games made by Philips/ Magnavox—*Conquest of the World*, *Quest for the Rings*, and *The Great Wall*

Street Fortune Hunt—required a board game to be used along with the video game itself.

Note: Most board games, though not all, can be cross-listed with Adaptation, and many can also be cross-listed with Strategy.

Examples: *Backgammon; Battleship; Clue; Conquest of the World; Fooblitzky; The Great Wall Street Fortune Hunt; Jones in the Fast Lane; Monopoly; Othello; Quest for the Rings; Scrabble; Stratego; Video Checkers; Video Chess*

Capturing

Games in which the primary objective involves the capturing of objects or characters that move away from and try to evade the player-character. This may involve stopping the object or character (as in *Gopher* or *Keystone Kapers*) or closing off their access to an escape route (as in *Surround* or in the light cycle section of the arcade game *Tron*). This term should not be used for games in which objects or characters do not move (see Collecting) or do not actively try to avoid the player-character (see Catching), nor should it be used for strategy games (such as Chess and Checkers) involving the capturing of pieces which are controlled by the player, but which are not player-characters directly representing the player in the game.

Note: Not necessary to cross-list with Chase as this is implied in Capturing. Many games with more than one player can be cross-listed with Escape, as gameplay often involves player-characters alternately trying to capture one another and escape from one another. Capturing objectives also occur briefly in some games; for example, in *Pac-Man* after eating a power pill when the ghosts can be chased and eaten, or the capturing of criminals in *Superman*.

Examples: *Gopher; Hole Hunter; Keystone Kapers; Surround* (with Escape); *Take the Money and Run; Texas Chainsaw Massacre;* the light cycle game in *Tron*

Card Games

Games which are adaptations of existing card games, or games which are essentially like card games in that they are primarily card based (such as various solitaire computer games). While most card games use the standard four-suit deck, some games use specialized cards (such as *1000 Miles,* a shareware game which is an adaptation of Parker Brothers' *Milles Bornes* racing card game). This term should not be used for trivia games, which are primarily question-and-answer games.

Note: Not necessary to cross-list with Adaptation, as that is implied in Card Games. Many card games which involve betting can also be cross-listed with Gambling.

Examples: *1000 Miles* (with Racing); *Blackjack* (with Gambling); *Casino* (with Gambling); *Eric's Ultimate Solitaire; Ken Uston Blackjack/ Poker* (with Gambling); *Montana; Video Poker* (with Gambling)

Catching

Games in which the primary objective involves the catching of objects or characters that do not actively try to evade the player-character. If the objects or characters are in motion, it is usually along a predetermined path and independent of the movements of the player-character. In some cases the player-character can affect the motion of the objects or characters (such as in *Stampede,* where the player-character can nudge the cattle forward), but at no time do the objects or characters try to actively avoid the player-character. This term should not be used for games in which objects or characters do not move (see Collecting) or games in which they actively try to avoid the player-character (see Capturing). Nor should the term be used for games that require timing in order to use moving objects, such as the moving logs in *Frogger* or the swinging vines in *Pitfall!* nor for sports games with balls which are thrown, bounced, or caught, as these objects are used and reused but not "caught" and removed from the game.

Examples: *Alpha Beam with Ernie* (with Educational); *Big Bird's Egg Catch; Circus Atari, Fishing Derby; Lost Luggage; Stampede; Quantum;* and games 21 through 27 in *Street Racer*

Chase

See Catching, Capturing, Driving, Escape, Flying, and Racing.

Collecting

Games in which the primary objective involves the collecting of objects that do not move (such as *Pac-Man* or *Mousetrap*) or the surrounding of areas (such as *Qix* or *Amidar*). Often scoring in these games is determined by the number of objects collected or areas bounded. "Collecting" here can mean simply running over or hitting objects which then disappear (like the dots in *Pac-Man* or the balloons in *Prop Cycle*). This term should not be used for games in which objects or characters sought by the player-character are in motion (see Catching) or games in which they actively try to avoid the player-character (see Capturing). Nor should the term be used

---

Genre and the Video Game

for games that require the use of objects (such as keys, currency, or weaponry) which are only indirectly used in the attainment of the game's objective. Some games involve the collecting of pieces of an object which can be assembled once all the pieces are found, such as the bridge in *Superman* or the urn in *Haunted House*, although these games often have objectives that involve more than simply collecting, and so should not be considered as belonging to this genre.

Examples: *Amidar* (with Abstract); *Mousetrap* (with Maze and Escape); *Pac-Man* (with Maze and Escape); *Spy Vs Spy* (with Adaptation, Combat, and Maze); *Prop Cycle* (with Flying); *Qix* (with Abstract)

Combat

Games which involve two or more players, or one player and a computer-controlled player, shooting some form of projectiles at each other, and in which all players are provided with similar means for a fairly balanced fight. These games usually emphasize maneuverability and sometimes the outwitting of the opponent. This term should not be used for shoot 'em up games in which the two sides are clearly unequal or not evenly balanced, or for fighting games which do not involve shooting. Although these games may range in the appearance of their content (for example, cowboys in *Outlaw*, tanks or planes in *Combat*, or paddles in *Warlords*), the basic play of the game—shoot the opponent while avoiding getting shot—remains essentially the same.

Note: For related games, see Fighting and Shoot 'Em Up.

Examples: *Battletech; Battlezone; Combat; Dactyl Nightmare; Outlaw; Spy Vs Spy* (with Adaptation, Collecting, and Maze); *Unreal Tournament; Warlords*

Demo

Cartridges, discs, or downloads designed to demonstrate games or a game system. Such cartridges were primarily used in store displays to demonstrate games. While they may not contain complete games themselves, these cartridges have the same appearance as game cartridges and are sometimes collected and traded as game cartridges, and they are often included in listings of cartridges. As discs or downloads, demos allow a player to try out a game for free without buying the full-sized game.

Note: Not necessary to cross-list with Utility, as that is implied in Demo.

Examples: *ADAM Demo Cartridge, Dealer Demo* (Bally Astrocade),

Demonstration Cartridge (RCA Studio II), *Music Box Demo* (Coleco ADAM)

Diagnostic

Cartridges designed to test the functioning of a system. While they are not games themselves, these cartridges have the same appearance as game cartridges and are sometimes collected and traded as game cartridges, and they are often included in listings of cartridges.

Note: Not necessary to cross-list with Utility, as that is implied in Diagnostic.

Examples: *Diagnostic Cartridge* (Identification number FDS100144) for the Atari 5200 system; *Diagnostic Cartridge* (Identification number CB101196) for the Atari 7800 system, *Final Test Cartridge* (Coleco ADAM), *Super Controller Test Cartridge* (Coleco ADAM)

Dodging

Games in which the primary objective is to avoid projectiles or other moving objects. Scoring is often determined by the number of objects successfully dodged or by the crossing of a field of moving objects that must be dodged (as in *Freeway* or *Frogger*). This term should not be used for games in which players avoid getting shot at and are able to shoot (see Combat and Shoot 'Em Up). In many games like *Asteroids* or *Space Invaders*, avoidance of objects or projectiles is important for the player to remain in the game, but points are not awarded for merely avoiding them, and players usually have the option of shooting at obstacles, which is not the case in dodging games.

Examples: *Dodge 'Em* (with Driving), *Freeway* (with Obstacle Course); *Frogger* (with Obstacle Course); *Journey Escape;* and some games in *Street Racer* (with Driving and Racing)

Driving

Games based primarily on driving skills, such as steering, maneuverability, speed control, and fuel conservation. This term should not be used for games in which racing or the winning of a race is the main objective (see Racing), or for games which are essentially obstacle courses in which a player's main objective is to hit or avoid touching a series of objects or characters (see Obstacle Course), unless driving skills are essential to play and to the winning of the game. In most cases, driving games involve vehicles, whereas obstacle course games generally do not. Scoring in driving games is often based on how fast a particular course is completed, rather than whether or not an opponent is beat in a race, and these games are often single-player games.

Examples: *Dodge 'Em* (with Dodging); *Indy 500* (with Racing); *Night Driver; Pole Position* (with Racing); *Red Planet* (with Racing); *Street Racer* (with Dodging and Racing)

Educational

Games which are designed to teach, and in which the main objective involves the learning of a lesson. Rather than being structured as a straightforward set of lessons or exercises, these programs are structured like games, with such elements as scoring, timed performances, or incentives given for correct answers. The degree to which these programs can be considered games varies greatly.

Note: Not necessary to cross-list with Utility, as this is implied in Educational.

Examples: *Alpha Beam with Ernie* (with Catching); *Basic Math; Mario's Early Years: Fun with Numbers; Mario Teaches Typing; Math Blaster: Episode 1; Math Grand Prix; Morse; Number Games; Playschool Math; Spelling Games; Word Games*

Escape

Games whose main objective involves escaping pursuers or getting out of some form of enclosure. Games can be open-ended, with the game ending when a player escapes from an enclosure or enters a place safe from the pursuers, or closed, in which a player escapes pursuers for as long as possible but always succumbs in the end (as in *Pac-Man*). This term should not be used for games in which the player-character battles the opponent instead of fleeing (see Combat and Shoot 'Em Up), or for games like *Adventure* or *Haunted House*, in which the player-character is only occasionally pursued by characters.

Examples: *Pac-Man* (with Collecting and Maze); *Maze Craze* (with Maze); *Mousetrap* (with Collecting and Maze); *Ms. Pac-Man* (with Collecting and Maze); *Surround* (with Capturing)

Fighting

Games involving characters who fight usually hand-to-hand, in one-to-one combat situations without the use of firearms or projectiles. In most of these games, the fighters are represented as humans or anthropomorphic characters. This term should not be used for games which involve shooting or vehicles (see Combat and Shoot 'Em Up), or for games which include fighting, like *Ice Hockey*, but which have other objectives (see Sports).

Note: Many fighting games can also be cross-listed with Sports. For related games, see also Combat.

Examples: *Avengers; Body Slam; Boxing* (with Sports); games in the *Mortal Kombat* series; *Soul Edge;* games in the *Tekken* series; *Wrestle War*

Flying

Games involving flying skills, such as steering, altitude control, takeoff and landing, maneuverability, speed control, and fuel conservation. This term should not be used for games in which shooting an opponent is the main objective (see Combat and Shoot 'Em Up), unless flying skills are essential to gameplay and to the winning of the game. Flying games can involve airplanes, birds, or spaceships, and movement can take place in the sky (as in *A-10 Attack* and *Prop Cycle*), through caverns (as in *Descent*), or in outer space (as in *Starmaster* and *Star Ship*).

Note: See also Combat, Shoot 'Em Up, Sports, and Training Simulation.

Examples: *A-10 Attack* (with Training Simulation); *Descent* (with Maze and Shoot 'Em Up); *F/A-18 Hornet 3.0* (with Training Simulation); *Flight Unlimited* (with Training Simulation); *Prop Cycle* (with Collecting); *Solaris; Starmaster* (with Shoot 'Em Up)

Gambling

Games which involve the betting of a stake, which increases or decreases the player's total assets in the following round. These games usually involve multiple rounds of betting, allowing a player's stakes or money to grow or diminish over time. This term should not be used for games in which betting does not occur, or for games in which wins and losses do not carry over into the following round.

Note: See also Card Games and Table-Top Games.

Examples: *Blackjack* (with Card Games); *Casino* (with Card Games); *Slot Machine; Video Poker* (with Card Games); *You Don't Know Jack* (with Quiz)

Interactive Movie

Games which are made up of branching video clips or other moving images, the branching of which is decided by a player's actions. Players are often called to make decisions at points in the game where the action stalls or loops, or during action sequences that allow player input which can stop or change the course of action while the video clip is running. While the player may be given limited freedom of movement or action, revelation of the story is still largely linear in structure, with little or no variation possible in its overall sequence of events. This term should not be used for games which place a controllable player-character over backgrounds which are essentially video clips, like *Rebel Assault*, nor should the term be used to refer to games like *Myst*, which allow a player to wander and explore its "world" freely, but still limit outcomes and possible narrative paths to a series of video sequences and linear progression through a relatively predetermined narrative.

Examples: *Dragon's Lair; Space Ace; Gadget; Johnny Mnemonic; Star Trek: Borg*

Management Simulation

Games in which players must balance the use of limited resources to build or expand some kind of community, institution, or empire, while dealing with internal forces (for example, the crime and pollution in *SimCity*) or external forces such as those of nature or chance (for example, natural disasters and monsters in *SimCity*, or planets that require various amounts of terraforming as in *Spaceward Ho!*), and often competition from other players as well. Single-player games are often open-ended, where the community or institution grows and develops over time and continues changing, while multiple-player games usually have the objective of dominating all of the other players, at which point the game ends. In some cases, these games can take on an educational function as well, for example, games found in museum displays which simulate supply and demand or other economic principles.

Note: See also Educational and Utility.

Examples: *Aerobiz; Caesar II; Sid Meier's Civilization; M.U.L.E.; Monopoly; Railroad Tycoon; SimAnt; SimCity; SimFarm; SimTower; Spaceward Ho!*

Maze

Games in which the objective requires the successful navigation of a maze. What can be called a maze is, of course, a matter of degree, though it is usually possible to discern whether a configuration of rooms or hallways was intended to deliberately cause difficulties in navigation (consider, for example, the difference in complexity between the mazes found in *Berzerk*, *Pac-Man*, and *Doom*). Mazes may appear in an overhead view (as in *Pac-Man*), a side view (as in *Lode Runner*), or first-person perspective (as in *Doom*) or be hidden from view (as in certain games in *Maze Craze*). In some cases, the player-character can alter the maze, such as opening or closing passageways (as in *Mousetrap*) or even digging holes or passageways (as in *Lode Runner* or *Dig Dug*). Some mazes, such as those found in *Lode Runner*, focus less on navigation and more on how to gain access to certain portions of the screen in order to achieve certain results or obtain objects. Often the player-character must navigate the maze under the pressure of pursuers, although this is not always the case. Mazes are also often imbedded within other games, such as the Blue Labyrinth in *Adventure* or the underground maze of the Selenetic Age in *Myst*.

Examples: *Descent* (with Flying and Shoot 'Em Up); *Dig Dug; Doom* (with Shoot 'Em Up); *K. C. Munchkin* (with Collecting and Escape); *Lode Runner* (with Platform); *Maze Craze; Mousetrap* (with Collecting and Escape); *Pac-Man* (with Collecting and Escape); *Tunnel Runner; Tunnels of Doom* (with Adventure); *Ms. Pac-Man* (with Collecting and Escape); *Spy Vs Spy* (with Collecting and Combat); *Take the Money and Run*

Obstacle Course

Games in which the main objective involves the traversing of a difficult path or one beset with obstacles, through which movement is essentially linear, often involving running, jumping, and avoiding dangers. This term should not be used for games which do not require more than simply steering down a clear path (see Driving) or avoiding objects or characters without a linear progression of movement (see Dodging), nor should it be used for games which involve chasing or being chased (see Chase), shooting at opponents or getting shot at (see Combat and Shoot 'Em Up), for games with complex objectives (see Adventure), or for games involving more than traversing a path of obstacles (see Platform).

Note: While obstacle courses are generally linear in design as far as the player-character's advancement through them is concerned, this degree of linearity can vary somewhat; for example, in games allowing a character to backtrack or choose an alternate route.

Examples: *Boot Camp; Clown Downtown; Freeway* (with Dodging); *Frogger* (with Dodging); *Pitfall!; Jungle Hunt*

Pencil-and-Paper Games

Games which are adaptations of games usually played by means of pencil and paper (see Adaptation). This term should not be used for drawing or doodling programs (see Utility), or for games like those in the *Dungeons & Dragons* series, whose adaptations are very different from the version of the game played with pencil and paper.

Note: Not necessary to use with Adaptation as this is implied in Pencil-and-Paper Games.

Examples: *3-D Tic-Tac-Toe; Effacer: Hangman from the 25th Century: Noughts and Crosses; Tic-Tac-Toe;* and the version of *Hangman* which appears as a cartridge in several game systems.

Pinball

Games which simulate the play of a pinball game. Although these games could be considered as Table-Top Games, there is a tradition of video pinball games and a wide enough variety of them to warrant categorizing them in a genre of their own.

Note: Not necessary to cross-list with Table-Top Games as that is implied in Pinball.

Examples: *Arcade Pinball; Astrocade Pinball; Electronic Pinball; Extreme Pinball; Flipper Game; Galactic Pinball; Kirby's Pinball Land; Midnight Magic; Pachinko!; Pinball; Pinball Challenge; Pinball Dreams; Pinball Fantasies; Pinball Jam; Pinball Quest; Pinball Wizard; Power Rangers Pinball; Pro Pinball; Real Pinball; Sonic Spinball; Spinball; Super Pinball: Behind the Mask; Super Sushi Pinball; Thunderball!; True Pinball; Video Pinball*

Platform

Games in which the primary objective requires movement through a series of levels, by way of running, climbing, jumping, or other means of locomotion. Characters and settings are seen in side view as opposed to top view, thus creating a graphical sense of "up" and "down," as is implied in the category "Platform." These games can also often involve the avoidance of dropped or falling objects, conflict with (or navigation around) computer-controlled characters, and often some character, object, or reward at the top of the climb which provides narrative motivation. This term should not be used for games which do not involve ascending heights or advancement through a series of levels (see Adventure), or for games which involve little more than traversing a path of obstacles (see Obstacle Course).

Note: For related games, see also Adventure and Obstacle Course.

Examples: *Crazy Climber; Donkey Kong; Donkey Kong Jr.; Lode Runner* (with Maze); *Spiderman* (Atari 2600); *Super Mario Bros.* (with Collecting); *Warioland; Yoshi's Island*

Programming Games

Games in which the player writes short programs that control agents within a game. These agents then compete and react to situations based on the player's programming. This term should not be used for games in which a player must learn to operate a machine, such as *Riven* (see Puzzle), or for games in which the player controls the player-characters directly. Depending on what the programmed agents do, games may be cross-listed with other genres.

Examples: *AI Fleet Commander; AI Wars; CoreWar; Crobots; Omega; RARS (Robot Auto Racing Simulator); Robot Battle*

Puzzle

Games in which the primary conflict is not so much between the player-character and other characters, but rather the figuring out of a solution, which often involves solving enigmas, navigation, learning how to use different tools, and the manipulating or reconfiguring of objects. Most often there is a visual or sonic element to the puzzles as well, or at least some verbal description of them. This term should not be used for games which only involve the answering of questions (see Quiz). Many text adventures also contain puzzles and use text to describe their sights and sounds.

Examples: *The 7th Guest; Atari Video Cube; Block Out* (with Abstract); *Dice Puzzle; Hitchhiker's Guide to the Galaxy* (with Text Adventure); *Jigsaw; Myst* (with Adventure); *Rubik's Cube* (with Adaptation); *Sokoban; Suspended Animation* (with Text Adventure); *Tetris* (with Abstract)

Quiz

Games in which the main objective is the successful answering of questions. Scoring is usually based on either how many questions are answered correctly or on the amount of money players have after betting on their answers. Some of these games are adaptations of board games or quiz shows from television.

Note: Games in which players can place a bet on their answers should be cross-listed with Gambling.

Examples: *$25,000 Pyramid* (with Adaptation); *Fax; Jeopardy* (with

Adaptation); *NFL Football Trivia Challenge '94/'95; Name That Tune* (with Adaptation); *You Don't Know Jack* (with Gambling); *Sex Trivia; Trivial Pursuit* (with Adaptation); *Trivia Whiz; Triv-Quiz; Video Trivia; Wizz Quiz.*

Racing

Games in which the objective involves the winning of a race or the covering of more ground than an opponent (as in *Slot Racers*). Often these games involve driving skills and can also be cross-listed with Driving. One-player games can be considered as Racing if there are other computer-controlled cars or vehicles competing on the race track; however, if they are not competitive and act only as obstacles, use Driving.

Note: See also Driving. Not necessary to cross-list with Sports as this is implied in Racing. Although most of these games involve driving skills and can be cross-listed with Driving, some of them, like *1000 Miles*, do not.

Examples: *1000 Miles* (with Card Games); *Daytona U.S.A.* (with Driving); *High Velocity* (with Driving); *Indy 500* (with Driving); *Mario Kart 64* (with Driving); *Math Grand Prix* (with Educational); *Pole Position* (with Driving); *Red Planet* (with Driving); *Slot Racers* (with Dodging); *Street Racer* (with Dodging and Driving); *Super GT* (with Driving)

Rhythm and Dance

Games in which gameplay requires players to keep time with a musical rhythm. These games may employ a variety of controllers beyond the usual video game hardware, including controllers simulating drums (as in *DrumMania*), turntables (as in *Beatmania*), guitars (as in *Guitar Freaks*, or even maracas (as in *Samba de Amigo*).

Examples: *Beatmania; Bust-a-Groove; Dance Dance Revolution; Guitar Freaks; PaRappa the Rapper; Pop'n'Music; Samba de Amigo; Space Channel 5; Um Jammer Lammy; Vib-Ribbon* (with Obstacle Course)

Role-Playing Games

Games in which players create or take on a character represented by various statistics, which may even include a developed persona. The character's description may include specifics such as species, race, gender, and occupation, and may also include various abilities, such as strength and dexterity, usually represented numerically. The games can be single player, such as *Ultima III: Exodus* (1983), or multiple player, such as those which are networked. This term should not be used for games like *Adventure* or

Raiders of the Lost Ark, in which identity is not emphasized or important, or where characters are not represented statistically.

Note: Many networked games, including MUDs (Multi-User Dimensions), MOOs (MUD, Object-Oriented), and MUSHs (Multi-User Shared Hallucination), fall into this category, although the degree to which they can be considered games may vary depending on the players and system operators, and whether or not objectives are set for the players and competition occurs.

Examples: *Anvil of Dawn; Diablo; Dragon Lore 2; Fallout; Mageslayer; Phantasy Star; Sacred Pools;* games from the *Ultima* series or *Dungeons & Dragons* series. Networked games include *Interstate '76; Ivory Tower; JediMUD; Northern Lights; OutlawMOO; PernMUSH; RiftMUSH; Rivers of MUD; Sunflower; Unsafe Haven; VikingMUD; Zodiac.*

Shoot 'Em Up

Games involving shooting at, and often destroying, a series of opponents or objects. As opposed to Combat games, which feature one-on-one battles with opponents of roughly equal attributes and means, Shoot 'Em Up games usually feature multiple opponents (the "'Em" is short for "them") attacking at once (as in *Space Invaders* or *Galaga*) or multiple objects which can be destroyed (as in *Centipede*), which are often potentially harmful to the player-character (as in *Asteroids*). In many cases, the player-character and opponents of the player-character have unequal attributes and means and do not even resemble one another (as in *Yar's Revenge*), and the games usually require quick reflexes. Do not use this term for games like *Stellar Track*, in which the player-character and opponents fire at each other, but in such a way that quick reflexes are not necessary (see Strategy). There are three types of Shoot 'Em Up games which are common: in one, the player-character moves horizontally back and forth at the bottom of the screen shooting upward while opponents moving around above shoot downward (as in *Space Invaders*); in the second, the character moves freely about the screen, encountering opponents from all sides (as in *Berserk* or *Robotron: 2084*), and the third features a first-person perspective (as in *Doom*). This term should not be used for fighting games which do not involve shooting (see Fighting), for games in which opponents are fairly evenly matched (see Combat), or for games in which none of the objects the player-character fires upon can harm the player-character (see Target). In a few cases, the player-character is primarily defending rather than attacking, as in *Atlantis, Commando Raid, Missile Command,* and *Missile Defense 3-D*.

Examples: *Asteroids; Berzerk; Centipede; Doom; Duckshot; Galaga; Millipede; Missile Command, Robotron: 2084; Space Invaders; Yar's Revenge; Zaxxon*

Simulation

See Management Simulation and Training Simulation.

Sports

Games which are adaptations of existing sports or variations of them.

Note: No need to cross-list with Adaptation as this is implied in Sports. See also Driving, Fighting, Obstacle Course, Racing, and Table-Top Games.

Examples: *American Football; Atari Baseball; Bowling; Boxing* (with Fighting); *Fishing Derby* (with Catching); *Hot Shots Tennis; Golf; Human Cannonball* (with Target); *Ice Hockey; Madden Football 97; Miniature Golf; NHL Hockey 97; PONG* (with Table-Top Games); *Skeet Shoot* (with Target); *Track & Field; Summer Games; Video Olympics; RealSports Soccer; RealSports Tennis; RealSports Volleyball; SimGolf; Sky Diver; Tsuppori Sumo Wrestling; World Series Baseball '98*

Strategy

Games emphasizing the use of strategy as opposed to fast action or the use of quick reflexes, which are usually not necessary for success in these games.

Note: See also management simulation games like *M.U.L.E.* and *Spaceward Ho!* as well as many board games, card games, and combat games.

Examples: *Ataxx* (with Abstract); *Checkers* (with Board Games), *Chess* (with Board Games); *Monopoly* (with Board Games); *M.U.L.E.* (with Management Simulation); *Othello* (with Board Games); *Spaceward Ho!* (with Management Simulation); *Stellar Track*

Table-Top Games

Games involving adaptations of existing table-top games requiring physical skill or action (such as pool or pinball). This term should not be used for games involving little or no physical skill or action (see Board Games and Card Games), nor should it be used for games which cannot be played on a table-top of some sort (see Sports). For games which resemble pinball games, see Pinball.

Note: Not necessary to cross-list with Adaptation, as this is implied in Table-Top Games.

Examples: *Battle Ping Pong; Electronic Table Soccer!; Parlour Games; Pocket Billiards!; PONG* (with Sports); *Sure Shot Pool; Trick Shot; Virtual Pool*

Target

Games in which the primary objective involves aiming and shooting at targets which are not moving or which are in motion. Occasionally the targets may be harming the player-character's property (as in *Wabbit*). This term should not be used for games in which the player-character can be fired upon by opponents (see Combat and Shoot 'Em Up), for games that do not involve shooting (see Catching and Collecting), or for games in which the objects or characters actively elude the player-character.

Examples: *Air-Sea Battle; Carnival; Human Cannonball; Marksman/ Trapshooting; Shooting Gallery; Skeet Shoot* (with Sports); *Wabbit*

Text Adventure

Games which rely primarily on text for the player interface, and often for the description of the game's "world" and the action which takes place there. Some games may use images, but these are usually noninteractive illustrations which are not central to the play of the game. Games range from allowing free movement throughout the game's "world" (usually by commands such as north, south, east, west, up, and down) with a variety of options for interaction, to more linear, branching narratives. Players often are able to carry objects which are kept track of by an inventory function, and are able to converse with computer-controlled players/characters through a very limited vocabulary. Although some games may incorporate text-based informational screens (as in *Stellar Track*), rely on text for description (such as the books in the library in *Myst*), or even use text as a graphic element (such as *Rogue*), this term should only be used for games in which the "world" of the game is primarily experienced through text which describes the world of the game and the events occurring in it.

Note: Not necessary to cross-list with Adventure since that is implied in Text Adventure. Multiple-player Text Adventures which are networked are considered to be role-playing games (see Role Playing). Almost all Text Adventures can also be cross-listed with Puzzle.

Examples: *The Hitchhiker's Guide to the Galaxy; Planetfall; Leather Goddesses of Phobos; Suspended; Zork*

Training Simulation

Games or programs which attempt to simulate a realistic situation, for the purpose of training, and usually the development of some physical skill such as steering (as in driving and flight simulators). This term should not be used for simulations which focus on management (see Management Simulation) or the employment of strategy (see Strategy). These games can range from realistic simulations used by institutions, such as those used to train astronauts, tank drivers, or airline pilots, to simplified gamelike approximations of them used mainly for entertainment, such as *Police Trainer* or *A-10 Attack*.

Note: Not necessary to cross-list with Utility or Simulation, as that is implied in Training Simulation.

Examples: *A-10 Attack; Comanche 3* (with Flying); *F/A-18 Hornet 3.0* (with Flying); *Flight Unlimited* (with Flying); *Police Trainer;* military and airline flight simulators; and driving simulations used in driver education.

Utility

Cartridges or programs which have a purpose or functional beyond that of entertainment, although they may be structured in a manner similar to games (such as *Mario Teaches Typing*) or contain elements of entertainment. While they are often not games themselves, some of these programs have the same appearance as game cartridges and are sometimes collected and traded as game cartridges, and they are usually included in listings of cartridges.

Note: See also Demo, Diagnostic, Educational, and Simulation.

Examples: *Basic Programming; Beginning Algebra; Beginning Math; Computer Programmer; Diagnostic Cartridge* (Identification number FDS100144) for the Atari 5200 system (with Diagnostic); *Home Finance; Infogenius French Language Translator; Mario Teaches Typing; Music Box Demo* (with Demo); *Number Games; Speed Reading; Spelling Games; Touch Typing, Word Games*

....

Notes

1. Thomas Schatz, *Hollywood Genres* (New York: McGraw-Hill, 1981), p. 15.

2. Ibid., p. 30.

3. Ed Buscombe, "The Idea of Genre in the American Cinema," *Screen* 11.2 (1970), pp. 33–45.

4. Andrew Tudor, "Genre and Critical Methodology," in *Movies and Methods*, vol. 1, ed. Bill Nichols (Berkeley: University of California Press, 1976), pp. 118–126.

III

The Video Game
in Society
and Culture

7

Hot Circuits

Reflections on the 1989 Video Game Exhibition of the
American Museum of the Moving Image

Rochelle Slovin

n 1989, I proposed that the American Museum of the Moving Image,
of which I am founding director, mount a retrospective exhibition of
video games. This became *Hot Circuits: A Video Arcade*, which was
presented by the museum from June 6, 1989, through May 20, 1990.

Reaction from peers and trustees was, in the beginning, mixed. Within
and without the museum, the idea was met with raised eyebrows. Our
institution, after all, was founded in 1981 as the first museum in the United
States devoted to the art, history, technique, and technology of motion pictures and television. To that end, it is both a screening and a collecting
institution. When the museum opened its doors in September 1988, it presented to the public the core exhibition *Behind the Screen*, the film series
Glorious Technicolor, and the video series *The Media and the Vietnam War*.
How then, would video games fit into this mandate? What was there worth
saying about them? And would anyone be interested in what we found?

As we set about answering those questions, we became the first
museum to call for a reconsideration of the very notion of the moving
image. Assessing video games was a crucial step in making the first links
between old and new media—between television and film, and the video-
computer mix that dominates current "new media." The establishment of
these relationships led naturally to the creation of a valuable archive of
video arcade games, the first genuinely mass-market digital entertainment.
Looking back at it today—when new media is an everyday subject, and
early video games are enjoying not only increased critical attention but are
being repackaged for nostalgic use on home computers—the exhibition
seems to have been a decade ahead of its time.

Nonetheless, my original question was apt: What exactly do video games tell us about the moving image?

On a general level, I knew that video games were not, as many dismissed them, a trend or fad, but, on the contrary, the beginning of something significant. Exactly *what*, I wasn't sure. I sensed that digital media were not about to go away, and would in fact increase in importance. It seemed that the merging of the computer and the CRT was creating a genuine form of interactivity—a much-hyped concept even back then. Not least, I realized that video games were acclimating a whole generation of young Americans to computers.

What struck me most about early video games was that they enacted the mind-set, if you will, of computers. This is partly due to their genesis in ballistics and military simulation of movement. In their earliest forms, computers and chips were designed to deal exclusively with pure mathematics: force and vectors. When they were recruited into service as video games, there was still a strong trace of pure mathematics about them. It was a unique moment in visual entertainment: technology became both the enabling force and the content of the games. This was a useful orientation for the museum, because we meant, as I saw it, to show how technology affected the content and technique of the entertainment industry. Video games innovated a way of visualizing and feeling, almost sensually, the laws of physics.

The game *Asteroids* is an elegant example of this. With its evocation of a weightless, almost frictionless environment, the game is a virtual enactment of Newton's first laws of motion. For instance, Atari programmed the game to include the principle of conservation of motion, whereby small rocks breaking from exploded asteroids would move more quickly than the original, larger rock. And though the game operates in accordance with only a few of these very simple rules of movement, they are as intractable as the theory behind them. That rigidity—that sense of a super-rational, almost platonic ideal—is a defining feature of early video games. They are thus, as the poet Charles Bernstein wrote in his essay commissioned for the exhibition, something like a glimpse into the mind of a microchip. "Video games are the purest manifestation of computer consciousness," he wrote. "Liberated from the restricted economy of purpose or function, they express the inner, nonverbal world of the computer."[1] Bernstein's essay, reprinted as Chapter 8 of this book, has the uncanny sense of seeming prescient in spite of—and in some cases perhaps paradoxically *because* of—its being so dated.

That super-rational element is reflected in the early games' graphics, which have a spare, modernist feel. This again became another point of interest because, considered as moving images, the aesthetics of these pioneering games are unique in digital media. Their pixellation is so chunky and low resolution that it seems at times mosaic. If you look closely at, say, a character like Pac-Man, you can see individual pixels, the atomic building blocks of visualized computer space. This effect, of course, came about less by design than by necessity. Video game programmers, fighting against the limitations of the chips' tiny memory, were forced to compress their ideas. But that compression had a creative edge—it functioned much in the way a sonnet necessitates a compression of language and an economy of metaphor. In contrast to today's intensely realistic three-dimensional computer environments, the early games bear a resemblance to post-abstract- expressionist paintings by artists such as Larry Poons. The stripped-down feel of the early games also suggests early black-and-white films before sound. Here, too, the art is defined by its limitations. And while later innovations in film, as in computer games, produced arguably "better" graphics, color, and effects, there is a poetic spareness about the early moments in each technology.

My interest in early video games also stemmed from other parallels with the history of early cinema. Both video games and movies were presented to audiences in a coin-operated, arcade format. Although Auguste and Louis Lumière introduced Parisian audiences to projected moving images in 1895, Americans' first view of motion pictures was Edison's Kinetoscope, a peep-show-type viewer first marketed in 1894, which exhibitors lined up arcade-style in Kinetoscope parlors. The Mutoscope, a hand-cranked flipbook apparatus, was patented in 1894 and became a long-running arcade hit. Mutoscopes were still to be found in the beachfront boardwalk penny arcades of my childhood in the 1940s. From these inauspicious beginnings, the movie business grew at explosive rates, so that less than twenty years later major studios had emerged, individual actors were famous, and the film industry was becoming a financial powerhouse.

Video games have seen almost precisely the same evolution. In spite of almost continual public outcry about their on-screen violence, their importance is unwavering: they too have developed, in only two decades, into an industry whose annual revenues outstrip Hollywood's box office take. Meanwhile, individual video game companies have become the Hollywood "studios" of digital gaming; the best example of this is probably Id Software, maker of the phenomenally popular games *Doom* (1993) and

Edison Kinetoscope, c. 1896.

Quake (1996). Similarly, creators of individual games have gained fame as "directors." Within the core gaming community, everyone follows the career of John Romero, famous for designing the original *Quake.*

In many ways, assembling the intellectual justification for the exhibition was the easy part. Assembling the games themselves was another thing altogether.

My goal was to present the games themselves—this was to be a museum exhibition, after all, and the museum's first responsibility is to offer the public a direct encounter with the objects of study. I wanted to select the games that had somehow stood apart from the mass—because they had broken new ground in graphic design, introduced a new type of gameplay, or perhaps been unpredictably popular. However, in 1989, there was little interest on the part of academics or consumers in the early video games. Although there were articles from time to time in the popular press on the effects of video games in general, there was no archival work being done, and thus virtually no recording of the details of any individual games.

In this void, word of mouth became extremely important. To generate a list of the "top" games of museological interest, I approached Roger Sharpe, author of a history of pinball games, long-time video game reviewer for *Play Meter* magazine, and marketing executive at Williams/Bally. On the basis of his own knowledge and experience in the field, Sharpe produced a list of games he considered milestones. It began with the "founding" games. The two key ones here were Nutting's 1971 *Computer Space*—which grew out of *Spacewar!* a game developed by programmers at MIT in the early 1960s—and Atari's 1972 *PONG*, the first massively successful video game. The list continued with the second wave of "space invasion" games, such as Bally/Midway's 1978 *Space Invaders* and Gremlin's 1979 *Galaxian*. It carried on through the explosion of character-driven, right-brained games—such as Namco's 1980 *Pac-Man* and Gottlieb's 1982 *Q*bert*—touching on the increasingly realistic driving games (Sega's 1986 *Out Run*), and finishing at the then-present with *NARC*, a 1988 offering by Williams, and a rather surreal reflection of the war on drugs.

With that list in hand, Sharon Blume, then the deputy director of the museum, and David Draigh, the publications editor, began the search. After six months, they had located forty-seven of the games on Sharpe's list. In many ways, the hunt was similar—and thus presented similar challenges—to work we had previously done in collecting licensed merchan-

Computer Space *(Nutting, 1971). Collection of the American Museum of the Moving Image. Photograph © Peter Aaron/Esto. All rights reserved.*

dise and tie-ins. A central part of the museum's mandate is to collect the material culture of motion pictures and television. This includes dolls, games, coloring books, and other manifestations of the impact of the moving image on the objects of everyday life. Locating such materials often involved research in obscure locations; Blume and I collected much of this material from country flea markets.

However, with this exhibition, the dynamics of game consumption made for some unexpected problems. Older did not always mean harder to find, although it was generally true that the older games were difficult to locate. In fact, our protracted hunt for *PONG* led, at one point, to a New York City game dealer who apparently had twenty-one games in his basement; upon arrival, we discovered that the building had been demolished three months earlier. In the end, we located a *PONG* machine only one-and-a-half weeks before the exhibition opened. As the oldest game of the lot, *Computer Space* was even more challenging to locate; Draigh stumbled upon one only by accident, while searching for other games in a warehouse.

Surprisingly, many newer games were equally difficult to find. This was partly because anything produced more than a few years before 1989 was regarded by the dealers as "ancient," and was thus likely out of commission and out of repair. Moreover, because we were focusing on the games in their entirety, and because I intended them to become part of the permanent collection of the museum, we required games with pristine cabinets, which were rare under the best of circumstances. Finding quality cabinets was further complicated by the fact that arcade owners would regularly put the board for a new game into an old cabinet whose decals had been removed or painted over.

This modular treatment of the chips is interesting. It mirrors the unfortunate "content focus" of most video game criticism, which too often concerns itself solely with what is happening on the screen. Just as jaded arcade owners would often regard the game cabinet as irrelevant (and the game program itself of prime importance), too many academics and psychologists had hitherto ignored the rich cultural value of the games' context—cabinets, arcades, and the like.

With *Hot Circuits*, I hoped to correct that mistake. I commissioned an exhibition design that would allow the games to be presented in our 6,200-square-foot third floor, elegantly but in classic arcade style, lined up against the wall. Museum visitors were given five free tokens to encourage them to play the games; they could also purchase more tokens. This strat-

egy was even reflected in the naming of the exhibition: *Hot Circuits: A Video Arcade.* The title evoked two of the most important issues we were showcasing—the "circuit"-based computer origins of these moving images and the dynamics of the arcade, the social sphere in which the world first experienced them. The designer, Stephanie Tevonian, placed the games seven or eight feet apart and at a precise 45-degree angle from the wall, the better to allow visitors to appreciate the cabinet art. Between each game she placed a large rectangular text panel. Together, these elements produced an effect of both distance and intimacy, a mix between the raucous dynamics of the arcade and the objectifying nature of a museum. Video game critic J. C. Herz described the sensation as a visitor in her book *Joystick Nation:*

> Yes, you get to play with all the old machines, and they're aligned almost the same way they were when you were a teenager. But not quite, because the consoles are much farther apart than an arcade owner would plant them. They are privileged with space, like statues or really expensive clothing, and thus become Design Objects.
>
> And this is when you realize, for the first time, that these cabinets, apart from containing your favorite video games, are really just god-

damn beautiful . . . Playing a 1980s video game on an arcade machine is like viewing a 1930s Hollywood extravaganza on the silver screen rather than watching it at home on a VCR. It's a public rather than private experience.[2]

Herz's comparison here is particularly acute, insofar as it illustrates another point of contact between video games and film history. As industries, both have slowly moved away from a concern with the environmental issues of presentation. The lavishly appointed picture palaces, with their uniformed ushers, stage shows, and full orchestras, have given way to shabbily constructed small-screen multiplexes and, more importantly, home video. Video games, driven by major technological shifts, have similarly shifted from immersive, social experiences in arcades (where, according to some academic studies, more than half the time participants would watch, "hang out," and socialize rather than play[3]) to solitary, home-based entertainment. Herz' astonishment at reappreciating the *context* of the games was precisely the effect at which we aimed.

In this sense, observing the dynamics of our visitors became illuminating. What was particularly notable was that the exhibition attracted an unusually large number of older visitors—people who clearly would have had no previous contact with video games. Doubtless, it is partly due to the fact that our "arcade" was the first time they had felt socially sanctioned to enter a video game space; they would have felt none of the intimidation that keeps many adults (and social critics) from successfully exploring arcades.

Indeed, the number of older visitors provided us with a chance to observe the interaction of the non-digital generation with the digital world. Devoid of contact with video games for most of their lives, the older visitors had never acquired fluency in the basic disconnect of computer space. By "disconnect," I mean the ability of a video game player to intuit the link between the physical movement of a joystick and the corresponding movement of the on-screen "player." For most people under the age of forty, this is an almost embarrassingly easy feat, of course. Nevertheless, it was—and still is—a profound feature of our relation to computers, as *Hot Circuits* re-illustrated. Steven Johnson discusses the importance of this disconnect with regard to windows-style computer interfaces in his recent book *Interface Culture*. As he argues it, the concept of a visual computer interface is the pivotal moment in modern human-computer relations.

The original creation of the windows interface was the translation of computer logic and thought into a form—a representative metaphor—that everyday humans could find livable. "There are few creative acts in modern life more significant than this one, and few with such broad social consequences," he writes. He goes on to describe the historic impact of the first windows-style graphical user interface, demonstrated in 1968:

> The pointer darting across the screen was the user's virtual doppelganger. The visual feedback gave the experience its immediacy, its directness: move the mouse an inch or two to the right and the onscreen pointer would do the same. . . . The mouse allowed the user to enter that world and truly manipulate things inside it, and for that reason it was much more than just a pointing device.[4]

Though he does not discuss the early video games, his argument can easily extend. Far in advance of windows computers, in fact, video games functioned as the first and most popular interface. The games gave us mass training in how to "live" inside the pure, weightless, scientific space of the computer.

The older players, who had missed out on this training, would normally interact only with certain games. For example, they would almost entirely avoid *Robotron 2084*—a game that requires a relatively complex, simultaneous manipulation of two joysticks (one for movement, one for firing). In contrast, they would stick to "driving simulations," where the disconnect was more familiar, because real-life driving demands its own type of disconnect: the wheel and accelerator are extensions of our body, allowing us to interact with the "virtual" world that, outside the car, scrolls by us.

Younger visitors to the exhibition, in contrast, were instantly fluent in the language of the games. But their reactions were also revealing, though for completely different reasons. With them, it had more to do with illustrating the extreme speed at which digital entertainment had developed.

As Blume—an extraordinarily gifted museum educator—noted, *Hot Circuits* was one of the first museum exhibitions that gave children and adolescents *a sense of history passing*. This was an important, if unexpected, aspect of the success of the exhibition, as it is often difficult for museums to communicate a sense of history to young people. Time, for them, is peculiarly compressed; the events of the present seem infinitely more real than those of even the very recent past. When children visited the exhibition then, even the games that were only few years old—such as *Time Pilot* (1982) or *Karate Champ* (1984)—seemed "ancient" and "old-fashioned" to them. Their reactions closely paralleled those of the dealers from whom we had bought the machines. For them, too, any machine more than a year or two old had been hopelessly back-dated by newer technology. Yet these same younger visitors were old enough to have played those games back when they were new. They could thus viscerally recall the excitement that the games had generated at the time. They experienced this as a sort of imploded nostalgia—a remembrance of things past, even though that past was barely three or four years ago.

On the one hand, of course, this reaction seems amusingly naive. But on the other, it is perfectly understandable—the young attendees were reacting to the exponential pace at which digital media had evolved in such a very short time. Which is to say, the older games could be considered both new *and* old: "new," in strict measures of human history, yet, in terms of digital media, stunningly antiquated. This is a conundrum that the American Museum of the Moving Image has experienced many times; we develop new exhibitions featuring the newest of the new media, knowing that technology put on display as cutting-edge quickly becomes anything but. Indeed, it is a problem faced by everyday consumers of technology, who, caught on the treadmill of digital planned obsolescence, buy new computers every two years.

It is worth noting the central role of video games in creating this culture of ever-expanding computer needs. Many computer-industry critics have argued that it was the demand for graphically rich video games that fueled the development of faster computers and CD-ROM drives. After faster computers came out, the gaming industry took full advantage of them, producing ever-faster games that pushed the cycle further, requiring ever-faster computers; that cycle continues to this day. In fact, some observers have explained the success of Cyan's 1993 game *Myst*—the best-selling computer game of all time—by noting that it was released at the exact moment that CD-ROMs became standard peripherals for computers. Consumers would buy *Myst*, an acoustically and visually rich adventure game, not so much to play as to showcase the capabilities of their high-end computers. "Everybody buys *Myst*," one video game reviewer once commented. "Nobody *plays Myst*."[5]

While the re-enactment of the social sphere of the games was illuminating, we also aimed, with *Hot Circuits*, to present technological and cultural analysis. We commissioned texts on each game from John Berton,

Tron *(Bally/Midway, 1982). Collection of the American Museum of the Moving Image. Photograph © Peter Aaron/Esto. All rights reserved.*

who was then a computer expert with the Ohio Supercomputer Graphics Project. The texts noted which features had made each game unique, as both digital medium and cultural artifact. In the case of Atari's 1980 *Missile Command*, for example, Berton pointed out that it was the only game ever to use a separate sighting device for aiming—a large trackball. At the same time, *Missile Command* was important for its powerful evocation of nuclear dread, with the final words "THE END" closing up each lost game: "The Atomic Age lesson is apparent: the only way to win is not to play." Though the goal was not to "overintellectualize" the games, the texts often succeeded in exposing the elements of each game that, while central to its appeal, had remained previously unnoted. *Pole Position*'s (1982) unique features included its realistic mapping of an actual racetrack in Japan, a fact that would have been lost on even the most avid player. *Tron*'s (1982) singularity came from its rather postmodern origins: "*Tron* is a great self-referential icon: a video game based on a movie based on a computer based on a video game," Berton wrote. "The game has probably been played by more people than ever saw the movie."

In the end, *Hot Circuits* was a huge success for the museum. It received an extraordinary amount of press, partly because reporters had the same reaction as the children—how strangely "old" these games seemed. From June 1990 to September 1993, the show traveled to ten science centers across the country, with similarly warm receptions. In the process of traveling, though, the show conflated even further the nature of arcade and exhibition, and not always in desirable ways. A number of the venues unwittingly placed the games in increasingly arcade-like settings—a consequence of galleries too small for the volume of games in the show—which resulted in many cabinets and text panels being significantly harmed. When the balance of "museum" and "arcade" was disturbed, and the sense of "museum" lost, visitors clearly felt greater freedom to behave with the games as they would in an arcade: sticking gum on the underside of the cabinets or causing damage to decals.

By the time *Hot Circuits* closed at the Museum in May 1990, there was no longer any question as to whether video games "fit" at the American Museum of the Moving Image. And we have in the years since almost always had video games on view (*Hot Circuits II* in 1993, *Computer Space* in 1995, *Expanded Entertainment* in 1996, and *Computer Space 98* in 1998). In retrospect, it was astonishing how groundbreaking the exhibition was in recognizing the importance of digital media. It even precipitated a shift in the museum's focus. When we opened in 1988, our stated mission was to

---

Expanded Entertainment Exhibition, 2000. Super PONG Model C-140 (Atari, 1975), center and PONG (Atari, 1972), right, from the collection of the American Museum of the Moving Image. Photograph © Peter Aaron/Esto. All rights reserved.

educate the public about "the art, history, technique, and technology of motion pictures, television, and video." Four years later, the board of trustees approved the addition of "digital media," recognizing the importance of the computer to the production, delivery, and content of the moving image. In 1991, I appointed Carl Goodman Curator of Digital Media—the first such curatorship, I believe, in any museum.

Rapidly advancing digital technologies, as well as the growing number of people who devise and apply them, are changing the way existing media are made, distributed, and experienced. Through collections, exhibitions, seminars, and software development, Goodman and the museum play crucial roles in the public dialog about the use, value, and promise of these new technologies. The museum's website, for example, at http://www.ammi.org, features an online gallery presenting exhibitions curated by Goodman about the history, technology, and uses of digital media—including video games. Goodman believes it is likely that the term "curator of digital media" itself may soon become anachronistic: all media will be digital, with differences based more on the type of delivery.

Today, *Hot Circuits* seems even more apposite, since the early arcade games are enjoying a consumer resurgence. The young people who grew up with the games are now adults, and, like generations before them, they are having their childhood obsessions duly marketed back to them. Williams, Midway, Bally, Atari, and other game companies are repackaging the early arcade hits for consoles, computers, and even Nintendo's Game Boy. Critics have particularly hailed the Game Boy versions, because the format's low-resolution pixellation and relatively low-power hardware approximates the limitations of the early arcade cabinets. It is pleasing to consider that, since the main target consumers for Game Boys are children, these rereleases may be the youngest players' initial encounter with the aesthetics and mind-space of early computer gaming.

This nostalgia for the recent past has had the positive effect of preserving original copies of the early games. For example, recent years have seen the rise of arcade game auctions. In dozens of major cities across North

Expanded Entertainment Exhibition, 2000. Photograph © Peter Aaron/Esto. All rights reserved.

America, dealers and collectors now gather monthly to trade, buy, and sell early arcade games. As supply has increased to match demand, prices have remained surprisingly low: at a recent Philadelphia-area auction, a copy of Nintendo's 1983 *Mario Bros.*, with a mint-condition cabinet, was sold for only $100, about the same price we would have paid in 1989. Collectors are particularly eager to obtain unblemished cabinets, indicating that a concern for the context of the games is also resurgent. The auctions themselves function partly as ad hoc exhibitions. At each auction, a significant minority of attendees will come as observers, solely to examine and play games (and indeed, crammed into small and dirty auction warehouses, with the games lined up closely together, the events often unintentionally mimic the intimidating dynamics of early arcades).

Most significant, though, is the sense of custodianship that is coming from the field of digital media itself. In 1997, a collection of computer programmers worldwide launched a collaborative project to preserve early-arcade computer code on the Internet. It began with two programmers in Italy, Mirko Buffoni and Nicola Salmoria. They decided, as an engineering exercise, to write a program that would emulate the chip architecture of the most common arcade cabinets. They were fascinated by the same thing that originally intrigued me about early arcade games: the way that programs, so constrained by the old chips, acted out the "consciousness" of physics and science. Yet the emulator also had a practical element to it: it would allow anyone to play original early-arcade games on his or her own computer. After Buffoni and Salmoria finished their emulator, they placed it on their website for anyone to download for free. Other coders who personally owned original arcade cabinets began posting on-line, free, of course, the original code they electronically removed from the machines. The program—called the Multiple Arcade Machine Emulator (MAME)—has become wildly popular. Over 1 million Internet users have downloaded the emulator program and are using it to play up to three hundred available games. (There are, of course, legal issues here. It is a violation of copyright for anyone to download the emulator and play pirated game code on it.)

Museologically, the MAME project is important in its own way. In fact, both Buffoni and Salmoria explicitly describe their emulator as a type of archival work. "Our goal was to document the inner workings of the arcade machines. Most of them are left abandoned in big storages. We're preserving the treasure for future generations," Buffoni told the Canadian magazine *Shift*.[6] In fact, he notes that the Internet is, by virtue of its highly networked architecture, a foolproof storage mechanism for the early arcade code. Once the code has been released, playable, into cyberspace, it becomes a cultural *meme*, replicating itself through people's desire to play the games. And, unlike the physical chips and cabinets of the original games, the code will not decay or vanish—particularly since thousands of additional users are downloading it every day, and dozens of programmers worldwide are now debugging and maintaining the program.

It is a singularly self-referential moment in the evolution of digital media. Arcade games were among the first completely digital media; their widespread use gave rise to the very computer literacy—and digital-media literacy—that encouraged the Internet. Now the Web is being used to archive and preserve those very games. There is a pleasing symmetry in this evolution. When creators of digital media seek their roots, it seems, they are inevitably drawn to the early arcade games. It points again to the fact that these games were important not just for their technological novelty. It was their cultural import, their value as entertainment—as moving images, if you will—that created the idea that computers could be more than just industrial machines. Technology critic Sherry Turkle has described this moment in technological history as "the movement from a culture of calculation to a culture of simulation"—the beginnings of the computer as an imaginative space.[7] As *Hot Circuits* ultimately showed, it is the moment when we stopped using computers as tools, and started using them as culture.

An essential part of the exhibition *Hot Circuits: A Video Arcade* was the essay the museum commissioned from poet and critic Charles Bernstein. Drawing on a wide range of intellectual sources, Bernstein offered up strikingly original ways of thinking about what early arcade games *meant*, socially, technologically, and politically. The exhibition aimed to present the original games as physical, playable artifacts, allowing visitors to experience viscerally—or re-experience—their peculiar allure. Bernstein's ruminations complemented that aim, offering crucial analysis as to why that allure exists. In the essay, he evokes the similarities between computer "thought" and the narrative logic of the games. It is an analysis that was unique at the time, and, ten years later, still seems fresh—pinpointing nicely the means by which computers became instruments of culture.

The essay is reprinted here in full, in the following chapter.

Notes

1. Charles Bernstein, *Play It Again, Pac-Man*, written as the catalogue essay for the American Museum of the Moving Image exhibition *Hot Circuits: A Video Arcade* (1989). Published in Charles Bernstein, *A Poetics* (Cambridge, Mass., and London: Harvard University Press, 1992), pp. 128–141. Also published in *Postmodern Culture* (1991).

2. J. C. [Jessie Cameron] Herz, *Joystick Nation: How Videogames Ate Our Quarters, Won Our Hearts, and Rewired Our Minds* (Boston: Little, Brown, 1997), pp. 61–62.

3. For an early, untitled, study showing this result, see, e.g., B. D. Brooks, in *Video Games and Human Development: A Research Agenda for the 80's*, ed. S. S. Baughman and P. D. Clagett (Cambridge, Mass.: Monroe C. Gutman Library, Harvard Graduate School of Education, 1983). See also E. A. Eli and L. S. Meyers, "The Role of Video Game Playing in Adolescent Life: Is There Reason to Be Concerned?" *Bulletin of the Psychonomic Society* 22.4 (1984).

4. Steven Johnson, *Interface Culture: How New Technology Transforms the Way We Create and Communicate* (San Francisco: HarperEdge, 1997), p. 22.

5. "Riding the Tail of the *Myst* Meteor," *Globe and Mail* (Oct. 4, 1997), p. C27.

6. "Black Market Arcade," *Shift* on-line (Jan. 1998), http://www.shift.com/shiftonline/sitemap/frames/features.asp?searchfor=game.

7. Sherry Turkle, *Life on the Screen: Identity in the Age of the Internet* (New York: Simon and Schuster, 1995), p. 20.

8

Play It Again, Pac-man

Charles Bernstein

Your quarter rolls into the slot and you are tossed, suddenly and as if without warning, into a world of controllable danger. Your "man" is under attack and you must simulate his defense, lest humanity perish and another quarter is required to renew the quest.

Drop in, turn on, tune out.

The theories of video games abound: poststructuralist, neomarxian, psychoanalytic, and puritanical interpretations are on hand to guide us on our journey through the conceptual mazes spawned by the phenomenon. Acting out male aggression. A return, for adolescent boys, to the site of mom's body. Technological utopia. As American as autoeroticism. The best introduction to computer programming. No more than an occasion for loitering in seedy arcades. A new mind-obliterating technodrug. Marvelous exercise of hand-eye coordination. Corrupter of youth. Capital entertainment for the whole family. Not since the advent of TV has an entertainment medium been subjected to such wildly ambivalent reactions or such skyrocketing sales.

If the Depression dream was a chicken in every pot, today's middle-class adolescent's dream is a video game in every TV.

More and faster: better graphics and faster action, so fast you transcend the barriers of gravity, so vivid it's realer than real.

A surprising amount of the literature on video games has concerned the social context of the games: arcade culture, troubled youth, vocational training for tomorrow's Top Gun. So much so that these scenarios seem to have become a part of video game culture: Nerdy kid who can't get out a full sentence and whose social skills resemble Godzilla's is the Star of the arcade: as taciturn as a Gary Cooper Sheriff, he gets the job done without designer sweaters or the girl.

In the Saturday Night Fever of Computer Wizardry, achievement with your joystick is the only thing that counts; success is solitary, objectively measured, undeniable.

Or, say, a 1980 Horatio Alger. A failure at school, marginal drug experimenter, hanging out on the wrong side of the tracks with a no-future bunch of kids, develops $30-a-day video game habit, can't unplug from the machine without the lights going out in his head. Haunts the arcade till all hours, till the cops come in their beeping cruisers, bounding into the mall like the beeping spaceships on the video screen and start to check IDs, seems some parents complained they don't know where Johnny is and it's pushing two. Cut to: Young man in chalk-striped suit vice-prez for software development of Data Futurians, Inc. of Electronic Valley, California: pulling down fifty thou in his third year after dropping out of college. (Though the downside sequel has him, at thirty, working till two every morning, divorced, personal life not accessible at this time, waiting for new data to be loaded, trouble reading disk drive.)

Like the storyboards of the games, the narratives that surround video games seem to promise a very American ending: redemption through the technology of perseverance and the perseverance of technology. Salvation from social degeneracy (alien menace) comes in the form of squeaky clean high tech (no moving parts, no grease). Turns out, no big surprise, that the Alien that keeps coming at you in these games is none other than Ourselves, split off and on the warpath.

The combination of low culture and high technology is one of the most fascinating social features of the video game phenomenon. Computers were invented as super drones to do tasks no human in her or his right mind (much less left brain) would have the patience, or the perseverance, to manage. Enter multitask electronic calculators which would work out obsessively repetitive calculations involving billions of individual operations, calculations that if you had to go by hand would take you centuries to finish, assuming you never stopped for a Coke or a quick game of *Pac-Man*. Now our robot drones, the ones designed to take all the boring jobs, become the instrument for libidinal extravaganzas devoid of any socially productive component. Video games are computers neutered of purpose, liberated from functionality. The idea is intoxicating; like playing with the help on their night off, except the leisure industry begins to outstrip the labors of the day as video games become the main interface between John Q. and Beth B. Public and the computer.

Instruments of labor removed from workaday tasks, set free to roam the unconscious, dark spaces of the imaginary—dragons and assault asteroids, dreadful losses and miraculous reincarnations.

If a typewriter could talk, it probably would have very little to say; our automatic washers are probably not hiding secret dream machines deep inside their drums.

But these microchips really blow you away.

Uh, err, um, oh. TILT!

Okay, then, let's slow down and unpack these equations one by one, or else this will begin to resemble the assault on our ability to track that seems so much at the heart of the tease of the games themselves.

Spending Time or Killing It?

The arcade games are designed, in part, to convince players to part, and keep parting, with their quarters. This part of the action feels like slot-machine gambling, with the obvious difference that there is no cash payoff, only more time on line. Staying plugged in, more time to play, is the fix. The arcade games are all about buying time and the possibility of extending the nominal, intensely atomized, thirty-second (or so) minimum play to a duration that feels, for all impractical purposes, unbounded. Clearly the dynamic of the ever-more popular home games is different enough that the two need to be considered as quite distinct social phenomena, even though they share the same medium.

Like sex, good play on an arcade video game not only earns extra plays but also extends and expands the length of the current play, with the ultimate lure of an unlimited stretch of time in which the end bell never tolls: a freedom from the constraints of time that resembles the temporal plenitude of uninterrupted live TV (or closed-circuit video monitoring) as well as the timeless, continuous present of the personal computer (PC). In contrast, a film ticket or video rental buys you just 90 or 120 minutes of "media," no extensions (as opposed to reruns) possible. Meanwhile, the home video game, by allowing longer play with greater skills, simulates the temporal economy of the arcade product while drastically blunting the threat of closure, since on the home version it costs nothing to replay.

Video games create an artificial economy of scarcity in a medium characterized by plenitude. In one of the most popular genres, you desperately fight to prolong your staying power, which is threatened by alien objects that you must shoot down. There's no intrinsic reason that the threat of premature closure should drive so many of these games; for example, if your quarter always bought two minutes of play the effect of artificial scarcity would largely disappear. Is this desire to postpone closure a particular male drive, suggesting a peculiarly male fear? It may be that the emphasis on the overt aggression of a number of the games distracts from seeing other dynamics inherent in video game formats.

Another dynamic of the arcade games is the ubiquitous emphasis on scoring. These games are not open-ended; you try to accumulate the most points not only to extend play and win bonus games, but also to compete with the machine's lifetime memory of best-ever scores. If achievement-directed scoring suggests sex as opposed to love, games more than play, then it seems relevant to consider this a central part of the appeal of video games.

An economy of scarcity suggests goal-oriented behavior: the desire for accumulation; this is what George Bataille has dubbed a "restricted" economy in contrast to an unrestricted or "general" economy, which involves exchanges or loss or waste or discharge. The drive to accumulate capital and commodities is the classic sign of a restricted economy. Potlatch (the festive exchange of gifts) or other rituals or carnivals of waste ("A helluva wedding!" "Boy, what a Bar Mitzvah!") suggest a general economy.

While the dominant formats and genres of video games seem to involve a restricted economy, the social context of the games seems to suggest features of a general, unrestricted economy. For while the games often mime the purposive behavior of accumulation/acquisition, they are played out in a context that stigmatizes them as wastes of time, purposeless, idle, even degenerate.

These considerations link up video games with those other games, in our own and other cultures, whose social "function" is to celebrate waste, abandon, excess; though the carnival or orgiastic rite is clearly something that is repressed in a society, like ours, where the Puritan ethic still holds powerful sway. What redeems many sports from being conceived as carnivals of waste is the emphasis on athletics (improvement of the body) and the forging of team or group or community spirit (building a community, learning fair play)—two compensatory features conspicuously absent from solitary, suggestively antiphysical video gaming.

In a society in which the desire for general economy is routinely sublimated into utilitarian behaviors, the lure of video games has to be understood as, in part, related to their sheer unproductivity. Put more simply, our unrestricted play is constantly being channeled into goal-directed games; how appealing then to find a game whose essence seems to be totally useless play. Yet it would be a mistake to think of the erotic as wed to de-creative flows rather than pro-creative formations; both are in play, at work. Thus the synthesis of play and games that characterizes most available video games addresses the conflictual nature of our responses to eros and labor play and work.

So what's really being shot down or gobbled up in so many of the popular games? Maybe the death wish played out in these games is not a simulation at all; maybe it's time that's being killed or absorbed—real-life productive time that could better "spent" elsewhere.

If the Message Is the Medium and the Genre Is the Message, Who's Minding the Store?

Like movies, especially in the early period, video games are primarily characterized by their genre. *PONG*, from 1972, is an arcade version of ping-pong, and so the progenitor of a series of more sophisticated games based on popular sports, including *Atari Football*, *Track & Field*, *720°* (skateboarding), and *Pole Position* (car racing). (Perhaps driving simulation games are a genre of their own; they certainly have the potential to be played in an open-ended way, outside any scoring: just to drive fast and take the curves.)

Quest or "fantasy" adventures, typically using a maze format, is another very popular genre, especially in the home version. Arcade versions include *Dragon's Lair*, *Gauntlet*, and *Thayer's Quest*. Dragons, wizards, and warriors are often featured players, and each new level of the game triggers more complex action, as the protagonist journeys toward an often magical destination at the end of a series of labyrinths. In the home versions, where there may be up to a dozen levels, or scenes, the narratives can become increasingly elaborate. Still, the basis of this genre is getting the protagonist through a series (or maze) of possibly fatal mishaps. In their simplest form, these games involve a single protagonist moving toward a destination, the quest being to complete the labyrinth, against all odds. So we have Pac-Man gobbling to avoid being gobbled, or *Donkey Kong's* Mario trying to save his beloved from a family of gorillas who roll barrels at him, or, in *Berzerk*, humanoids who must destroy all the pursuing robots before reaching the end of the maze.

But the genre that most characterizes the arcade game is the war games, in which successive waves of enemy projectiles must be shot down or blown up by counterprojectiles controlled by joystick, push button, or trackball. Some of the more famous of these games include *Star Wars* (a movie tie-in), *Space Invaders* (squadrons of alien craft swoop in from outer space while the player fights it out with one lone spacecraft), *Asteroids* (weightless, drifting shooter, lost in space, tries to blast way through meteor showers and occasional scout ship), *Defender* (wild variety of space aliens to dodge/shoot down in spaceman rescue), *Galaxian* (invaders break ranks and take looping dives in their attacks), *Stratovox* (stranded astronauts on alien planet), *Centipede* (waves of insects), *Missile Command* (ICBM attack), *Robotron: 2084* (robots against humanity), *Seawolf* (naval action), *Zaxxon* (enemy-armed flying fortress), *Battlezone* (which so accurately simulated tank warfare, so the press kit says, that the Army used a version of it for training), and, finally, the quite recent "total environment" sit-down pilot's-view war games—*Shrike Avenger, Afterburner*, and *Out Run.*

A related, newer genre is the martial arts fighting-man video games, such as *Double Dragon* and *Karate Champ*, where star wars have come home to earth in graphically violent street wars reminiscent of Bruce Lee's mystically alluring Kung Fu action movies: another example of film and video game versions of the same genre.

Discussions of video games rarely distinguish between media and genre, probably because the limited number of genres so far developed dominate the popular conception of the phenomenon. But to imagine that video games are restricted to shoot 'em ups, quest adventures, or sports transcriptions would be equivalent to imagining, seventy years ago, that the Perils of Pauline or slapstick revealed the essence of cinema.

A medium of art has traditionally been defined as the material or technical means of expression; thus, paint on canvas, lithography, photography, film, and writing are different media, while detective stories, science fiction, rhymed verse, or penny dreadfuls are genres of writing. This is altogether too neat, however. Since we learn what a medium is through instances of its use in genres, the cart really comes before the horse, or anyway, the medium is a sort of projected, or imaginary, the constant that is actually much more socially and practically constituted than may at first seem apparent.

In trying to understand the nature of different media, it is often useful to think about what characterizes one medium in a way that distinguishes it from all other media—what is its essence, what can it do that no other medium can do? Stanley Cavell has suggested that the essential elements of the two predominant moving-image media—TV and movies—are quite distinct. The experience of film is voyeuristic—I view a world ("a succession of automatic world projections") from a position of being unseen, indeed unseeable. TV, in contrast, involves not viewing but monitoring of events as its basic mode of perception—live broadcast of news or sports events being the purest examples of this property.

It's helpful to distinguish the video display monitor from TV-as-medium. Several media use the video monitor for non-TV purposes. One distinction is between broadcast TV and VCR technologies, which, like PCs, use the television screen for non-event-monitoring functions. Video games, then, are a moving-image medium distinct from TV and film.

In distinguishing medium and genre, it becomes useful to introduce a middle term, "format." Coin-op and home video games feature differences in hardware format; scored versus open-ended games (or time-constrained versus untimed play) feature different software formats. Similar or different genres could then be imagined for these different formats.

....

The Computer Unconscious

The medium of video games is the CPU—the computer's central processing unit. Video games share this medium with PCs. Video games and PCs are different (hardware) formats of the same medium. Indeed, a video game is a computer that is set up (dedicated) to play only one program.

The experimental basis of the computer-as-medium is prediction and control of a limited set of variables. The fascination with all computer technology—gamesware or straightware—is figuring out all the permutations of a limited set of variables. This accounts for the obsessively repetitive behavior of both PC hackers and game players (which mimes the hyper-repetitiveness of computer processing). As a computer game designer remarked to me, working with computers is the only thing she can do for hours a day without noticing the time going by: a quintessentially absorbing activity.

Computers, because they are a new kind of medium, are likely to change the basic conception of what a medium is. This is not because computers are uniquely interactive—that claim, if pursued, becomes hollow quite quickly. Rather, computers provide a different definition of a medium: not a physical support but an operating environment. Perhaps it overstates the point to talk about computer consciousness, but the experiential dynamic in operating computers—whether playing games or otherwise—has yet to receive a full accounting. And the fascination of relating to this alien consciousness is at the heart of the experience of PCs as much as video games.

Video games are the purest manifestation of computer consciousness. Liberated from the restricted economy of purpose or function, they express the inner nonverbal world of the computer.

What is this world like? Computers, including video games, are relatively invariant in their response to commands. This means that they will always respond in the same way to the same input but also that they demand that the input be precisely the same to produce the same results. For this reason, any interaction with computers is extremely circumscribed and affectless (which is to say, all the affect is a result of transference and projection). Computers don't respond or give forth, they process or calculate.

Computers are either on or off, you're plugged in or you're out of the loop. There is a kind of visceral click in your brain when the screen lights up with "System Ready," or your quarter triggers the switch and the game comes on line, that is unrelated to other media interactions such as watching movies or TV, reading, or viewing a painting. Moreover—and this is crucial to the addictive attraction so many operators feel—the on-ness of the computer is alien to any sort of relation we have with people or things or nature, which are always and ever possibly present, but can't be toggled on and off in anything like this peculiar way. The computer infantilizes our relation to the external, re-presenting the structure of the infant's world described by Piaget, where objects seem to disappear when you turn your back to them or close your eyes. For you know when you turn your PC on it will be just like you left it: nothing will have changed.

TV is for many people simulated company, freely flowing with an unlimited supply of "stuff" that fills up "real time." Computers, in contrast, seem inert and atemporal, vigilant and self-contained. It's as if all their data are simultaneously and immediately available to be called up. It is unnecessary to go through any linear or temporal sequence to find a particular bit of information. No searching on fast forward as in video, or waiting as in TV, or flipping pages as in a book: you specify and instantly access. When you are into it, time disappears, only to become visible again during "down time." Even those who can't conceive that they will care about speed become increasingly irritated at computer operations that take more than a few seconds to complete. For the non-operator, it may seem that a ten-second wait to access data is inconsequential. But the computer junkie finds such waits an affront to the medium's utopian lure of timeless and immediate access, with no resistance, no gravitational pull—no sweat, no wait, no labor on the part of the computer: a dream of weightless instantaneousness, continuous presentness. The fix of speed for the computer or video game player is not from the visceral thrill of fastness, as with racing cars, where the speed is physically felt. The computer ensnares with a Siren's song of time stopping, ceasing to be experienced, transcended. Speed is not an end in itself, a roller coaster ride, but a means to escape from the very sensation of speed or duration: an escape from history, waiting, embodied space.

The Anxiety of Control/The Control of Anxiety

Invariance, accuracy, and synchronicity are not qualities that generally characterize human information processing, although they are related to certain idealizations of our reasoning processes. Certainly, insofar as a person embodied these characterizations he or she would frighten: either lobotomized or paranoid. In this sense, the computer can again be seen as an alien form of consciousness; our interactions with it are unrelated to the forms of communication to which we otherwise are accustomed.

Many people using computers and video games experience a surprisingly high level of anxiety; controlled anxiety is one of the primary "hooks" into the medium.

Since so may of the video game genres highlight paranoid fantasies, it's revealing to compare these to the paranoia and anxiety inscribed in PC operating systems. Consider the catastrophic nature of numerous PC error messages: invalid sector, allocation error, sector not found, attempted write-protect violation, disk error, divide overflow, disk not ready, invalid drive specification, data error, format failure, incompatible system size, insufficient memory, invalid parameter, general failure, bad sector, fatal error, bad data, sector not found, track bad, disk unusable, unrecoverable read error; or the ubiquitous screen prompts: "Are you sure?" and "Abort, Retry, Ignore?"

The experience of invoking and avoiding these sometimes "fatal" errors is not altogether unlike the action of a number of video games. Just consider how these standard PC software operating terms suggest both scenarios and actions of many video games and at the same time underscore some of the ontological features of the medium: escape and exit and save functions ("You must escape from the dungeon, exit to the next level and save the nuclear family"), path support (knowing your way through the maze), data loss/data recovery (your "man" only disappears if he gets hit three times), defaults are not in the stars but in ourselves, erase (liquidate, disappear, destroy, bombard, obliterate), abandon (ship!), unerase (see data recovery), delete (kill me but don't delete me), searches (I always think of John Ford's *The Searchers*, kind of the opposite of perhaps the most offensive of video games, *Custer's Revenge*), and of course, backups (i.e., the cavalry's on its way, or else: a new set of missiles is just a flick of the wrist away).

The pitch of computer paranoia is vividly demonstrated in the cover copy for a program designed to prevent your hard drive from crashing: "Why your hard disk may be only seconds away from total failure! Be a real hero! Solve hard disk torture and grief. You don't need to reformat. You don't need to clobber data. How much these errors already cost you in unrecoverable data, time, torture, money, missing deadlines, schedule delays, poor performance, damage to business reputation, etc."

Loss preventable only by constant saving is one PC structural metaphor that seems played out in video games. Another one, though perhaps less metaphoric than phenomenological, revolves around location. Here it's not loss, in the sense of being blipped out, but rather being lost— dislocation—as in how to get from one place to another, or getting your bearings so that the move you make with the controls corresponds with what you see on the far-from-silver screen. Or else the intoxicating anxiety of disorientation: vertigo, slipping, falling, tumbling . . .

What's going on? The dark side of uniformity and control is an intense fear of failure, of crashing, of disaster, of down time. Of not getting it right, of getting lost, of losing control. Since the computer doesn't make mistakes, if something goes wrong, it must be something in you. How many times does an operator get a new program and run it through just to see how it works, what it can do, what the glitches are, what the action is. Moving phrases around in multiple block operations may not be so different from shooting down asteroids. Deleting data on purpose or by mistake may be something like gobbling up little illuminated blips on the display screen of a game. And figuring out how a new piece of software works by making slight mistakes that the computer rejects—because there's only one optimum way to do something—may be like learning to get from a thirty-second Game Over to bonus points.

If films offer voyeuristic pleasures, video games provide vicarious thrills. You're not peeking into a world in which you can't be seen—you are acting in a world by means of tokens, designated hitters, color-coded dummies, polymorphous stand-ins. The much-admired interactiveness of video games amounts to less than it might appear given the very circumscribed control players have over their "men." Joysticks and buttons (like keyboards or mice) allow for a series of binary operations; even the most complex games allow for only a highly limited amount of player control. Narrowing down the field of possible choices to a manageable few is one of the great attractions of the games, in just the way that a film's ability to narrow down the field of possible vision to a view is one of the main attractions of the cinema.

Video games offer a narrowed range of choices in the context of a predictable field of action. Because the games are so mechanically predictable, and context invariant, normal sorts of predictive judgments based on situational adjustments are unnecessary and indeed a positive hindrance. The rationality of the system is what makes it so unlike everyday life and therefore such a pleasurable release from everyday experience. With a video game, if you do the same thing in the same way it will always produce the same results. Here is an arena where a person can have some real control, an illusion of power, as "things" respond to the snap of our fingers, the flick of our wrists. In a world where it is not just infantile or adolescent but all too human to feel powerless in the face of bombarding events, where the same action never seems to produce the same results because the contexts are always shifting, the uniformity of stimulus and response in video games can be exhilarating.

In the social world of our everyday lives, repetition is near impossible if often promised. You can never utter the same sentence twice—not only technically, in the sense of slight acoustic variation, but also semantically, in that it won't mean the same thing the second time around, won't always command the same effect. With video games, as with all computers, you can return to the site of the same problem, the same anxiety, the same blockage and get exactly the same effect in response to the same set of actions.

In the timeless time of the video screen, where there is no future and no history, just a series of events that can be read in any sequence, we act out a tireless existential drama of "now" time. The risks are simulated, the mastery imaginary; only the compulsiveness is real.

....

Paranoia or Paramilitary

"Paranoia" literally means "being beside one's mind." Operating a computer or video game does give you the eerie sensation of being next to something like a mind, something like a mind that is doing something like responding to your control. Yet one is not in control of the computer. That's what's scary. Unlike your relation to your own body—that is, being in it and of it—the computer only simulates a small window of operator control. The real controller of the game is hidden from us, the inaccessible system core that goes under the name of Read Only Memory (ROM), that's neither hardware that you can touch nor software that you can change but rather, "firmware." Like ideology, ROM is out of sight only to control more efficiently.

We live in a computer age in which the systems that control the formats that determine the genres of our everyday life are inaccessible to us. It's not that we can't "know" a computer's mind in some metaphysical sense; computers don't have minds. Rather, we are structurally excluded from having access to the command structure: very few know the language, and even fewer can (re)write it. And even if we could rewrite these deep structures, the systems are hardwired in such a way as to prevent such tampering. In computer terms, to reformat risks losing all your data: it is something to avoid at all costs. Playing video games, like working with computers, we learn to adapt ourselves to fixed systems of control. All the adapting is ours. No wonder it's called good vocational training—but not just for Air Force Mission Control or, more likely, the word processing pool: the real training is for the new regulatory environment we used to call 1984 until it came on line without an off switch. After that we didn't call it anything.

In the machine age, a man or woman or girl or boy could fix an engine, put in a new piston, clean a carburetor. A filmgoer could look at a piece of film or watch each form being pulled by sprockets across a beam of light at a speed that he or she could imagine changing. A person operating a threshing machine may have known all the basic principles, and all the parts that made it work. But how many of us have even the foggiest notion—beyond something about binary coding and microchips and overpriced Japanese memory—about how video games or computers work?

Yet, isn't that so much Romantic nonsense? Haven't societies always run on secrets, hidden codes, inaccessible scripture?

The origins of computers can be traced to several sources. But it was military funding that allowed for the development of the first computers. Moreover, the first video game is generally considered to be *Spacewar!*, which was developed on mainframes at MIT in the 1960s, a by-product of "strategic" R&D (research and development), and a vastly popular "diversion" among the computer scientists working with the new technology.

The secrecy of the controlling ROM cannot be divorced from the *Spacewar!* scenario that developed out of it, and later inspired the dominant arcade video game genre. Computer systems, and the games that are their product, reveal a military obsession with secrecy and control, and the related paranoia that secrets will be exposed or control lost. Computers were designed not to solve problems, per se, not to make visually entertaining graphics, not to improve manuscript presentation or production, not to do bookkeeping or facilitate searches through the *Oxford English Dictionary*. Computers have their origins in the need to simulate attack/respond scenarios. To predict trajectories of rockets coming at a target and the trajectory of rockets shot at these rockets. The first computers were developed in the late 1940s to compute bombing trajectories. When we get to the essence of the computer consciousness, if that word can still be stomached for something so foreign to all that we have known as consciousness, these origins have an acidic sting.

Which is not to say other fantasies, or purposes, can't be spun on top of these origins. Programs and games may subvert the command and control nature of computers, but they can never fully transcend their disturbing, even ominous, origins.

So one more time around this maze. I've suggested that the Alien that keeps coming at us in so many of these games is ourselves, split off; that what we keep shooting down or gobbling up or obliterating is our temporality: which is to say that we have "erring" bodies, call them flesh, which is to say we live in time, even history. And that the cost of escaping history is paranoia: being beside oneself, split off (which brings us back to where we started).

But isn't the computer really the Alien—the robot—that is bombarding us with its world picture (not view), its operating environment—that is always faster and more accurate than we can ever hope to be, and that we can only pretend to protect ourselves from, as in the Pyrrhic victory, sweet but unconvincing when we beat the machine, like so many John Henrys in dungarees and baseball hats, hunching over a pleasure machine designed to let us win once in a while?

The Luddites wanted to smash the machines of the Industrial Revolution—and who can fail to see the touching beauty in their impossible dream. But there can be no returns, no repetitions, only deposits, depositions. Perhaps the genius of these early video games—for the games, like computers, are not yet even toddlers—is that they give us a place to play out these neo-Luddite sentiments: slay the dragon, the ghost in the machine, the berserk robots. What we are fighting is the projection of our sense of inferiority before our own creation. I don't mean that the computer must always play us. Maybe, with just a few more quarters, we can turn the tables.

9

Archetypes on Acid

Video Games and Culture

Rebecca R. Tews

The room is dark save for the flickering images on the 35-inch TV screen. The figures on the screen weave and dart as they wage the battle between good and evil to the throbbing bass beat of the sound track. The room is consumed by the battle being fought. All eyes are on the epic struggle of the heroine as she tries to vanquish the evil warrior sent to destroy her. The player, a young woman of twenty, seated in this amphitheater, is joined in the battle by her mesmerized five-month-old infant. In the shadowy light, the baby girl's eyes glow with dual images of the battle her mother is fighting. Her tiny hands wave in the air as they try to mimic her mother's hand movements. This duo pauses only briefly to handle "baby business," barely interrupting the flow of the game. As the baby nurses at her mother's breast she continues to keep one eye on the images that pass before her on the screen, pausing only occasionally to eat with seriousness. She is oblivious to all else. They play in this quiet time before dawn because competition for the game is less during the hours when the husband/father is asleep. These vital hours of practice are required to be able to keep up with the "pro" when he is ready to play later in the day. They also unite mother and daughter in a unique bond of shared experience, emotion, and competition.

Understanding and explaining the impact of video game experiences is essential to understanding the cultural experience of this young family. The parents play for their own reasons and inevitably their young child will soon play as well. We know that early experiences strongly affect our sense of the world, our sense of self and ability to adapt to the environment. The role that video games play in affecting these senses is an issue that must be addressed in greater depth by the field of psychology because the games have as great a potential to impact behavior, problem solving, and social coping as any other form of media. Unlike other approaches to understanding the video game phenomenon, psychology's response must be viewed in the context of the major philosophical approaches commonly used by the field to make sense of human behavior. The purpose of this discussion is threefold. First, an overview of the psychologically related research and application of the major approaches is provided as a foundation for understanding the immense impact these games may have on society as a whole. Second, out of this overview comes the suggestion that Jung's approach to understanding cultural archetypes may provide the best expression of the social impact of these games. Finally, Jungian theory is applied to specific games.

Modern psychology, as a scientific discipline, favors taking a step-by-step approach to defining and measuring less tangible aspects of human experience and behavior. Systematic research that addresses the cultural phenomenon of video games one step at a time is essential if we are to understand the processes at work. This modern scientific approach flies in the face of the old standard, the psychoanalytic legacy. Combining the philosophical insights of the psychoanalytic tradition with the more empirical research may be what is ultimately required to understand the complex role of video gaming and its impact on the psyche of individual and society.

The video game era certainly dawned with little fanfare in the academic and clinical world of psychological research. Frequently, video games were dismissed in the early literature as a fad and a passing fancy played by only a few advantaged children. Video gameplay was only addressed as school and behavior problems appeared, suggesting that some kids had significant difficulties related to gameplay. Under these circumstances it really is not very surprising that the handful of books and articles related to the behaviors and cultural impact of video games are sprinkled sparsely through the thirty years that encompass the video game era.

Brief History of Related Research and Assumptions on Video Gameplay

Early versus Later Demographic Research

Tom Panelas published the earliest systematic commentary on the world and culture of video gaming, arguing that these games would profoundly change the culture of youth. Additionally, Panelas noted that the video game culture of the early 1980s was dominated by the battle between arcade and home play games for market share supremacy. The winner in this battle was predicted to strongly influence the role that video games would eventually play in youth culture because the home market would bring the games into the everyday experience of the entire household rather than staying a free-standing, youth-centered entertainment venue.[1]

Time has demonstrated that the home market has outstripped the arcade market.[2] While some might argue this point, it is important to consider the overall impact of the home market, including resale sales figures and total hours of use, when one is calculating the overall impact of each venue. Further, new generations of technology allow the home games to have graphics and thrills which rival those of arcade games. From an economic perspective, hours of home gameplay can be had for significantly less cost than an equal number of arcade play hours. Continuously improving home technologies such as large-screen TVs and super-surround sound speakers often result in a home gameplay experience that equals the arcade experience (and there is no line behind you). As video gameplay has moved increasingly to the privacy of the home, an accurate measurement of how long people play and how they respond is much harder to achieve.

The earliest research looks at gaming as almost entirely a youth phenomenon. Perhaps in the early 1980s this was true. Research suggests that children were much more receptive to the new technology than their adult counterparts and that they seemed to see more value in the play experience.[3]

While we believe that gaming peaks in adolescence, between age thirteen and seventeen, there is no evidence to suggest that it is outgrown or that people do not continue to play into adulthood.[4] In fact, it appears that adults who played as adolescents continue to be avid users. Although most general research looks only at childhood players, marketing research suggests that adults play as well. Time has shown that many of those who began playing in childhood continue to play as adults and to share the experience with their young children as soon as they are old enough to play. In fact, direct observation suggests that infants and very young children are mesmerized by the flashing images and sound effects commonly found in games available on the home game market and watch their parents' play with rapt attention on a daily basis.[5] In other words, for many younger families gaming is a form of interactive family entertainment and a cultural tradition shared between generations from infancy on.

The earlier systematic research on this phenomenon also looks primarily at usage rates and the impact of arcade play on the grades and behavior of adolescent boys, reportedly because girls were not playing in the arcades.[6] It appears that girls have always played at home but preferred not to do so in the male-dominated arcade environments or for the purpose of competing with others. Instead they play as a social activity and when lonely.[7] Additionally, anecdotal research suggests that females believe video gameplay is a male-dominated activity and are reticent to admit the frequency of their game use.

Early versus Recent Research on Affective Impact

The majority of psychological research on the affective impact of video games, both early and recent, focuses on aggression. Generally, this research hypothesizes that video game violence and competition significantly affects player behavior. This is attributed to the level of interaction between player and game rather than passive observation. With some mixed results, these hypotheses have generally been supported.[8]

As video game realism has increased, so has the amount of affect generated in response to gameplay. Collateral to research on video games and aggression, anxiety and self-esteem have been examined in a less intensive manner.[9] The results of these studies have also supported the notion that realistic games produce more intense behavioral and emotional responses in the player.

Research on affective, behavioral, and physiological responses to the games suggest that people do play at different intensity levels. It is suggested that perhaps 11–25 percent of players feel a compulsion to play.[10] These players are more intense, more competitive, less able to cope with distractions, and more likely to fantasize about and role-play their favorite characters when not playing the game.[11] No research to date has addressed the impact of the compulsion to play on family dynamics. Clinical observation suggests that this is a problem that cuts across several generations.[12]

The problem with the early research is that it did little to encourage additional research on the complexities of the gaming world. For example, researchers often failed to distinguish between home and arcade play. The more recent research is characterized by a more focused emphasis on affective and physiological responses to gameplay. This research is a significant improvement in understanding the experience of gameplay and how it reinforces us; however, studies still often suffer greatly from methodological problems and small subject sets (fewer than fifty subjects) which limit generalizability and accuracy.

Overview of the Psychological Theories Related to Gameplay

Three main theoretical perspectives—behaviorism, social learning theory, and psychoanalysis—have dominated the field of psychology. A brief overview of each approach puts the related research in context and demonstrates why the research has been less than successful at explaining the video game experience.

Behaviorism and Video Games

The behavioral perspective suggested by B. F. Skinner[13] focuses primarily on human behavior as the result of complex interactions between the various punishments and rewards we receive from the environment. Through various studies on behavior (utilizing pigeons and a contraption now known as a Skinner box, which provided corn as an immediate reinforcement), Skinner demonstrated that most organisms will perform repetitive behaviors for very little randomly distributed reinforcement. Skinner's theories are used to explain why we gamble or play the lottery when we know we have little chance of winning and a large chance of losing. Behavioral psychologists are interested in video gameplay because the game unit is perceived as the ultimate Skinner box. The game environments reinforce the player for improving responses with additional points or movement on to higher levels (differential reinforcement of successive approximations, also known as "shaping"). In the case of violent, aggressive, or antisocial games, we are also reinforced for aggressive, quick-thinking, and bloodthirsty behavior.

But do we play solely to move on to higher levels, gain more points, or get to the end of the game? Is this simplified approach enough to account for this multi-billion-dollar mega-industry and the ever-increasing demand for new, interesting, and challenging games? It is doubtful that reinforcement alone accounts for intense interest and response to these games. It certainly cannot account for emotional responses to the games or the rapt attention of the small, non-playing observers.

Social Learning Theory: A Plausible Explanation of Gameplay Behavior?

Social learning theory, first articulated by Albert Bandura,[14] demonstrates that we learn from observing models and mimicking their behaviors. Children in these studies were placed in a room with a "Bobo Doll"(a blow-up punching doll). What the children did with the doll depended on what they had seen prior to being placed in the room. Those that watched someone hit the doll and yell at it copied that behavior. Through research with the now-infamous "Bobo Doll," Bandura concluded that children learn from watching others. Live models are most effective, but children also learn from behavior observed in TV, cartoon and book characters of all types,[15] and from behaviors they are told about. In fact, we all do to some extent. Nearly all of the psychological research on video gameplay has been built on the foundation laid by Bandura's research on the contribution that TV and media make in our social development. In other words, Bandura's work on how we learn culture is a predominant influence in the psychologically related research on video game culture.

This approach does make significant contributions toward our understanding of play behavior and multigenerational interest. It explains why a small child would pay attention and mimic a parent's or older child's interest in the games and grow up to value playtime. It also raises issues about what the game characters are teaching as we interact with the fantasy world. Again, however, as with behaviorism, this approach provides an oversimplified answer for how we become emotionally involved in the gameplay experience and why it becomes such an influential part of our lives. It is unreasonable to believe that all affective game response and cultural influence is based solely on observation and expectation of reward.

Psychoanalysis and the Subconscious Connection

Psychoanalysis is one of the foundational schools of thought in psychological philosophy. Based on the work of Freud and Jung, this approach emphasizes the conflict between our pleasure-seeking subconscious and our more conservative conscious minds. Reassessment of the global cultural impact of the games through the use of Jung's unique psychoanalytic view may be more helpful in understanding the complex connections of these interactive media experiences to our sense of self.

Carl Jung argued that all societies share a primitive and basic understanding of the world.[16] These understandings, depicted through symbols or archetypes, most often appear in our art, dreams, analogies, metaphors, and nonverbal communications. They are the backbone of our primitive knowing, affective responses, fears, aspirations, and sense of progress through life's stages. These archetypes are translated into standard symbols that tell the collective story of our human experience and our search for meaning.

There are those who argue that our legends, myths, fairy-tales, and even modern stories work because they touch that primitive archetypal self.[17] In effect we are drawn to these stories because they connect with our own experiences in the real world. Video games may have such a powerful influence because they connect on many levels with these same primitive symbols.

Jungian-Focused Theory of Game Culture

These archetypes may have some innate connections, but they are solidified in our subconscious sense of self in early childhood—through the stories we see and hear and through our early experiences. These archetypes, then, exist for us on two levels. On a subconscious level, accessed mostly through dreams and unspoken images, these symbols affect our interpretation of environmental stimuli. Later, with practice, we may become consciously aware of these symbols in our quest to bring meaning to our experiences and to share with others our sense of these experiences.[18] Often this occurs through storytelling. All cultures use the retelling of myths and fables in this way. They also use art, song, and dance in a similar way.[19] Video media and interactive video are recent newcomers to this traditional world of symbols, but they are no less significant in their content.

In modern society, we spend little time engaged in telling the stories of old. Gone are the fireside stories of the ancient heroes and their successes and mistakes. Gone are the symbolic trappings of their journey toward self-actualization; the weapon, the talisman, the quest. In their place we watch our new heroes on television and listen to them tell their own stories, *or* we become them, writing the script through our experiences in the video game world. The most popular games provide us with the opportunity to join the quest to conquer evil villains, protect the weak, or develop the skill to gain the highest honor or most points. This is true of all games, whether they are action, fantasy, sports, or skill games. We like them because they temporarily transport us to another reality.

The interactive medium of video games allows us to join the story in progress and become one with the quest. Stimulating our curiosity, desire to succeed, and desire for other reinforcements, these games transport us to an alternate reality where we can learn to succeed. Regardless of whether the game involves dueling adversaries, a quest for treasure, or simply perfection of a skill—the games themselves become symbolic of our own quest to self-actualize, our quest to become better than we currently are. With endless "do-overs" and plenty of chances to learn what comes next and what reinforcers we can expect, these games are the best Skinner box ever invented. However, these games also contain the basic symbols of the human experience. The most common of these archetypes are the villain, the threats to self from seemingly "safe" objects (like trees, rocks, or "safe" animals), the power for resurrection (through food, power pellets, rings, or other energy sources), the voluptuous and often dangerous *anima*, in Jung's terminology (the archetype of the female, who symbolizes both birth and death), and so on (as opposed to the *animus*, or male figure). These symbols exist in all cultures through history. All stories created by humans contain elements of these images. Western thought and Christianity have modified the way our society perceives these images, but they have not left us.[20] They are alive and well in the video game world. Here they appear as if on LSD—caricatures of the traditional images, highly transformed by technology, color, speed, and sound, but elementally the same.

From a psychological point of view what is most intriguing about the games isn't that people gravitate toward them, use them for long periods of time, have trouble ending their play before successful completion of a game, or become disinterested in the games as soon as they have conquered them. Rather, what is most fascinating is that the gameplay may modify the player's behavior in interpersonal relationships. Gameplay, particularly with violent or frustrating games, seems to elicit increased perception of threat, increased physiological arousal in game threat situations (which may translate to other perceived threat situations), and less use of traditional verbal problem-solving strategies and appropriately assertive person-to-person conflict resolution. Again, there may be an archetypal connection here. The human "nuisance" becomes one and the same with the game adversary on the subconscious level. The individual responds with the feelings and the problem-solving behaviors learned in gameplay. In effect, the video game world teaches responses to problems that may be effective in the surreal symbolic world of gameplay but may not be as effective in the highly structured, over-controlled modern society in which we now live.

Jungian Archetype Theory Applied to Gaming and Specific Games
The gaming world as a whole generates its own language and shared understanding of the symbolism behind the "effects" in a game. One need only

visit game players' websites or pick up the latest copy of their favorite gaming magazine to observe this phenomenon. The games also speak to the inner self in a way that releases inhibitions against basic affective responses. Observing game players behind a one-way mirror has suggested that they ride the roller-coaster of their successes and failures in quick succession—cursing at a failure, berating their poor choice of solutions, praising themselves for their successes, acting out frustration on the equipment when progress is slow.[21] Behavior of this type has been observed with all types of games from fantasy to action to skill. Interestingly enough, this affective response is what is needed to ensure the popularity of a game. Games that don't engage the user on an emotional level are considered "boring," "dumb" and "for babies."[22]

Almost intuitively, the game creators know what will strike that personal chord for their audience. The heroes and villains they create come from their own subconscious, which reflects the broader culture in which they were raised. Market research further fine-tunes the selection of these themes. Themes that strike a universal chord are more likely to succeed. Without the game player consciously realizing it, these archetypes are entering their lives.

A Few Specific Archetypes in Popular Games

With the exception of *PONG* (1972), all of the early games showed evidence of the archetypes to one degree or another. A classic example of this is *Pac-Man* (1980). The sun-shaped Pac-Man represents the animus or male presence on a quest to survive various trials. As this character progresses through the game, the shadow world threatens his existence as the ghosts try to take his lives. Pac-Man's defense against this threat is the nurturance of various foods left on the path and the occasional pellet, which transforms the ghosts and allows him to however briefly place them in bondage. The maze is an archetype of the quest to find meaning in life. The holding area for the ghosts typifies the symbolic notion of the netherworld. Granted, the technology of the period limits the detail and realism, but many action games from this point forward are essentially variations on this theme. Examples of these later games include all of the Sonic the Hedgehog games, the James Pond series, *Diddy Kong Racing* (1997), and *Bubble Bobble* (1986)—to name a few. They all include the conflict between the "good" characters seeking fulfillment from the environment and avoiding the marauding evil characters.

Centipede (1980) represents yet another set of symbolic themes. The game pits a descending snake-like creature against the vigilant protagonist armed only with a finite supply of magic bullets. Snakes, dragons, and reptilian creatures have long represented humanity's struggle with the animal world. In mythology these animals also represent evil incarnate, a scourge from the bowels of the earth. The challenge here isn't to negotiate the journey but to defend the self from personal destruction. Again, the cutesy graphics and lack of realism obscure this theme. Nevertheless, it does exist and in later games becomes a much more embedded and fully developed theme. So many of the more recent games include themes of reptilian evil that it seems almost a requirement for an interesting game. Games including this typical theme include *Shadow Madness* (1999) and *Hercules: The Legendary Journeys* (1999), to name but a few. Interestingly, these characters are often mutations of their real-world counterparts, which suggests a transformational process. Henderson argues that this alchemy represents the evolution of the beast of the underworld as it transitions to supernatural status through its experiences in our reality.[23] This may reflect an innate belief in the presence of evil or negative energies that exist beyond our conscious knowing.

Action games of the early period are also replete with the archetypes of threat, conquest, and death. Even such favorites as *Frogger* (1981) and *Defender* (1980) contain themes emphasizing survival of the species against formidable odds. We need that sense of "us" against the unpredictable being from on high to maintain our sense of human identity.[24]

With the advent of games containing female (anima) figures, other common archetypes begin to emerge. These figures tend to fall into one of three categories. She may be the weak damsel in distress awaiting rescue (*Donkey Kong* [1981], *Night Trap* [1992], *Gex 3: Deep Pocket Gecko* [1999]), the villainess, seductive but deadly (*Mortal Kombat III* [1995]), or a more recent development, the powerful female warrior who can both defend herself and be sexually erotic at the same time (the *Tomb Raider* Series). This pattern is consistent with our understanding of the anima as having both positive and negative aspects. These characters represent the age-old conflict typically experienced by men trying to individuate from the nurturing protective mother and become connected on an adult level to a female sexual partner. At once protective and resentful of the female, men expressing this conflict often create the image of woman as a helpless creature in need of rescue who is ultimately under their control. If men fail to rescue her, she perishes without fulfilling her sexual potential, freeing them from the need to connect with the female aspect.[25]

THE VIDEO GAME IN SOCIETY AND CULTURE

Symbolic of the male need to believe himself powerful and independent, Jung argues that the weaker woman archetype is designed to protect man from his deepest fear.[26] Jung suggests that men throughout the centuries have had an intense fear of losing the self to the strong, controlling, procreative female presence. This deep fear is more honestly symbolized by the dark anima. Voluptuous and violent, she stands for creative power, sensuality, and control of man. Receiving gratification and nurturance from her means giving up freedom and male identity. This anima force stands as a direct opposite to the animus or male force and is perceived as the ultimate threat to male selfhood. She must be dominated either in combat or through other symbolically sexual means if the animus is to survive.[27]

The darker anima themes are more prevalent in recent games in the *Mortal Kombat* series, *Parasite Eve* (1998), *Bust-a-Groove* (1998), *Virtua Fighter 3: Team Battle* (1998), *Giants* (2000), *Shenmue* (1999), and *Apocalypse* (1998). While the games vary in content, they include the standard anima characters either as the main villain or as ancillary characters. Even games such as those in the *Tomb Raider* series that contain strong female characters (e.g., Lara Croft) as the main protagonists often cast those characters in a more negatively focused anima form.

Lara Croft, for example, is a highly idealized anima form. She is novel to the male player because of her highly sexualized body, and the angles from which it is viewed during gameplay obscure the more intensely threatening possibility that she might turn her weapons on any man that tries to sexually dominate her. Through Lara, voyeurism is elevated to a new level, allowing the male player to hide once again behind a protective woman as he formerly hid behind his mother. For female players, on the other hand, Lara represents a powerful warrior icon that empowers them to express their strength and sensuality.

Games have also explored both the positive and negative aspects of the animus. The valiant warrior overcoming the obstacles of his quest symbolizes the positive aspects of the animus.[28] Popular games with this theme include *Golden Eye 007* (1997), *Banjo-Kazooie* (1998), games in the *Zelda* series, and many others. Win or lose, in these games the hero succeeds in achieving a legendary status that overcomes the negative aspects of the animus.[29] The conflict between positive and negative animus aspects is the subject of most hand-to-hand combat games like *Mortal Kombat* (all versions), *Final Fantasy* (all versions), and *Tekken 3* (1997). The games emphasize the destruction of the antisocial and evil animus forms by the positive animus in hero form.

Rings, power crystals, perfect squares, and mandala-like spirals are also believed to be archetypes of the spiritual quest. Jaffe argues that these symbols emphasize the human quest for peace, spiritual centeredness, and an emerging sense of self.[30] The inclusion of these symbols in nearly all games suggests a preoccupation with themes of overcoming adversity, finding meaning, and becoming self-aware. Archetypes like these strongly connect to the most private aspects of the subconscious, causing emotional changes on a deeper and more personal level.

Only a brief summary of the possible interpretations of the rich imagery and embedded archetypal themes, this overview suggests an immense area for continued research and analysis. The games themselves have become an art form containing the cultural archetypes of all human knowledge. Because these themes connect with the innermost sense of self and the world, they perpetuate a distinctive culture and interpretation of reality that stands in stark contrast to the rigidity of our scientific, rational, modern world.

These archetypes are translated by the player's perception and adapted into his or her own personal archive of knowledge and interpretation. Admittedly, there are differences in how the archetypes are processed. Processing of this information is a product of age and physical development. Regardless of developmental level, however, video games have a profound power to draw us into an alternate reality and teach us to think in a different way.

While each player takes something unique away from the situation, games are also a democratic equalizer. Each copy of a game spreads a particular experience and alternate reality to each person who plays it. Because the sequence and resolution are identical (within certain parameters), the games become an acculturating force. The fact that gamers experience this archetypally enriched world sets them apart from non-gamers. With popular games selling millions of copies per year, it is easy to see how these become a part of collective social consciousness.

Questions still remain. Future research needs to systematically evaluate archetypal themes and content in all games. Gender differences in perception of the meaning of archetypes and awareness of their presence should also be evaluated. Empirical research also needs to be done in assessing the role of archetypally enriched games in affective response. The impact of game play in early childhood development, marital satisfaction, and parenting issues should also be closely examined. Finally, second-generation players should be carefully compared to first generation players in all areas. It is particularly the latter areas which will shed the most light on understanding the role that the video game archetypes play in video game culture.

....

Notes

1. T. Panelas, "Adolescents and Video Games," *Youth and Society* 15.1 (1983), pp. 51–65.

2. E. F. Provenzo, *Video Kids: Making Sense of Nintendo* (Cambridge, MASS.: Harvard University Press, 1991); P. M. Greenfield and R. R. Cocking, "Interacting with Video," *Advances in Applied Developmental Psychology* (1996), p. 11.

3. R. F. McClure, "Age and Video Game Playing," *Perceptual and Motor Skills* 61 (1985), pp. 285–286; R. F. McClure and F. G. Mears, "Video Game Players: Personality Characteristics and Demographic Variables," *Psychological Reports* 55 (1984), pp. 271–276.

4. Media Analysis Laboratory, "Video Game Culture: Leisure and Play Preferences of B.C. Teens" (Burnaby, B.C.: Simon Fraser University, 1998). Available from: www.media-awareness.ca/eng/issues/violence/resource/reports/vgames.html.

5. Based on the author's anecdotal and case study observation.

6. G. D. Gibb, J. R. Baily, T. T. Lambirth, and W. P. Wilson, "Personality Differences between High and Low Electronic Video Game Users," *Journal of Psychology* 114 (1983), pp. 159–165; E. A. Egli and L. S. Meyers, "The Role of Video Game Playing in Adolescent Life: Is There a Reason to Be Concerned?" *Bulletin of the Psychonomic Society* 22.4 (1984), pp. 309–312.

7. C. A. Anderson and M. Morrow, "Competitive Aggression without Interaction: Effects of Competitive vs. Cooperative Instructions on Aggressive Behavior in Video Games," *Personality and Social Psychology Bulletin* 28.10 (1995), pp. 1020–1030; M. D. Griffiths and N. Hunt, "Computer Game Playing in Adolescence: Prevalence and Demographic Indicators," *Journal of Community and Applied Social Psychology* 5 (1995), pp. 189–193.

8. J. H. Chambers and F. R. Ascione, "The Effect of Prosocial and Aggressive Video Games on Children's Donating and Helping," *Journal of Genetic Psychology* 148.4 (1987), pp. 499–505; J. Cooper and D. Mackie, "Video Games and Aggression in Children," *Journal of Applied Social Psychology* 16.8 (1986), pp. 726–744; J. R. Dominick, "Video Games, Television Violence and Aggression in Teenagers," *Journal of Communication* (Spring 1984), pp. 136–147; D. Graybill, M. Strawniak, T. Hunter, and M. O'Leary, "Effects of Playing versus Observing Violent versus Non-violent Video Games on Children's Aggression," *Psychology: A Quarterly Journal of Human Behavior* 24.3 (1987), pp. 1–8; N. S. Schutte, J. M. Malouff, J. C. Post-Gordon, and A. L. Rodasta, "Effects of Playing Video Games on Children's Aggressive and Other Behaviors," *Journal of Applied Social Psychology* 18.5 (1988), pp. 454–460; D. Scott, "The Effect of Video Games on Feelings of Aggression," *Journal of Psychology* 129.2 (1995), pp. 121–132.

9. C. A. Anderson and M. Morrow, "Competitive Aggression without Interaction: Effects of Competitive vs. Cooperative Instructions on Aggressive Behavior in Video Games," *Personality and Social Psychology Bulletin* 28.10 (1995), pp. 1020–1030; M. D. Griffiths and I. Dancaster, "The Effects of Type A Personality on Physiological Arousal While Playing Computer Games," *Addictive Behaviors* 20.4 (1995), pp. 543–548.

10. Ibid.

11. G. I. Kerstenbaum and L. Weinstein, "Personality, Psychopathology and Developmental

Issues in Male Adolescent Video Game Use," *Journal of the American Academy of Child Psychiatry* 24.3 (1985), pp. 329–337; M. D. Griffiths and I. Dancaster, "The Effects of Type A Personality on Physiological Arousal While Playing Computer Games," *Addictive Behaviors* 20.4 (1995), pp. 543–548; M. D. Griffiths and N. Hunt, "Computer Game Playing in Adolescence: Prevalence and Demographic Indicators," *Journal of Community and Applied Social Psychology* 5 (1995), pp. 189–193; S. Kline (Aug. 1998), "One in Four Young People Addicted to Video Games," *Globe and Mail*. Available: www.media-awarenesss.ca/eng/news/news/two/vidgame.html.

12. Based on the clinical issues brought up by the author's clients in outpatient psychotherapy.

13. B. F. Skinner, "Superstition in the Pigeon," *Journal of Experimental Psychology* 38 (1948), pp. 168–172.

14. A. Bandura, D. Ross, and S. A. Ross, "Transmission of Aggression through Imitation of Aggressive Models," *Journal of Abnormal Psychology* 63.3 (1961), pp. 575–582.

15. The author's research with four- and five-year-old preschoolers suggests that they will copy the behavior of picture-book characters they have heard about in recent stories. This is in keeping with Bandura's hypotheses but was not actually a part of Bandura's research. Bandura focused predominantly on live vs. media models.

16. C. J. Jung, ed., "Approaching the Unconscious," in *Man and His Symbols* (New York: Dell, 1968), pp. 1–94. (Original work published in 1964)

17. A. Jaffe, "Symbolism in the Visual Arts," in *Man and His Symbols*, ed. C. J. Jung (New York: Dell, 1968), pp. 255–322. (Original work published in 1964)

18. The preceding material draws heavily from C. J. Jung, "Approaching the Unconscious," in *Man and His Symbols*, ed. C. J. Jung (New York: Dell, 1968), pp. 1–94. (Original work published in 1964)

19. J. L. Henderson, "Ancient Myths and Modern Man," in *Man and His Symbols*, ed. C. J. Jung (New York: Dell, 1968), pp. 95–156. (Original work published in 1964)

20. C. J. Jung, "Approaching the Unconscious," in *Man and His Symbols*, ed. C. J. Jung (New York: Dell, 1968), pp. 1–94. (Original work published in 1964)

21. These behaviors have been systematically observed from behind a one-way mirror during the author's research on video gameplay behavior and physiological arousal in aggressive and skill gameplay.

22. These statements are from the personal communications of numerous clients and research subjects regarding educational, skill, or unengaging video games.

23. J. L. Henderson, "Ancient Myths and Modern Man," in *Man and His Symbols*, ed. C. J. Jung (New York: Dell, 1968), pp. 95–156. (Original work published in 1964)

24. C. J. Jung, "Approaching the Unconscious," in *Man and His Symbols*, ed. C. J. Jung (New York: Dell, 1968), pp. 1–94. (Original work published in 1964)

25. Ibid.

26. Ibid.; M. L. Von Franz, "The Process of Individuation," in *Man and His Symbols*, ed. C. J. Jung (New York: Dell, 1968), pp. 157–254. (Original work published in 1964)

27. Ibid.

28. J. L. Henderson, "Ancient Myths and Modern Man," in *Man and His Symbols*, ed. C. J. Jung (New York: Dell, 1968), pp. 95–156. (Original work published in 1964)

29. Ibid.

30. A. Jaffe, "Symbolism in the Visual Arts," in *Man and His Symbols*, ed. C. J. Jung (New York: Dell, 1968), pp. 255–322. (Original work published in 1964)

Appendix

Resources for Video Game Research

Mark J. P. Wolf

As with film or other media, firsthand experience is the best for research, yet while many video games can be purchased or rented, older ones can be more difficult to find. Arcades may feature a few older games which are still commercially viable and in working condition, but they are typically few and far between. Old home video games require old home game systems, and some old computer games can only be played on out-of-date computers (some games on the old Macintoshes, for example, cannot be run on today's models). Even finding such information as the year of release for an older video game can be hard. Some of the *PONG* imitations do not even feature a copyright date on the box of the game. But the number of resources for the video game researcher is growing. Below is a list of some of the better sources, a number of which were useful in doing the research for this book.

Videotopia

Keith Feinstein's Videotopia is a traveling museum exhibit including a wide range of arcade video games which patrons are able to play in an arcade-like setting. Historical information and displays put the games into context, and the collection of games represents all periods of arcade video game history, including *Computer Space*, the first arcade video game from 1971, an assortment of vector games, and laserdisc games, as well as new games. Videotopia is perhaps the only place where one can get firsthand experience of such a wide range of games and an overview of video game history. More information on the exhibit can be found at http://www.videotopia. com.

Home Video Games: The First Twenty-Five Years

This is an extensive list of home video games and game systems available from the author by e-mailing mark.wolf@cuw.edu.

World Wide Websites

The Internet is perhaps one of the best and most up-to-date sources for video game research. Company websites are useful, but do not always list games and are, not surprisingly, rather limited informationally beyond advertising themselves and their products. Other sites vary in their reliability and usefulness. The term "video games" also appears sometimes as a single word ("videogames"), so web searches often must include both spellings. Although there are thousands of websites relating to video games, there are a number of sufficient quality to be of use to video game researchers. Web addresses change and websites come and go, so I have tried to limit the list to the most stable sites with lasting value.

http://www.dmoz.org/Games/Video_Games
> Part of the Open Directory Project, this page lists thousands of websites on video games, neatly arranged and categorized hierarchically by topic and subject matter, making searches easier than a search engine style of search. Includes annotations with listings of websites.

http://www.klov.com
> The homepage of the Killer List of Videogames (KLOV) offers a growing list of arcade games including technical information, images, and some video clips of the games. It is the largest single collection of arcade video game information gathered into one site. For a sample of the detailed information available on the games, see http://www.klov.com/P/Pac-Man.html, the page for *Pac-Man*.

http://www.gamedex.com
> This website is a search engine for finding information on computer games and has a variety of other resources.

http://www.vaps.org
> The Video Arcade Preservation Society is an international group of arcade video game collectors and has a membership of over 1,600 collectors. Contact information is provided for many of these collectors, along with what games they own, which is useful to video game researchers wishing to do primary research or for anyone interested in learning more about arcade games.

http://www.videogames.org
> This website is a good source for information about home systems and contains links to lists and photographs of early systems, all collected together in a timeline format.

http://fly.hiwaay.net/~lkseitz/cvg/cvglit.shtml
> The Classic Video Games Literature List is an extensive list of books and published essays relating to video games and one of the most extensive bibliographies assembled on the subject.

http://nav.webring.yahoo.com/hub?ring=cvgs&list

> Lee K. Seitz's Classic Video Game Syndicate Webring features over 250 websites dealing with video games.

http://www.videotopia.com

> The website for videotopia includes essays on video games, information on Videotopia and The Electronics Conservancy, as well as assorted video game links.

http://www.pong-story.com

> David Winter's pong-story site contains an enormous amount of information on dozens of PONG systems and imitators both in the United States and Europe, as well as some of the history behind them. The site is well organized and features many pictures of these early systems, as well as images of their boxes, cartridges, and even their chips.

http://www.gamearchive.com

> A searchable archive of material relating to video games.

http://games.yahoo.com/top/lot123.html

> A searchable glossary of video game and computer game terminology.

http://www.retrogames.com

> A source of information on older video games as well as emulators which run them.

http://www.atari2600.com

> A good place to buy old Atari goods as well as other early home video game systems.

http://dougphelps.com/ryan/index2.htm

> Maps of Atari 2600 games complete with walkthroughs and explanations of how to win various games.

http://www.digipen.com

> This is the homepage of DigiPen, the first school in the world to offer degree-granting programs for video game programming.

http://www.vgf.com

> Video Gamers' First Network features news for platforms including Sony, Nintendo, Sega, and Microsoft. Features many articles and a news archive; a good source for game-company-related news items.

http://www.gamegirlz.com

> A magazine-format website with material of interest to women gamers, and with connections to women gamers' on-line communities.

http://cgi.gaming-age.com/gaming/front/index.pl

http://www.gameinformer.com

http://www.happypuppy.com

http://www.zdnet.com/gamespot

> These websites are magazine-style formats featuring gaming news, reviews, previews, and some downloads. Though most of the material pertains to newer games, some sites have archives as well.

Emulators

Emulators are computer applications that simulate the graphics and gameplay of a particular video game or video game system. For researchers trying to track down hard-to-find games, emulators can sometimes give a good idea what certain early games were like. However, not all emulators give exact renditions of the games they are emulating; graphics may not appear at their original ratios, and the experience of watching a computer screen is often quite different from that of a television screen, or better still, a period television of the sort on which the games would have been played. Emulators can be of use in video game research, but users should beware of the differences and get firsthand experience whenever possible.

http://www.pong-story.com/odyemu.htm
>   The story and status of ODYEMU, an emulator of the Magnavox Odyssey, can be found on this page.

http://www4.ncsu.edu/~bwmott/2600/
>   Stella is an Atari 2600 emulator available for several operating systems. Although I have found Stella to work well on my Macintosh, there are many other emulators for the Atari 2600, and a comparison chart for them can be found at http://members.tripod.com/skintigh/atari/EmuReview.html.

http://www.classicgaming.com/vault/
>   Scroll down this page for a list of emulators of home game systems, including the Arcadia 2001, Atari 2600, Atari 5200, Atari 7800, Coleco Systems, MSX, Neo Geo, NES, Odyssey 2, Sega Genesis, Sega Master System, TurboGrafx16, and Vectrex.

http://www.mame.net/
>   Probably the largest collection of games for one emulator, the Multiple Arcade Machine Emulator (MAME) is said to able to run over two thousand arcade games, and its homepage shows more than 8 million visitors since May 12, 1997. The list of supported games can be found at http://www.mame.net/gamelist.html.

http://hive.speedhost.com/
>   Homepage of the High Velocity Emulator (HiVE), an arcade game emulator which can be run on a Windows 95/98/NT computer. Runs a variety of arcade games and has downloadable ROM images.

http://www.applewoodhouse.com/
>   Another emulator for arcade game is the Superb Arcade Game Emulator (SAGE), which can run over twenty-five arcade games on a Windows 95 computer.

Video

Game Over: Gender, Race, & Violence in Video Games, thirty-five minutes, 2000. Available from the Media Education Foundation, (800) 897-0089, or at http://www.mediaed.org. An educational documentary which addresses questions of gender, race, and violence in video games.

Books

ISBN numbers are given for locating the book faster on electronic search systems. Contact information is given for unpublished theses.

Cassell, Justine, and Henry Jenkins, eds. *From Barbie to Mortal Kombat: Gender and Computer Games*. Boston: MIT Press, 1988. ISBN: 0262531682

Chiang, Bor-Yang. "Involvement and Motive in Sports Video Game Playing, Televised Sports Viewing, Live Sports Attendance and Team Sports Participation." Archival/Manuscript Material, Thesis (M.A. in Mass Communication), University of Wisconsin-Milwaukee, 1996.

Greenfield, Patricia Marks. *Mind and Media: The Effects of Television, Video Games, and Computers*. Cambridge, Mass.: Harvard University Press, 1984. ISBN: 0674576217

Herman, Leonard. *ABC to the VCS*. Springfield, NJ: Rolenta Press, 1996.

Herman, Leonard. *Phoenix: The Fall and Rise of Video Games*. 2d ed. Springfield, NJ: Rolenta Press, 1997. ISBN: 0964384825

Herz, J. C. *Joystick Nation: How Videogames Gobbled Our Money, Won Our Hearts and Rewired Our Minds*. London: Abacus. New York: Little, Brown, 1997. ISBN: 0316360074

Jaffe, Martin S. *Regulating Videogames*, with appendix by Edward H. Ziegler. Chicago: American Planning Association, Planning Advisory Service, 1982.

Kafai, Yasmin Bettina. *Minds in Play: Computer Game Design as a Context for Children's Learning*, Hillsdale, N.J.: Erlbaum, 1995. ISBN: 0805815139

Kent, Steven L. *Electronic Nation: A History of Video Games*. Forthcoming.

Kinder, Marsha. *Playing with Power in Movies, Television, and Video Games: From Muppet Babies to Teenage Mutant Ninja Turtles*. Berkeley: University of California Press, 1991. ISBN: 0520075706

Loftus, Geoffrey R. *Mind at Play: The Psychology of Video Games*. New York: Basic Books, 1983. ISBN: 0465046096

Poole, Steven. *Trigger Happy: Video Games and the Future of Entertainment Revolution*. Arcade Publishing, 2000. ISBN: 1559705396

Provenzo, Eugene. *Video Kids—Making Sense of Nintendo*. Cambridge, Mass.: Harvard University Press, 1991. ISBN: 0674937090

Saltzman, Marc. *Game Design: Secrets of the Sages.* 2d ed. Indianapolis: Brady Games. ISBN: 1566869870

Sheff, David, and Andy Eddy. *Game Over Press Start to Continue.* Game Press, 1999. ISBN: 0966961706

Sheff, David. *Game Over: Nintendo's Battle to Dominate an Industry.* London: Hodder and Stoughton, Vintage Books, 1990. ISBN: 0679736220

Skurzynski, Gloria. *Know the Score: Video Games in Your High-Tech World.* New York: Bradbury Press. Toronto: Maxwell Macmillan Canada. New York: Maxwell Macmillan International, 1994. ISBN: 0027829227

Southern, Matthew Jon. *The Cultural Study of Videogames,* Unpublished thesis, available from Liverpool John Moores University, School of Media, Critical and Creative Arts, Dean Walters Building, St. James Road, Liverpool L1 7BR, England. The author may be contacted by e-mailing: m.southern @livjm.ac.uk, or through the university website: http://www.livjm.ac.uk.

Sullivan, George. *Screen Play: The Story of Video Games.* New York: F. Warne, 1983. ISBN: 0723262519

....

Periodicals

Articles on video games appear in *The Reader's Guide to Periodicals* as early as 1970 (under the heading "Electronic Games"), and a complete bibliography of the medium would be a book-length work. A small selection of articles is given below, representing a variety of angles including technology, business, aesthetics, psychology, art, and culture. There are also several periodicals devoted to video games, including *Videogame Advisor, Arcade, Game Fan, NEXT Generation, Ultimate Gameplayers, Computer Games Magazine,* and *2600 Connection Magazine,* as well as others, like *Computer Graphics World,* which feature articles on video games from a graphics standpoint in almost every issue. ISSN numbers are given for locating the periodicals faster on electronic search systems.

Ackerman, Elise. "The Pinball Wizard Blues." *U.S. News & World Report* 127.19 (Nov. 15, 1999), p. 56. ISSN: 0041-5537

Anderson, Craig A., and Dill, Karen E. "Video Games and Aggressive Thoughts, Feelings, and Behavior in the Laboratory and in Life." *Journal of Personality and Social Psychology* 78.4 (April 2000), p. 772. ISSN: 0022-3514

Asher, Mark. "Massive Multiplayer Entertainment." *Computer Games,* no. 126 (May 2001), pp. 52–68.

Bell, Carrie. "Acts Score Big with Vid Games." *Billboard* 111.46 (Nov. 13, 1999), p. 5. ISSN: 0006-2510

———. "Games Have Yet to Yield Hit Soundtrack." *Billboard* 111.46 (Nov. 13, 1999), p. 101. ISSN: 0006-2510

Blickstein, Jay, and John Soat. "When It Comes to Sexual Harassment, Play Carefully." *InformationWeek*, no. 774 (Feb. 21, 2000), p. 29. ISSN: 8750-6874

Croal, N'gai. "The Art of the Game." *Newsweek* 135.10 (March 6, 2000), p. 60. ISSN: 0028-9604

——. "Making a Killing at Quake." *Newsweek* 134.21 (Nov. 22, 1999), p. 104. ISSN: 0028-9604

Dominick, Joseph R. "Videogames, Television Violence, and Aggression in Teenagers." *Journal of Communication*, no. 34 (1984), p. 136.

Elkin, Tobi. "Dreamcast System Brings Sega Back into Contention." *Advertising Age* 71.7 (Feb. 14, 2000), p. 17.

——. "Sony Blitz Sets Stage for the Next PlayStation." *Advertising Age* 70.45 (Nov. 1, 1999), p. 24. ISSN: 0001-8899

Ellis, Desmond. "Video Arcades, Youth, and Trouble." *Youth and Society* 16.1 (Sept. 1984), p. 47.

Garrity, Brian. "Video-Game Console Makers Eye New Music-Download Applications." *Billboard* 111.42 (Oct. 16, 1999), p. 3. ISSN: 0006-2510

Gillen, Marilyn A. "Sega Bowing 'Backward-Compatible' Game." *Billboard* 106.35 (Aug. 27, 1994), p. 104. ISSN: 0006-2510

Goodale, Gloria. "Inside Video Games." *Christian Science Monitor* 92.20 (May 26, 2000), p. 13. ISSN: 0882-7729

——. "Video Games Get Smarter, Good-Looking." *Christian Science Monitor* 92.30 (March 17, 2000), p. 19. ISSN: 0882-7729

Guth, Robert A. "Inside Sony's Trojan Horse." *Wall Street Journal* (Eastern ed.) 235.40 (Feb. 25, 2000), p. B1. ISSN: 0099-9660

——. "Sony Gears Up to Ship One Million Units of PlayStation 2 for Next Month's Debut." *Wall Street Journal* (Eastern ed.) 235.25 (Feb. 3, 2000), p. A23. ISSN: 0099-9660

Haddon, Leslie. "Electronic and Computer Games, the History of an Interactive Medium." *Screen* 29.2 (1988), p. 52.

Hagiwara, Shiro, and Oliver, Ian. "Sega Dreamcast: Creating a Unified Entertainment World." *IEEE Micro* 19.6 (Nov./Dec. 1999), p. 29. ISSN: 0272-1732

Hara, Yoshiko. "Chip-Supply Kinks May Slow Volume Runs of Playstation 2." *Electronic Engineering Times*, no. 1102 (Feb. 28, 2000), p. 22. ISSN: 0192-1541

Horowitz, Mark. "A Dreamcast Deferred?" *New Yorker Magazine* 32.50 (Jan. 3, 2000), p. 68. ISSN: 0028-7369

Horton, C. "Videogames See Another Hot Year." *Advertising Age* 62.3 (Jan. 21, 1991), p. 55. ISSN: 0001-8899

——. "Zapping the Recession." *Advertising Age* 63.3 (Jan. 20, 1992), p. 56. ISSN: 0001-8899

Hosefros, Paul. "Flying the 'Big Iron,' No Experience Needed." *New York Times* 149.51266 (Jan. 13, 2000), p. G9. ISSN: 0362-4331

Ko, Marnie. "Mortal Konsequences." *Report/Newsmagazine* (Alberta ed.) 27.2 (Maybe 22, 2000), p. 47. ISSN: 1488-8092

Koerner, B. I. "How PONG Invented Geekdom." *U.S. News & World Report* 127.25 (Dec. 27, 1999), p. 67. ISSN: 0041-5537

Kroll, Jack. "Emotion Engine? I Don't Think So." *Newsweek* 135.10 (March 6, 2000), p. 64. ISSN: 0028-9604

Lefton, Terry. "Nintendo Rides Game Boy, N64 Openings with $25M+ in Q4." *Brandweek* 40.37 (Oct. 4, 1999), p. 4. ISSN: 0892-8274

Levy, Steven. "Here Comes PlayStation 2." *Newsweek* 135.10 (March 6, 2000), p. 55. ISSN: 0028-9604

Lohr, Steve. "Microsoft Plans to Try Its Hand at Video Games." *New York Times* 149.51323 (March 10, 2000), p. C1. ISSN: 0362-4331

Maiello, Michael, and Tom Post. "Game Boy." *Forbes* 165.11 (May 15, 2000), p. 328. ISSN: 0015-6914

Meloni, Wanda. "Gaming's Golden Age?" *Computer Graphics World* 23.4 (April 2000), p. 21. ISSN: 0271-4159

Menez, Gene, Kevin Cook, and Mark Mravic. "All That's Missing Is the Sweat." *Sports Illustrated* 91.23 (Dec. 13, 1999), p. 32. ISSN: 0038-822X

Messer, Ian. "Sega's Stock Climbs On Reorganization, Despite Wide Losses." *Wall Street Journal* (Eastern ed.) 234.105 (Nov. 29, 1999), p. B28. ISSN: 0099-9660

Miller, Stephen C. "Most-Violent Video Games Are Not Biggest Sellers." *New York Times* 148.51598 (July 29, 1999), p. G3. ISSN: 0362-4331

Nagourney, Adam. "Hillary Clinton Seeks Uniform Sex and Violence Rating for a Range of Media." *New York Times* 149.51744 (Dec. 22, 1999), p. B5. ISSN: 0362-4331

Neal, Victoria. "Pac-Man Fever." *Entrepreneur* 27.11 (Nov. 1999), p. 256. ISSN: 0163-3341

Oh, Susan, Danylo Hawaleshka, and Tanya Davis. "An Elaborate Hunt." *Maclean's* 113.4 (Jan. 24, 2000), p. 9. ISSN: 0024-9262

Oka, Masaaki, and Masakazu Suzuoki. "Designing and Programming the Emotion Engine." *IEEE Micro* 19.6 (Nov./Dec. 1999), p. 20. ISSN: 0272-1732

Rae-Dupree, Janet, and Irene M. Kunii. "Can Dreamcast Make Sega's Dreams Come True?" *Business Week*, no. 3661 (Dec. 27, 1999), p. 62. ISSN: 0007-7135

Rakoff, David. "Let the Games Begin." *New York Times Magazine* 149.51685 (Oct. 24, 1999), p. 38. ISSN: 0028-7822

Rash, Wayne. "The Little Graphics Engine That Could Change the Net." *Internetweek*, no. 803 (March 6, 2000), p. 53. ISSN: 1096-9969

Schmidt, C. James. "Sex-and-Violence Ratings: What's in Them for Libraries?" *American Libraries* 31.4 (April 2000), p. 44. ISSN: 0002-9769

Selnow, Gary W. "Playing Videogames: the Electronic Friend." *Journal of Communication* 34 (1984), p. 148.

Snyder, Beth. "FCB Puts Looking Glass on Kids' Digital World." *Advertising Age* 71.6 (Feb. 7, 2000), p. 26. ISSN: 0001-8899

Stevenson, Seth, and N'Gai Croal. "Not Just a Game Anymore." *Newsweek* 134.26 (Dec. 27, 1999), p. 94. ISSN: 0028-9604

Takahashi, Dean. "'Sonic' Boom Marks Sega's Comeback in Video Games." *Wall Street Journal* (Eastern ed.) 235.10 (Jan. 13, 2000), p. B6. ISSN: 0099-9660

Takahashi, Dean. "How Four Renegades Persuaded Microsoft to Make a Game Machine." *Wall Street Journal* (Eastern ed.) 235.50 (March 10, 2000), p. B1. ISSN: 0099-9660

———. "Sega Console Grabs Big Sales in First Three Days." *Wall Street Journal* (Eastern ed.) 234.560 (Sept. 20, 1999), p. B8. ISSN: 0099-9660

———. "The Real Video Game Wars." *Wall Street Journal* (Eastern ed.) 235.560 (March 20, 2000), p. R16. ISSN: 0099-9660

———. "Video Games Transcend Child's Play as the Industry Broadens Its Appeal." *Wall Street Journal* (Eastern ed.) 235.95 (May 12, 2000), p. B6. ISSN: 0099-9660

———. "Video-Game Violence Is under Attack as Issue Heats Up before Sales Season." *Wall Street Journal* (Eastern ed.) 234.103 (Nov. 24, 1999), p. B14. ISSN: 0099-9660

———. "With Sony in Its Sights, Microsoft Weighs Entry into Game Machines." *Wall Street Journal* (Eastern ed.) 234.82 (Oct. 26, 1999), p. B1. ISSN: 0099-9660

Taylor, Chris. "Game Wars." *Time* 155.11 (March 20, 2000), p. 44. ISSN: 0040-781X

———. "PlayStation Redux." *Time* 155.21 (May 22, 2000), p. 156. ISSN: 0040-781X

Townsend, Christian. "Getting the Oh-So-Real Feeling." *Business Review Weekly* 21.44 (Nov. 12, 1999), p. 206. ISSN: 0727-758X

———. "Sagging Sega Hopes for a Dreamcast Run." *Business Review Weekly* 21.44 (Nov. 12, 1999), p. 206. ISSN: 0727-758X

Traiman, Steve. "Shortstages Hurt Video, PC Game Sales." *Billboard* 112.5 (Jan. 29, 2000), p. 67. ISSN: 0006-2510

Wade, Will, Junko Yoshida, Anthony Cataldo, and Yoshiko Hara. "M'soft X-Box Takes on Sony." *Electronic Engineering Times*, no. 1104 (March 13, 2000), p. 1. ISSN: 0192-1541

Whitmore, Stuart. "Playing Hardware Hardball." *Asiaweek* 26.12 (March 21, 2000), p. 43. ISSN: 1012-6244

Wildstrom, Stephen H. "Boy, Can This Box Play Games." *Business Week*, no. 3650 (Oct. 11, 1999), p. 22. ISSN: 0007-7135

Wolf, Mark J. P. "Virtual Sub-Creation: Two Top Computer Games Were Made by Christians." *World* (Dec. 6, 1997), p. 23. ISSN: 0888-157X

———. "Book Notes: *Myst*." *Film Quarterly* 52.1 (Fall 1998), p. 98. ISSN: 0015-1386

———. "Inventing Space: Toward a Taxonomy of On- and Off-Screen Space in Video Games." *Film Quarterly* 51.1 (Fall 1997), p. 11. ISSN: 0015-1386

Yang, Dori Jones. "Bill Gates Has His Hand on a Joystick." *U.S. News & World Report* 128.11 (March 20, 2000), p. 54. ISSN: 0041-5537

Index

AAMA. *See* American Amusement Machine
    Association
abstraction, 30–31, 104, 110n2, 139
A Bug's Life, 6
Academy Awards, 2
action-based clock, 89
Activision, 57, 115
Adams, Robert, 60, 75n5
Adidas, 42
Adlum, Eddie, 40, 44
Adventure, 59–62, 79, 86, 94, 96–98
Adventures of Baron Munchausen, The, 90
Afterburner, 160
Alcorn, Alan, xiv, 37–38, 41–42
Alger, Horatio, 156
algorithms, 3, 79, 81
Alpine Racer, 24
Altman, Rick, 59–60, 75n3
ambience, 79, 81
American Amusement Machine Association
    (AAMA), 2
American Museum of the Moving Image
    (AMMI), 8, 137–153
AMMI. *See* American Museum of the Moving
    Image
Ampex, 36–37
Andy Capp's Tavern, 37–38
anima, 176, 178–179
animus, 176, 179
Antz, 6
Apocalypse, 179
Apple II computer, 43, 64
Aquazone, 110n1
Arakawa, Minoru, 46

Arcadia 2001, 186
archetypes, 174–182
art installations, 31
Asteroids, 21, 44, 56, 75n7, 138, 160
Astron Belt, 22
Atari, xv, 30, 37–39, 41–46, 58, 64, 75n7, 138, 141,
    149–151, 159, 185
Atari 400, 26
Atari 800, 26
Atari 2600. *See* Atari VCS CX2600
Atari 5200, 186
Atari 7800, 186
Atari Jaguar, 17
Atari Lynx, 18, 20, 26
Atari Tank, 25
Atari VCS CX2600, 5, 17, 23, 25–26, 43–45, 56,
    59–60, 62–64, 71–72, 79, 82, 88–90, 95–96,
    102–104, 115, 186
Ataxx, 114
Atlus, 64

Baer, Ralph, ix–xvi, 25, 32n2, 38, 48
BAE System, xiii
Bally Corporation, 29–30, 38–39, 141, 148, 151
Bandai, 18
Bandura, Albert, 173–174
Banjo-Kazooie, 179
Basic Programming, 16
Basketball, 95
Battletech, 74
Battlezone, 21, 44, 64, 66–67, 72, 74, 99,
    104–105, 160
Behaviorism, 173
Behind the Screen, 137

Belson, Jordan, 31
Benedikt, Michael, 74
Berlin Alexanderplatz, 91
Bernstein, Charles, 138, 153–168
Berton, John, 147, 149
Berzerk, 59, 159
Bingo Novelty Company, 29
Black Imp, The, 55
Blade Runner, 115
Blockbuster Video, 2
Blume, Sharon, 141, 143, 146
Bobo Doll, 174
Bordwell, David, 75n9
bouncing ball demonstration, xi
Bram Stoker's Dracula, 90
Breakout, 55, 81, 110
Brookhaven National Labs, xi
Bubble Bobble, 177
Buffoni, Mirko, 152
Burch, Noël, 60–61, 63, 75n6,7
Buscombe, Ed, 114
Bushnell, Nolan, xi–xii, xiv–xv, 1, 5, 23, 29, 36–41, 43–44, 48
Bust-a-Groove, 179

Caesar II, 68
Cage, John, 31
Carnival, 81
Carrie, 65
cartridge-based games, xiv, 25–26, 42–43, 95, 102
Casablanca, 66
Cavell, Stanley, 160
CBS Electronics, 1
CD-ROMs, 1–2, 22, 26–27, 67, 71, 74, 82–84, 100–103, 147
Centipede, 44, 103, 160, 177
Chopper Command, 115
Christianity, 176
Chuck E. Cheese restaurants, 44
cinematic conventions, 3
Circus Atari, 81
Classic Video Games Literature List, 184
Classic Video Game Syndicate Webring, 184
Clue VCR Game, 17
Coca-Cola, 2
"cocktail" console, 24
coin-operated arcade games, 23
coin-operated machines, 29
Coleco (Connecticut Leather Company), 42, 45, 81

Coleco ADAM, 26
ColecoVision, 45, 186
Combat, 56, 90, 95, 115
Commodore 64 home computer, 64
computer as player, 15, 106
"computer games" as a subset of video games, 17, 27
Computer Space, xii, 1, 5, 23, 29, 37, 40, 56, 141–143, 183
Computer Space (museum exhibition), 149
Computer Space 98 (museum exhibition), 149
"connect the dots," ix, xii, xv
Conquest of the World, 17
console-based games, xiii, 25, 45, 46, 95
Corner in Wheat, A, 59–60
credit sequences, 82–83
Crime and Punishment, 107
Croft, Lara, 179
CRT (cathode ray tube), x–xi, xiv, 16–18, 20–21, 28, 138; resolutions of, 16
Crystal Castles, 69
Custer's Revenge, 164
"cut scenes," 82, 84
Cyan, 147. *See also* Myst *and* Riven
Cyberspace: First Steps, 74

Dabney, Ted, 37, 39
Dactyl Nightmare, 24–25, 65, 74
Danielewski, Mark Z., 61
Dark Chambers, 58
Dark Forces, 52, 66–67, 74, 86, 100
Daytona USA, 22, 65, 74, 105
Day with the Gypsies, A, 58
Death Race (also known as *Death Race 98*), 40, 95, 97, 110n3
DEC-1 computer, x
dedicated system, 17, 27, 161
Deep Blue, 15
Deep Thought, 15
Defender, 44, 57–58, 67, 115, 160, 178
Demons to Diamonds, 95
Descent, 52, 66, 74
diagnostic and test cartridges, 16
Diddy Kong Racing, 177
DigiPen, 185
Digital Pictures, 48
dioramas, 58
"disconnect," 145–146
Doctor Who, 61
Dodge 'Em, 81
Donahue, 40

Donkey Kong, 44, 46, 97, 159, 178
Donkey Kong Country, 47
Donkey Kong Jr., 19, 26, 44, 97
Doom, 1, 22, 52, 66–67, 74, 86, 100, 139
DOS, ix
Double Dragon, 63, 160
Dragon's Lair, 22, 66, 73, 81, 97, 159
Draigh, David, 141, 143
Dr. Zhivago, 88
Duke Nukem: Music to Score By, 2
Dungeons & Dragons (D&D), 54
DVD-ROMs, 1–2, 19, 22–23, 27
Dyer, Rick, 22, 26

E. T., The Extraterrestrial, 45, 82, 96–97
"Easter eggs," 7
Edison, x, 139
Edwards, Dan, 35
electronic games. *See* hand-held electronic
    games
electronic music, 30–31
Electronics Conservancy, The, 184
Empire Strikes Back, The, 21
emulators, 27, 152, 186
error messages, 163
Escape from the Devil's Doom, 18
Euclidean 2-torus, 56
Exidy, 40, 110n3
Expanded Cinema, 31, 33n7
Expanded Entertainment, 149–151
Exterminator, The, 18

Fairchild Camera and Instrument, 42
Fairchild/Zircon Channel F, 17, 25, 32n2, 42–43
Fairchilde, Lady Elaine, 61
Fassbinder, Rainer Werner, 91
Feinstein, Keith, 15, 183. *See also* Electronics
    Conservancy, The, *and* Videotopia
"film look," 79
Final Fantasy series, 7, 91, 179
Final Furlong, 24
Final Lap, 65
Firefox, 22
Fireman Fireman, 18
First Star Software, 8, 64
flight simulators, 75n10
Football, 58, 95, 104, 159
Ford, John, 164
freeze frame, 78
Freud, Sigmund, 174
Frogger, 81, 178

Front Line, 44
Fun With Numbers, 16

Gadget, 22, 73, 83–84, 100, 106–108
Galaga, 95
Galaxian, 141, 160
"game," defined, 14
Game Boy Color. *See* Nintendo Game Boy
    Color
Game Gear. *See* Sega Game Gear
*Game Over: Gender, Race, & Violence in Video
    Games,* 187
Gance, Abel, 65
Gateway 2000, 48
Gauntlet, 58, 159
GCE/Milton Bradley Vectrex, 17, 21, 25, 186
genre: abstract, 93, 117; adaptation, 116–118;
    adventure, 87, 96, 116, 118–119; artificial life,
    119; and film, 113–114; board games, 119–120;
    capturing, 120; card games, 93, 120–121;
    catching, 121; categorization by, 113–116;
    chase, 116, 121; collecting, 121–122; combat,
    122; demo, 116, 122; diagnostic, 116, 123;
    dodging, 123; driving, 86, 123–124; educa-
    tional, 116, 124; escape, 116, 124; fighting,
    101, 124–125; flying, 125; gambling, 125;
    iconography of, 114–116; interactive movies,
    85, 100, 125–126; management simulation,
    126; maze, 116, 126–127; obstacle course, 86,
    89, 127; pencil-and-paper games, 128; pin-
    ball, 128; platform, 128–129; programming
    games, 129; puzzle, 87, 93, 116, 129; quiz, 93,
    129; racing, 86, 89, 130; rhythm and dance,
    130; role-playing, 130–131; shoot 'em up, 116,
    131; simulation, 116, 132; sports, 89, 132;
    strategy, 132; table-top games, 132; target,
    133; text adventures, 53–54, 75n11, 87, 95–96,
    104, 110n4, 133; training simulation, 134;
    utility, 116, 134
"Genre and Critical Methodology," 115
Gex 3: Deep Pocket Gecko, 178
Giants, 179
Glorious Technicolor, 137
Godard, Jean-Luc, 58
Godzilla movies, 30, 155
GoldenEye 007, 179
Goodman, Carl, 150
Gorin, Jean, 58
Gottlieb, 30, 141
Graetz, J. Martin, 23, 30, 32n1, 33n6
graphical user interface, 146

graphics. *See* raster graphics, three-dimensional graphics, two-and-a-half-dimensional graphics, *and* vector graphics
Great Wall Street Fortune Hunt, The, 17
Gremlin (game company), 141
"gremlins," 40, 95, 97
Griffith, D. W., 59–60, 65–66, 75n3,5
Groundhog Day, 80
Gun Fight, 39–40

Halcyon (laserdisc home game system), 22, 26
Half-Life, 27
hand-held electronic games, 18–20, 23, 26
"happenings," 31
"hard-edge" painting style, 30
Haunted House, 96
Henderson, J. L., 178
Hepworth, 58
Hercules: The Legendary Journeys, 178
Herz, J. C., 144–145
Higginbotham, Willy, xi
High Velocity, 64, 75n8
High Velocity Emulator (HiVE), 186
Hingham Institute, 23
Hitchhiker's Guide to the Galaxy, The, 53, 96
Hoff, Marcian E., 29
Hoffman, Judi, 117
Hollywood Genres, 113
home video games: invention of, xii–xiv; list available, 183; patent for, xii–xvi; types of, 25
Hot Circuits: A Video Arcade, 137–153
Hot Circuits II, 149
"hourglass timer," 89
House of Leaves, 61

"Idea of Genre in the American Cinema, The," 114
id Software, 139
illusion of depth. *See* space: representing three dimensions
illusion of power, 165
imaging technologies. *See* DVD-ROM, graphics, laserdisc, light-emitting diode, and liquid-crystal display, raster graphics, vector graphics
Intel Corporation, 29
interactive movies, 85. *See also* genre: interactive movies
Interface Culture, 145–146

Internet, 152–153. *See also* LAN *and* Ultima Online
Invaders of the Mummy's Tomb, 18
I, Robot, 22, 69, 99

James Bond films, 90
James Pond game series, 177
Johnny Mnemonic, 6, 22, 100
Johnson, Steven, 145–146
Joystick Nation, 144
Jr. Pac-Man, 97
Judd, Donald, 30
Jung, Carl, 170, 174–176
Jungle Hunt, 44

Kalinske, Tom, 46
Kaprow, Allen, 31
Karate Champ, 147, 160
Kassar, Ray, 43–45
Kauffman, Pete, 110n3
Kee Games, 30
Kelly, Ellsworth, 30
Keystone Kapers, 57–58
Killer List of Videogames, 184
"kill-or-be-killed" mentality, 109
kinetoscope, 29, 139, 140
Kohl, Herb, 47
Krull, 90

LAN. *See* Local Area Network
Lara Croft, 102
laserdisc, 19, 22, 25, 100, 183
LCD. *See* liquid-crystal display
LED. *See* light-emitting diode
Lee, Bruce, 160
Leiberman, Joseph, 47
level editors, 1
Lewitt, Sol, 30–31
Liberman, Alexander, 30
Library of Congress Moving Imagery Genre-Form Guide, 116–117
Life of an American Fireman, The, 58
light-emitting diode (LED), 18, 20, 26
Lind, Carl, 42
liquid-crystal display (LCD), 16, 18–20, 26
Local Area Network (LAN), 27, 87
Lockheed, xiii
Lonely Villa, The, 59, 75n3
Longest Journey, The, 7
Loral, xii

Luddites, 167–168
Lumiere, Louis and Auguste, 55–56, 91n2, 139
Lunar Lander, 21
Lund, Karen, 117

Macintosh computers, 183, 186
Magnavox, xiv–xv, 28, 38–39, 41
Magnavox Odyssey, xiv, 17, 25, 28, 32n2, 38–41, 186
mainframe games, 23. *See also* Russell, Steve *and* Spacewar!
MAME. *See* Multiple Arcade Machine Emulator
Mario, Mario, 46, 97, 159
Mario Bros., 152
Mario's Cement Factory, 26
Mario Teaches Typing, 16, 116
M*A*S*H, 116
Mattel Electronics, 45–47
Mattel Electronics Basketball, 18
Maxis Software, 15
Media and the Vietnam War, The, 137
Media Education Foundation, 187
Mega Corp, 18
Méliès, George, 55
Merlin, 18
Microsoft, 48, 185
microprocessor, 28–29, 32n2
Microvision. *See* Milton Bradley Microvision
Midway Manufacturing, 38–40, 43–44, 141, 148, 151
Milton Bradley Microvision, 18, 20, 26
Milton Bradley Vectrex. *See* GCE/Milton Bradley Vectrex
minimalist art, 30–31
Missile Command, 44, 149, 160
Mister Roger's Neighborhood, 61
MIT (Massachuestts Institute of Technology), 28, 35–36, 141, 166
Moby Dick, 107
Moon Patrol, 22
MOOs (MUD, Object-Oriented), 54
Morpheus, 77
Mortal Kombat series, 1, 47, 84, 101, 105, 178–179
Motion Picture Producers and Distributors Association (MPPDA), 2
Mouse, Mickey, 46
MPPDA. *See* Motion Picture Producers and Distributors Association
Mr. Do, 97

Mr. Do's Castle, 97
Ms. Pac-Man, 44, 97
MSX, 186
MUDs (Multi-User Dimensions), 54
Multiple Arcade Machine Emulator (MAME), 152, 186
Murrow, Edward R., 28
mutoscope, 29, 139
My Dinner with Andre, 91n2
Myst, 2, 8, 17, 22–23, 55, 66–69, 73, 75n12, 80, 86–87, 89, 91n5, 93, 98, 100, 106, 108, 115, 147
Myst III: Exile, 15, 91
mythology, 178

Namco, 141
Napoleon, 65
NARC, 141
narrative, 85, 93–111; branching, 108–109; extradiegetic narrative, 101–103; and interactivity, 107–110; narrational orientation and structure, 104–107; point of view, 105
navigation, 3–4, 66–67, 81, 86, 94
NEC, 48
Nelsonic, 19
Neo Geo, 186
Newman, Barnett, 30
Nick of Time, 91n2
Night Driver, 63–64, 72, 104
Night Trap, 48, 178
Nintendo Corporation, 5, 44, 46–47, 97, 152, 185
Nintendo Entertainment System (NES), 46, 186
Nintendo Game Boy, 16, 18, 20, 26, 151
Nintendo Game Boy Color, 20, 26
Nintendo Ultra 64, 17, 22, 47–48
Nintendo Virtual Boy, 18, 20, 25, 63, 84
Nutting, Bill, 37, 40
Nutting, David, 40
Nutting Associates, 30, 37, 141–142

Oddworld: Abe's Exxodus, 2, 91
ODYEMU (Odyssey Emulator), 186
Odyssey. *See* Magnavox Odyssey
off-screen space. *See* space
Ohio Supercomputer Graphics Project, 149
on-screen space. *See* space
Open Directory Project, 184
Outlaw, 95, 115
Out Run, 141, 160

overlays (on the TV screen), 17–18
Oxford English Dictionary (OED), 167

Pac-Land, 97
Pac-Man, 21, 35, 44–45, 56, 84, 88, 96–97, 110n5, 111n8, 115–116, 139, 141, 155–156, 159, 177
Pac-Mania, 97
"paddle," 94, 102–103
Panelas, Tom, 170
"paranoia," defined, 165
Parasite Eve, 179
"pause" function, 87–88
PDP-1 computer, x, 23, 35–36
Perils of Pauline, 160
perspective, 104–105
Phantasmagoria, 27
Philips CD-I, 17
Philips Videopac
Pillow Talk, 65
pinball, 29–30, 33n5, 38, 44, 114, 141. *See also* genre: pinball
pixels defined, 19, 139
Pizza Time Theaters, 44
Planetfall, 53, 96
player input, 4
Play Meter magazine, 141
PlayStation®. *See* Sony PlayStation®
Pole Position, 72, 149, 159
PONG, xiv–xv, 25–26, 29, 37–43, 55–56, 64, 81, 104, 141, 143, 150, 159, 177, 183, 185
Poons, Larry, 139
Popeye, 44
Porter, Edwin S., 58
prerecorded video imagery, 22
"priority," 21
Prop Cycle, 24
psychoanalysis, 174–177

*Q*bert,* 19, 73, 84, 97, 141
Qix, 44, 53, 110n2
Quake games, 27, 74, 86, 141
Queribet, 58
Quest for the Rings, 17
QuickTime, 79
QuickTime VR, 74
Quinn, Tom, 41

Raiders of the Lost Ark, 82–83, 90, 96–97
"random scan," 21
raster graphics, 16, 19–21, 72

Reagan, Ronald, 44–45
"real time," 85, 91n3, 105
Rebel Assault. See Star Wars: Rebel Assault
Red Baron, 105
Red Planet, 74
RePlay magazine, 40, 44
ride-in console, 24
Riven, 2, 7, 15, 22–23, 27, 73, 80, 93, 98, 100, 106, 108
Robotron 2084, 146, 160
Robot Tank, 90
Rogue, 55, 60
role-playing games (RPGs), 27
Romero, John, 141
Rope, 91n2
Ross, Steve, 43, 45
Rothko, Mark, 30
RPGs. *See* role-playing games
Russell, Steve, x–xi, 23, 35–36, 48

Salmoria, Nicola, 152
Sampson, Pete, 35
Sanders Associates, xii–xiii, 38
Sanger, George Alistair, 82
"save" function, 87
Sceptre, 27
Schatz, Thomas, 113–114
Scrabble, 114
Scramble, 44
scrolling, 57–59
Searchers, The, 164
Sears, xv, 41
Seawolf, 160
See it Now, 28
Sega, 46–47, 97, 141, 185
Sega Game Gear, 18
Sega Genesis, 46–47, 186
Sega Master System (SMS), 186
Sega Saturn, 22, 47, 64
Seitz, Lee K., 184
7th Guest, The, 91
720° (skateboarding arcade game), 159
sex, 157
Shadow Madness, 178
Sharpe, Roger, 141
Shenmue, 179
Shift magazine, 152
"shock" cuts, 60
Shrike Avenger, 160
Sid Meier's Civilization, 58, 68, 88

SimCity, 15, 58, 68, 88, 91n4,5, 97, 109
SimCity 2000, 68
simulator games, 1
Single Wing Turquoise Bird, The, 31
sit-inside console, 24
60 Minutes, 40
Sketchpad, 28
Skiing, 57, 88–89
Skinner, B. F., 173
Skinner Box, 173, 176
slow-motion, 85, 88
Smith, E. E., 30
Smith, Tony, 30
SNES. *See* Super Nintendo Entertainment System
social learning theory, 173–174
Sonic the Hedgehog, 46, 97, 177
Sony Computer Entertainment of America, 5, 47–48, 185
Sony Playstation, 2, 17, 22, 27, 47–48
Soul Edge series, 84, 101
space: in film, 51–52; meaning of "off-screen," 54, 64; represented or "mapped," 67–70; representing three dimensions, 70–75, 75n10; scrolling, 57–59; types of, 53–69; in video games, 51–76; "wraparound," 56–57
Space Ace, 22, 66
Space Invaders, 21, 44, 55–56, 64, 95, 97, 104, 107, 110n8, 115, 141, 160
Space Jockey, 57
Spacewar!, xi-xii, 23, 28–30, 32n1, 33n6, 35–37, 55, 141, 166–167
Spaceward Ho! IV, 115
Spectre, 105
Spielberg, Steven, 45
sprites, 21
Spy Vs Spy, 8, 64–65, 67, 72–73, 75n8, 89, 106
Stampede, 57–58
stand-alone arcade video games, 1, 23–24
Starmaster, 72
Star Ship, 63, 71–72, 104
Star Trek: Borg, 6, 22, 26, 73, 81, 85, 100, 108
Star Trek: The Next Generation, 80
Star Wars, 21, 115, 160
Star Wars: Rebel Assault, 73, 83–85, 116
Stella (emulator), 186
Stellar Track, 55, 68, 89
Stern Electronics, 44
stillness. *See* time: stillness and movement
Stonekeep, 52, 66–67

"stopwatch" timer, 89
storytelling, 175
Stratovox, 160
Street Fighter, 1
Street Racer, 57–58
Streets of Rage, 63
Super Arcade Game Emulator (SAGE), 186
Super Breakout, 102, 104, 107, 110n7
Super GT, 74, 105
Superman, 59, 89, 96–97
Super Mario Bros., 1, 46, 61
Super Mario Bros. 3, 22
Super Nintendo Entertainment System (SNES), 18, 25, 47
Sutherland, Ivan, 28

Taito, 39, 43–44
Tallarico, Tommy, 82
Tank, 104
Taves, Brian, 117
Tech Model Railroad Club, 35–36
Tekken series, 75n9, 84, 101–102, 105, 179
television, 28, 161–162, 169, 171, 174, 186
Tempest, 21, 44, 53, 63–64, 72, 84, 104, 110n2
Tetris, 114
Tevonian, Stephanie, 144
Texas Instruments 99/4a, 26
text adventures. *See* genre: text adventures
Thayer's Quest, 159
Theory of Film Practice, 60, 75n6
three-dimensional graphics, 22, 67, 70–75, 75n10, 100, 104–105. *See also* space: representing three dimensions
3DO Interactive Multiplayer, 17
time: cyclical or looped time, 80–82; in interludes and title sequences, 82–85; sense of history passing, 146; stillness and movement, 77–80; time pressure and ticking clocks, 88–91; versus real time, 85–88; in video games, 77–91
Timecode, 65, 91n2
time-lapse, 85, 88
Time Pilot, 147
Time Traveler, 22
Toho Film Studios, 30
Tomb Raider, 1, 77, 84–87, 90, 178–179
Tomb Raider II, 7, 22, 67, 100, 102, 178–179
Tommy Tallarico: Virgin Games, Greatest Hits Volume One, 82
Top Skater, 2, 24

Tout Va Bien, 58, 75n1
Toy Story, 6
Track & Field, 159
"trade stimulators," 29, 33n4
Trip to the Moon, A, 55
Tron, 148–149
TSR Hobbies, 54
Tudor, Andrew, 115
TurboGrafx 16, 186
Turkle, Sherry, 153
20th-Century Fox, 1
Twinsen's Odyssey, 77
two-and-a-half-dimensional graphics, 21–23

Ultima Online, 27, 33n3, 99
Ultima series, 15, 58, 98–99, 111n6
Unreal Tournament, 27

VCR (video cassette recorder), 88, 145, 161
vector generator, 20
vector graphics, 16, 19–21, 63, 72, 104, 183
Vectrex. See GCE/Milton Bradley Vectrex
Video Arcade Preservation Society (VAPS), 184
"video" defined, x, 16
video game industry revenues, 5, 9n3
Video Gamer's First Network, 185
video games: and agression, 172, 174; auctions,
    152; based on TV shows, 9n1; characters in,
    98–99; as clinically addictive, 4, 9n2, 172;
    conflict-oriented, 105–106; cultural impor-
    tance of, 5; definition of, 14–19; as a demo-
    cratic equalizer, 180; diegetic worlds of, 6,
    31–32, 94–101; difficulties in studying, 6–7;
    emotional response to, 93, 110n1, 176–177;
    ending of, 106–107; female archetypes in,
    178–179; and film and TV theory, 2–4,
    13–14; invention of, ix–xvi, 28; Jungian
    analysis of, 175–180; modes of exhibition,
    23–27, 86; and older players, 145–146; and
    psychological research, 170–176; psycholog-
ical theories relating to, 173–180; research
    resources for, 183–191; and scoring, 82,
    105–106, 158; as a social experience, 145, 155,
    158, 169, 172; space in (see space); task-ori-
    ented, 106; threat of closure, 157–158; and
    worldviews, 4, 176; as a youth phenome-
    non, 171–172
video game studies, 6–8
Videopac. See Philips Videopac
Videotopia, 183–184
Virtua Fighter 3: Team Battle, 179
Virtual Boy. See Nintendo Virtual Boy
virtual reality, 1, 24–25. See also Dactyl Night-
    mare
Virtua Racing, 22, 65
Vortex Concerts, 31

Warioland, 22, 63, 67, 84
Warner Communications, 43, 45
Warrior, 18
Whirlwind mainframe computer, 28
Williams Electronics, 44, 141, 151
Wing Commander, 1
Winter, David, 185
Wonder Wizard, 25
Workers Leaving the Factory, 55
World Wide Web, 27, 53, 184–186
"wraparound" space, 56–57, 59

X-men, 118

Yar's Revenge, 103
Youngblood, Gene, 31, 33n7

z-axis, 61, 63–64, 70–73, 104
Zaxxon, 22, 61, 72, 160
Zelda series, 179
"zip mode," 80
Zork series, 15, 23, 53, 96

About the Contributors

Ralph H. Baer
Ralph H. Baer is the inventor of the *Odyssey*, the first home video game system, and has created numerous other toys and games. He has published numerous articles on electronic product design and development, and holds more than 50 U. S. patents and over 100 patents worldwide. He was an Engineering Fellow at Sanders/Lockheed from 1959–1975, and a Division Manager there from 1975–1987. In 1980 he was named Inventor of the Year by the New York Patent Law Association, and named Inventor of the Year in 1981 by the state of New Hampshire.

Charles Bernstein
Charles Bernstein's *My Way: Speeches and Poems* was published in 1999 by the University of Chicago Press. He is editor of *Close Listening: Poetry and the Performed Word* (Oxford) and *The L=A=N=G=U=A=G=E Book* (Southern Illinois University Press) and executive editor of the Electronic Poetry Center (http://wings.buffalo.edu/epc). Bernstein is David Gray Professor of Poetry and Letters at SUNY-Buffalo, where he teaches in the Poetics Program.

Steven L. Kent
Steven L. Kent is a journalist, video game historian, columnist for *The Seattle Times, The Los Angeles Times Syndicate, NEXT Generation* Magazine, and a correspondent on MSNBC, and is the author of the book *Electronic Nation: The History of Video Games.* His essay, "Super Mario Nation", originally appeared in *American Heritage* Magazine.

Rochelle Slovin

Rochelle Slovin has overseen all aspects of the development of *Behind the Screen* as producer and artistic director of AMMI, the Museum she founded in 1988. Ms. Slovin began her career as a performer in New York's avant-garde theater in the 1960s, appearing often at LaMama and other off-off-Broadway houses. Subsequently, she entered New York City government, working in municipal planning and cultural development while earning a master's degree from the Columbia University Graduate School of Business. In 1981, she joined the recently formed Astoria Motion Picture and Television Foundation as executive director, with the mission of setting policy for the Foundation and determining a proper use for its city-owned property. Ms. Slovin proposed converting part of the property into an American Museum of the Moving Image. She developed plans for exhibitions and programs, sought funding, assembled a staff, and worked with Gwathmey Siegel and Associates on the architectural renovation. She has directed the Museum since its opening in September 1988. Ms. Slovin is a member of the National Academy of Television Arts and Sciences, the Audio Visual Committee of the International Council on Museums, and the International Radio and Television Society. In 1992, she received the City of New York Mayor's Award of Honor for Arts and Culture. In 1993, she was appointed to the Committee on Art of the National Air and Space Museum, Smithsonian Institution. She was honored in 1993 by the Metropolitan Historic Structures Association "for her inspired leadership in the founding of the American Museum of the Moving Image, a site of national and international cultural significance."

Rebecca R. Tews

Rebecca R. Tews is a Ph. D. candidate in Counseling Psychology at Marquette University in Milwaukee, Wisconsin. She is an Assistant Professor of Pscyhology at Concordia University Wisconsin where she has been a part of the faculty since 1995. She is also a Child & Family Therapist with community agencies in Milwaukee area. Her areas of research interest include gender perceptions, image and propaganda, social learning theory, and media and video game play (why people play and how it affects them). She has been working with children and families since 1985. Throughout this period her interest in video games has been driven by the behavior problems and family conflicts observed in both educational and therapeutic settings. An avid "gamer," she is also intrigued by the impact that game content has on the psyche of the player. Currently she is completing dissertation research on the role that video games play in anxiety and physiological arousal of the game player.

Mark J. P. Wolf

Mark J. P. Wolf is an Assistant Professor in the Department of Communication at Concordia University Wisconsin. He has a Ph.D. from the Critical Studies Division of the School of Cinema/Television at the University of Southern California, and has made or worked on a number of film, video, and multimedia projects in addition to scholarly work. He has had work published in journals including *Film Quarterly*, *The Velvet Light Trap*, and *The Spectator*, and is the author of the book, *Abstracting Reality: Art, Communication, and Cognition in the Digital Age* from University Press of America. He has an anthology, *Virtual Morality: Morals, Ethics, and New Media*, forthcoming from Peter Lang Publishers, and is finishing his first novel. He lives in Wisconsin with his wife, Diane.